Debugging with Fiddler

The complete reference from the creator of the Fiddler Web Debugger

Eric Lawrence

ACKNOWLEDGEMENTS

This book, and Fiddler itself, would not have been possible without myriad contributions from hundreds of people around the world.

First, I'd like to thank my wife Jane, a source of inspiration, encouragement, and immense patience as I've spent innumerable nights and weekends working on Fiddler and authoring this book. Next, thanks to my parents and grandmother, who instilled in me a voracious appetite for books and the idea that one day I should try my hand at writing one. I beg my friends' forgiveness for declining so many gatherings over the years to stay home and write more code.

I'm grateful for the many contributions of colleagues too numerous to mention (they know who they are!), and to the broader Fiddler community for providing a steady stream of encouragement, suggestions and bug reports. My colleague Jim Moore warrants a special mention for his careful review of the draft version of this book, and his valuable feedback on Fiddler over the years. I'd also like to acknowledge the many dozens of donors who supported Fiddler financially as it became costly to maintain and distribute.

Lastly, I'd like to thank you, dear reader, for caring enough about Fiddler to pick up this book!

TABLE OF CONTENTS

Acknowledgements iii

Table of Contents iv

INTRODUCTION 1

Origins 3

    About this book 5

A Quick Primer 7

    Basic Concepts 7

    Usage Scenarios 8

        An Incomplete List of Things Fiddler Can Do 8

        An Incomplete List of Things Fiddler Cannot Do 9

EXPLORING FIDDLER 11

Getting Started 13

    System Requirements 13

    Installing Fiddler 13

        Permissions and XCOPY Deployment 14

    Updating Fiddler 14

    Uninstalling Fiddler 14

The Fiddler User-Interface 15

    The Web Sessions List 15

        Understanding Icons and Colors 16

        Keyboard Reference 18

    Web Sessions Context Menu 18

Fiddler's Main Menu 23

    The File Menu 23

    The Edit Menu 23

    The Rules Menu 24

        Performance Submenu 25

    The Tools Menu 26

    The View Menu 26

    The Help Menu 27

        Fiddler's About Box 28

Fiddler's Toolbar 29

   Fiddler's Status Bar 30

QuickExec 31

   QuickExec Selection Commands 31

   Default FiddlerScript Commands 33

Application Hotkeys 36

Statistics Tab 37

The Filters tab 39

   Hosts 39

   Client Process 40

   Request Headers 41

   Breakpoints 41

   Response Status Code 41

   Response Type and Size 42

   Response Headers 42

The Timeline tab 44

   Mode: Timeline 44

   Mode: Client Pipe Map 45

   Mode: Server Pipe Map 46

   Using the Timeline for Performance Analysis 46

The AutoResponder tab 47

   Specifying the Match Condition 48

      Matching Against Request Bodies 49

   Specifying the Action Text 50

   Using RegEx Replacements in Action Text 51

   Drag-and-Drop support 52

   FARX Files 52

The TextWizard 54

   Character Encodings 55

The Composer tab 56

   Request Options 56

   Raw Requests 57

   Parsed Requests 57

   Issuing Sequential Requests 57

File Upload Requests 58

Automatic Request Breakpoints 59

The Log tab 60

The Find Sessions Window 61

The Host Remapping Tool 63

TECHNIQUES AND CONCEPTS 65

Retargeting Traffic with Fiddler 67

Method #1 - Rewriting 67

Method #2 - Rerouting 67

Method #3 - Redirecting 68

Features to Retarget Requests 69

Comparing Sessions 70

UltraDiff 71

Comparing Multiple Sessions at Once 71

Debugging with Breakpoints 72

Setting Breakpoints 72

Tampering Using Inspectors 73

The Breakpoint Bar 73

Resuming Multiple Sessions 74

CONFIGURING FIDDLER AND CLIENTS 75

Fiddler Options 77

General Options 77

HTTPS Options 78

Extensions Options 79

Connections Options 79

Appearance Options 81

HeaderEncoding Setting 82

Preferences 83

Configuring Clients 84

Capturing Traffic from Browsers 84

Firefox 84

Opera 85

Other Browsers 85

Capturing Traffic from Other Applications 86

    WinHTTP 86

    .NET Framework 86

    Java 87

    PHP / CURL 88

Capturing Traffic from Services 88

Capturing Traffic to Loopback 88

    Loopback Bypasses 88

    Loopback Authentication 89

    Loopback Blocked from Metro-style Windows 8 Apps 90

Running Fiddler on Mac OSX 91

Capturing Traffic from Other Computers 93

Capturing Traffic from Devices 94

    Apple iOS Proxy Settings 95

    Windows Phone Proxy Settings 95

    Windows RT Proxy Settings 95

    Other Devices 96

Using Fiddler as a Reverse Proxy 96

    Acting as a Reverse Proxy for HTTPS 97

Chaining to Upstream Proxy Servers 97

Chaining to SOCKS / TOR 98

VPNs, Modems, and Tethering 99

DirectAccess 99

Memory Usage and Fiddler's Bitness 100

Buffering vs. Streaming Traffic 102

    Request Buffering 102

    Response Buffering 102

    COMET 103

HTML5 WebSockets 104

Fiddler and HTTPS 106

    Trusting the Fiddler Root Certificate 107

        Machine-wide Trust on Windows 8 108

        Manually Trusting the Fiddler Root 108

        Additional HTTPS Options 109

Configuring Clients for HTTPS Decryption 110

    Browsers 110

        Firefox 110

        Opera 110

    Cross-machine scenarios 110

    HTTPS and Devices 111

        Windows Phone 111

        Android and iOS 111

    Buggy HTTPS Servers 112

    Certificate Validation 113

    Certificate Pinning 113

Fiddler and FTP 115

Fiddler and Web Authentication 116

    HTTP Authentication 116

    Automatic Authentication in Fiddler 117

    Authentication Problems 118

        Channel-Binding 118

        WinHTTP Credential Release Policy 118

        Loopback Protection 119

    HTTPS Client Certificates 119

INSPECTORS 121

    Overview 123

    Auth 125

    Caching 127

    Cookies 128

    Headers 129

        Context Menu 130

        Keyboard Shortcuts 130

        Editing 130

    HexView 132

    ImageView 134

    JSON 135

    Raw 136

SyntaxView 137

TextView 139

Transformer 140

    Background on Response Encodings 140

    Adding and Removing Encodings using the Transformer 141

    Other Ways to Remove Encodings 142

WebForms 143

WebView 144

XML 145

EXTENSIONS 147

    Overview 149

        Popular 3rd Party Extensions 149

            Performance Add-ons 149

            Security Add-ons 149

        Extensions I've Built 150

    JavaScript Formatter 151

    Gallery 152

        Full-Screen View 152

    Content Blocker 154

    Traffic Differ 155

    FiddlerScript Editors 156

        FiddlerScript Tab 156

        ClassView Sidebar 157

        Fiddler2 ScriptEditor 157

    SAZClipboard 159

    AnyWHERE 160

STORING, IMPORTING, AND EXPORTING TRAFFIC 161

    Session Archive Zip (SAZ) Files 163

        Protecting SAZ Files 164

    FiddlerCap 165

        Capture Box 165

        Capture Options Box 166

        Tools Box 167

Fiddler's Viewer Mode..169

Importing and Exporting Sessions 170

    Import Formats 170

    Export Formats..170

        HTML5 AppCache Manifest...171

        HTTPArchive v1.1 and v1.2...172

        MeddlerScript..173

        Raw Files 173

        Visual Studio WebTest 174

        WCAT Script...174

FIDDLERSCRIPT 175

Extending Fiddler with FiddlerScript 177

    About FiddlerScript..177

    Editing FiddlerScript..178

        Updating FiddlerScript at Runtime 179

        Resetting to the Default FiddlerScript 179

FiddlerScript Functions...180

    Session Handling Functions 180

        OnPeekAtRequestHeaders 180

        OnBeforeRequest..180

        OnPeekAtResponseHeaders 180

        OnBeforeResponse 180

        OnReturningError...181

    General Functions 181

        Main 181

        OnRetire 181

        OnBoot...181

        OnShutdown...181

        OnAttach 181

        OnDetach..181

        OnExecAction(sParams: string[]) 182

FiddlerScript and Automation Tools..183

    Quiet Mode 183

Driving Fiddler from Batch Scripts 183

Driving Fiddler from Native or .NET Code 184

Extending Fiddler's UI - Menus 186

Extending the Tools Menu 186

Extending the Web Sessions Context Menu... 187

Extending the Rules Menu 187

Boolean-bound Rules 187

String-bound Rules 189

Creating New Top-Level Menus 190

Extending Fiddler's UI - Adding Columns to the Web Sessions List............... 192

Binding Columns using Attributes 192

Binding Columns using AddBoundColumn 194

FiddlerObject Functions 196

FiddlerObject.ReloadScript() 196

FiddlerObject.StatusText 196

FiddlerObject.log(sTextToLog) 196

FiddlerObject.playSound(sSoundFilename) 197

FiddlerObject.flashWindow() 197

FiddlerObject.alert(sMessage) 197

FiddlerObject.prompt(sMessage) 197

FiddlerObject.createDictionary() 197

FiddlerObject.WatchPreference(sPrefBranch, oFunc)..................................... 198

Referencing Assemblies... 199

Example Scripts 200

Request Scripts.. 200

Add (or Overwrite) a Request Header.. 200

Remove Request Headers 200

Flag Requests that Send Cookies 200

Rewrite a Request from HTTP to HTTPS 200

Swap the Host Header 201

Drop a Connection.. 201

Prevent Response Streaming 201

Response Scripts 202

Hide Sessions that Returned Images... 202

Flag Redirections..202

Replace Text in Script, CSS, and HTML..202

Remove All DIV Elements 202

More Examples..203

EXTENDING FIDDLER WITH .NET CODE 205

Extending Fiddler with .NET 207

Project Requirements and Settings 207

Debugging Extensions...207

Best Practices for Extensions 208

Best Practice: Use an Enable Switch...208

Best Practice: Use Delay Load 208

Best Practice: Beware "Big Data" 210

Best Practice: Use the Reporter Pattern for Extensions 210

Interacting with Fiddler's Objects...212

The Web Sessions List 212

Session[] GetAllSessions()...212

Session GetFirstSelectedSession() 212

Session[] GetSelectedSessions()..212

Session[] GetSelectedSessions(int iMax) 212

void actSelectAll()...212

void actSelectSessionsMatchingCriteria(doesSessionMatchCriteriaDelegate oDel) 212

void actRemoveSelectedSessions() 213

void actRemoveUnselectedSessions() 213

bool actLoadSessionArchive(string sFilename) 213

void actSaveSessionsToZip()...213

void actSaveSessionsToZip(string sFilename, string sPwd) 213

void actSessionCopyURL() 213

void actSessionCopySummary() 213

void actSessionCopyHeadlines()...213

int FiddlerApplication.UI.lvSessions.SelectedCount 214

SimpleEventHandler FiddlerApplication.UI.lvSessions.OnSessionsAdded 214

Session Objects 214

oRequest 214

requestBodyBytes 214

oResponse 214

responseBodyBytes 215

oFlags 215

void Abort() 215

bBufferResponse 215

bHasReponse 215

bypassGateway 215

clientIP 215

clientPort 215

bool COMETPeek() 216

fullUrl 216

PathAndQuery 216

port 216

host 216

hostname 216

bool HostnameIs(string) 216

bool HTTPMethodIs(string) 216

bool uriContains(string) 216

id 216

isFTP 216

isHTTPS 216

isTunnel 217

LocalProcessID 217

bool utilDecodeRequest() 217

bool utilDecodeResponse() 217

responseCode 217

state 217

BitFlags 218

Timers 219

Sending Strings to the TextWizard 220

Logging 220

Interacting with the FiddlerScript Engine 221

Programming with Preferences 223

Preference Naming 223

The IFiddlerPreferences Interface 223

Storing and Removing Preferences 224

Internally, all preference values are stored as strings; the...................................224

Retrieving Preferences..224

Watching for Preference Changes..225

Notifications in Extensions 225

Notifications in FiddlerScript 225

Building Extension Installers..226

Building Inspectors..229

Inspecting the Session Object 233

Dealing with HTTP Compression and Chunking 235

Decoding a Copy of the Body 235

Using the GetRe*BodyAsString Methods 236

Using the utilDecode* Methods 236

Inspector Assemblies...237

Building Extensions...238

Understanding Threading 239

Integrating with QuickExec...239

Example Extension 240

Extension Assemblies..245

Building Import and Export Transcoders...246

Direct Fiddler to load your Transcoder assemblies 246

The ProfferFormat Attribute..246

The ISessionImporter Interface...247

The ISessionExporter Interface 247

Handling Options 248

Providing Progress Notifications 249

Notes on Threading and Transcoders in FiddlerCore 250

Beyond Files...250

Example Transcoder 250

FIDDLERCORE 255

Overview...257

Legalities 257

Getting Started with FiddlerCore 258

Compiling the Sample Application 258

FiddlerCoreStartupFlags 260

The FiddlerApplication Class 262

FiddlerApplication Events 262

RequestHeadersAvailable Event 262

BeforeRequest Event 262

OnValidateServerCertificate Event 262

OnReadResponseBuffer Event 263

ResponseHeadersAvailable Event 263

BeforeResponse Event 264

BeforeReturningError Event 264

AfterSessionComplete Event 264

FiddlerAttach Event 264

FiddlerDetach Event 264

OnClearCache Event 264

OnNotification Event 265

FiddlerApplication Methods 265

Startup() 265

Shutdown() 265

IsStarted() 265

IsSystemProxy() 265

CreateProxyEndpoint() 265

DoImport() 266

DoExport() 266

GetVersionString() 266

GetDetailedInfo() 266

ResetSessionCounter() 266

FiddlerApplication Properties and Fields 266

isClosing... 266

Log 266

oDefaultClientCertificate 267

oProxy 267

oTranscoders...267

Prefs 267

The Rest of the Fiddler API 267

Common Tasks with FiddlerCore 268

Keeping track of Sessions 268

Getting Traffic to FiddlerCore 268

Trusting the FiddlerCore Certificate 269

Generating Responses 270

Other Resources..270

APPENDICES 271

Appendix A: Troubleshooting 273

Missing Traffic..273

Interference from Security Software...274

Problems Downloading Fiddler...274

Problems Installing Fiddler...274

Problems Running Fiddler...274

Corrupted Proxy Settings 275

Resetting Fiddler...275

Troubleshooting Certificate Problems...276

Wiping all traces of Fiddler 277

Fiddler crashes complaining about the "Configuration System"..277

Fiddler randomly stops capturing traffic...278

Fiddler stalls when streaming RPC-over-HTTPS traffic...278

Appendix B: Command Line Syntax...280

Option Flags 280

Examples 280

Appendix C: Session Flags 281

Session Display Flags 281

Breakpoint and Editing Flags...282

Networking Flags 283

Authentication Flags 284

Client Information Flags 285

Performance Simulation Flags 285

HTTPS Flags... 286

Request Composer Flags 288

Other Flags 288

Appendix D: Preferences.. 291

Network Preferences.. 291

HTTPS Preferences... 295

Fiddler UI Preferences 297

FiddlerScript Preferences... 300

TextWizard Preferences 301

Request Composer Preferences 301

Path Configuration 302

Miscellaneous.. 303

Extension Preferences 304

    Raw Inspector.. 304

    JavaScript Formatter.. 304

    Certificate Maker... 305

Index.. 307

Introduction

ORIGINS

First, a confession—the Fiddler Web Debugger is not the result of a grand vision or the ambition to develop the world's most popular debugging proxy. A tool born of necessity, I never set out to build a platform so flexible, powerful, and complicated that I'd be forced to spend nine months writing a book to explain how to fully take advantage of it. But here we are.

Before diving into the technical chapters, I will begin by sharing the story behind how Fiddler came to be.

As a student at the University of Maryland in the spring of 1999, I had the chance to interview for a Program Management position on a new team at Microsoft. One of my final interviewer's first questions was "How does HTTP work?" Knowing only the basics, I gave an incomplete and somewhat inaccurate answer, but didn't embarrass myself too badly. That summer and the following, I worked on features for the first version of SharePoint. On rare occasions, I found myself looking at web traffic in Microsoft Network Monitor (NetMon), a powerful but then primitive and difficult-to-use packet sniffer. In the early summer of 2001, I joined Microsoft full-time as the Program Manager for the Office Clip Art organizer client and web site.

At that time, most of the developers and testers working on my team were new to web development, having previously been responsible for writing native code applications in C and C++. It was quickly apparent that the debugging process was overly cumbersome—many of my colleagues were loath to use NetMon. I even watched some developers debugging HTTP requests by hovering over variables in Visual Studio, examining the raw traffic in hex:

Having authored a number of small utilities over the years, I was confident that I could code *something* to make web debugging simpler. My first simplistic effort was based on taking an existing C++ proxy server and making minor modifications to it so that it would spew HTTP traffic to the system console:

It's generous to call this effort primitive—the proxy couldn't handle secure traffic or authentication protocols. Non-text content was another problem—comically, the utility would try to render binary content as ASCII. Old-school console users may recall that the octet 0x07 represents the "bell" character, and when it's displayed in the console, a system beep is played. Soon after its release, the hallways of the Office Online team sounded like a Las Vegas casino, as binary content flowed through the debug proxies running in each tester's office.

Despite the very annoying limitations, this tool was still popular, and I was inspired to get started on the next version. I mocked up a quick little demo in Borland Delphi, a native code language used by most of my development work at the time. The colorful UI foreshadowed Fiddler's eventual appearance:

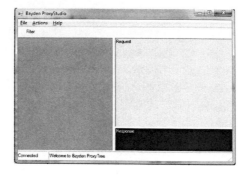

However, as I pondered the security and memory-management implications of writing a proxy server in native code, I soon decided that my next effort would be developed in C#, a new language being developed by the Visual Studio team that my best friend had just joined. The notion of writing a HTTP proxy server from scratch in .NET posed just two significant challenges: I didn't really know how HTTP worked, and I didn't know how to code in C#.

Fortunately, given a few bucks and a lot of spare weekends, both shortcomings would be remedied. Two books were my constant companions: HTTP: The Definitive Guide and the C# Cookbook. Chapter by chapter, I learned about HTTP and C# .NET, and week-by-week Fiddler came to life. About six months after I started, I had a basic version of Fiddler available:

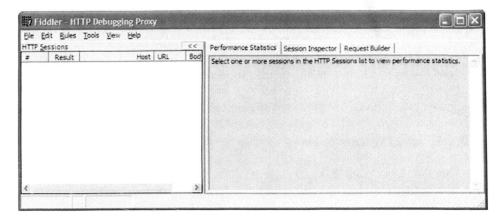

Like its predecessors, it too had a large number of limitations (and thousands of bugs) but it was eagerly adopted by colleagues whose PC speakers were in danger of burning out from the incessant beeps of my first proxy utility.

Over the subsequent years, Fiddler was progressively enhanced with two extensibility models, a mechanism to automatically generate and modify responses, and support for secure (HTTPS) traffic, FTP, and HTML5 WebSockets.

About this book

After nearly 9 years and one hundred version updates, Fiddler has evolved into a powerful utility and platform that can perform a wide variety of tasks. It has a rich extensibility model and a community of add-on developers who have broadened its usefulness as a performance, security, and load-testing tool. Questions in email, online discussion groups, and numerous conferences over the years made it overwhelmingly apparent that most users only exploit a tiny fraction of Fiddler's power. I came to realize that thousands of users would get a lot more out of Fiddler if there were a complete reference to the tool available. This book is the product of that realization.

As Fiddler's developer, I've found it both easy and challenging to write this book. It's easy, because I understand Fiddler deeply, down to its very foundation, and can consult the source code to research obscure details. On the other hand, it's been very challenging, as every time I choose an interesting scenario or feature to write about, I'm forced to think deeply about that scenario or feature. Commonly, I've found myself developing improvements to revise Fiddler and minimize or eliminate the need to write about the topic in the first place. As a result, I've rewritten large portions of both this book and Fiddler itself. It's been a slow process, but both projects have benefitted.

Publication of this book will roughly coincide with the release of Fiddler version 2.4.0.0 in the early summer of 2012. If you're using a later version of Fiddler, you will find some minor differences, but the core concepts will remain the same.

This book is deliberately limited in scope—it covers nearly every aspect of Fiddler and FiddlerCore, but it is not a tutorial on HTTP, SSL, HTML, Web Services or the myriad other topics you may want to understand to fully exploit Fiddler's feature set. If you want a deeper understanding of web protocols, I can recommend the references I consulted during the development of Fiddler:

- Hypertext Transfer Protocol -- HTTP/1.1 from `http://www.ietf.org/rfc/rfc2616.txt`

- HTTP: The Definitive Guide by David Gourley

- Web Protocols and Practice: HTTP/1.1, Networking Protocols, Caching, and Traffic Measurement by Balachander Krishnamurthy and Jennifer Rexford

- SSL & TLS Essentials: Securing the Web by Stephen A. Thomas

This book can be read either "straight through" or you can use the Table of Contents and Index to find the topics most interesting to you. Please consider skimming all of the chapters, even those that don't seem relevant to your needs, because each chapter often contains tips and tricks you might not find elsewhere.

I encourage you to begin by reading the primer in the next chapter, which lays out some terminology and the basic concepts that you'll need to understand to get the most out of Fiddler and this book.

Enjoy!

A Quick Primer

In this section, I'll provide some basic information about Fiddler that will help you get started and build a foundation for the rest of the book.

Basic Concepts

Fiddler is a special-purpose **proxy server** that runs on your Windows-based computer. Locally-running programs like web browsers, Office applications, and other clients send their HTTP and HTTPS **requests** to Fiddler, which then typically forwards the traffic to a web server. The server's **responses** are then returned to Fiddler, which passes the traffic back to the client.

Virtually all programs that use web protocols support proxy servers, and therefore Fiddler can be used with almost any app. When it starts **capturing**, Fiddler registers itself with the Windows Internet (WinINET) networking component and requests that all applications begin directing their requests to Fiddler.

Some applications do not automatically respect the Windows networking configuration and may require manual configuration in order for Fiddler to capture their traffic. Fiddler can be configured to work in more exotic scenarios, including server-to-server (e.g. Web Services) and device-to-server traffic (e.g. iPad or Windows Phone clients). By default, Fiddler is designed to automatically **chain** to any **upstream proxy** server that was configured before it began capturing—this allows Fiddler to work in network environments where a proxy server is already in use.

Because Fiddler captures traffic from all locally-running processes, it supports a wide range of **filters**. These enable hiding of traffic which is not of interest to you, as well as highlighting (using colors or font choice) of traffic deemed interesting. Filters can be applied based on the source of the traffic (e.g. the specific client process) or based on some characteristic of the traffic itself (e.g. what hostname the traffic is bound for, or what type of content the server returned).

Fiddler supports a rich extensibility model which ranges from simple **FiddlerScript** to powerful **Extensions** which can be developed using any .NET language. Fiddler also supports several special-purpose extension types, the most popular of which is called an **Inspector**, so named because it enables you to inspect a single request or response. Inspectors can be built to display all response types (e.g. the HexView Inspector) or tailored to support a type-specific format (e.g. the JSON Inspector). If you're a developer, you can build Fiddler's core proxy engine into your applications using a class library named **FiddlerCore**.

Fiddler can decrypt HTTPS traffic and display and modify the requests that would otherwise be inscrutable to observers on the network using a **man-in-the-middle** decryption technique. To permit seamless debugging without security warnings, Fiddler's **root certificate** may be installed in the Trusted Certificates store of the system or web browser.

A **Web Session** represents a single transaction between a client and a server. Each Session appears as a single entry in the **Web Sessions List** shown at the left side of the Fiddler interface. Each Session object has a **Request** and a **Response**, representing what the client sent to the server and what the server returned to the client. The Session object also maintains a set of **Flags** that record metadata about the session, and a **Timers** object that stores timestamps logged in the course of processing the session.

Proxy servers are not limited to simply viewing network traffic—Fiddler got its name from its ability to "fiddle" with outbound requests and inbound responses. Manual tampering of traffic may be performed by setting a request or response **breakpoint**. When a breakpoint is set, Fiddler will pause the processing of the session and permit manual alteration of the request and the response. Traffic rewriting may also be performed automatically by script or extensions running inside of Fiddler. By default, Fiddler operates in **buffering mode**, whereby the server's response is completely collected before any part of it is sent to the client. If the **streaming mode** is instead enabled, the server's response will be immediately returned to the client as it is downloaded. In streaming mode, response tampering is not possible.

Captured sessions can be saved in a **Session Archive Zip (SAZ)** file for later viewing. This compressed file format contains the full request and response, as well as flags, timers, and other metadata. A lightweight capture-only tool known as **FiddlerCap** may be used by non-technical users to collect a SAZ file for analysis by experts. Fiddler supports **Exporter** extensions that allow storing captured sessions in myriad other formats for interoperability with other tools. Similarly, Fiddler supports **Importer** extensions that enable Fiddler to load traffic stored in other formats, including the **HTTP Archive (HAR)** format used by many browsers' developer tools.

Usage Scenarios

Some of the most common questions I get are of the form: "*Can I use Fiddler to accomplish <x>?*" While there are a huge number of scenarios for which Fiddler is useful, and a number of scenarios for which Fiddler isn't suitable, the most common tasks fall into a few buckets. Here's a rough guide to what you can and cannot do with Fiddler:

An Incomplete List of Things Fiddler Can Do
- View web traffic from nearly any browser, client application, or service.
- Modify any request or response, either manually or automatically.
- Decrypt HTTPS traffic to enable viewing and modification.
- Store captured traffic to an archive and reload it later, even from a different computer.
- "Play back" previously-captured responses to a client application, even if the server is offline.
- Debug web traffic from most PCs and devices, including Mac/Linux systems, smart phones, and tablet computers.
- Chain to upstream proxy servers, including the TOR network.

- Run as a reverse proxy on a server to capture traffic without reconfiguring the client computer or device.
- Grow more powerful with new features added by FiddlerScript or the .NET-based extensibility model.

An Incomplete List of Things Fiddler Cannot Do

While Fiddler is a very flexible tool, there are some things it cannot presently do. That list includes:

- Debug non-web protocol traffic.
  - o Fiddler works with HTTP, HTTPS, and FTP traffic and related protocols like HTML5 WebSockets and ICY streams.
  - o Fiddler cannot "see" or alter traffic that runs on other protocols like SMTP, POP3, Telnet, IRC, etc.
- Handle huge requests or responses.
  - o Fiddler cannot handle requests larger than 2 gigabytes in size.
  - o Fiddler has limited ability to handle responses larger than 2gb.
  - o Fiddler uses system memory and the pagefile to hold session data. Storing large numbers of sessions or huge requests or responses can result in slow performance.
- "Magically" remove bugs in a website for you.
  - o While Fiddler will identify networking problems on your behalf, it generally cannot *fix* them without your help. I can't tell you how many times I've gotten emails asking: "What gives? I installed Fiddler but my website still has bugs!"

With that quick primer out of the way, let's dive in!

Exploring Fiddler

GETTING STARTED

Fiddler is available to download by visiting `http://getfiddler.com`. It is strongly recommended that you only download Fiddler from this official source, as some unscrupulous websites have repackaged the program using installers that will also install unwanted software (for instance adware or browser toolbars).

System Requirements

Fiddler is supported on all versions of Windows from XP to Windows 8. The only prerequisite to installing Fiddler is having the Microsoft .NET Framework version 2 or later installed. The .NET Framework is present by default on Windows Vista or later, and can be installed using WindowsUpdate on Windows XP. If your system has only .NET 4 installed (for instance, most Windows 8 systems do not have .NET 2.0, 3.0, or 3.5 installed) you will need to download the "Fiddler4" package which is compiled to run natively on the .NET v4 CLR. Like most .NET programs, Fiddler will run in 32bit mode on 32bit systems and 64bit mode on 64bit systems. Fiddler runs best on 64bit systems, even those with less than 4 gigabytes of RAM.

While not required, having Internet Explorer 9 or later installed provides Fiddler with a bit of extra functionality and is strongly recommended. In particular, when IE9+ is installed, Fiddler's WebView Inspector can display additional media types, and you will be able to see traffic sent to `http://localhost` without additional configuration steps. Additionally, a configuration change can be made to Internet Explorer to indicate, via the `X-Download-Initiator` request header, why each request was issued.

A basic install of Fiddler requires less than 5 megabytes of disk space, while installing the most popular additional plugins will require another 5 megabytes or so. Fiddler will run on systems with 512 megabytes of RAM, but performance dramatically improves on systems with 2 gigabytes or more of memory.

Installing Fiddler

Fiddler's installer is simple—you'll be asked to accept the terms of the End User License Agreement (short summary: don't do anything illegal, and keep in mind that I offer no warranties) and then to select a folder to which Fiddler will be installed. You should accept the default folder location unless there's a strong reason not too—some Fiddler add-ons will blindly assume Fiddler is in the default location and will not install properly if it's not. The default location is `%ProgramFiles%\Fiddler2`, which on most systems will be `C:\Program Files\Fiddler2\`, or `C:\Program Files (x86)\Fiddler2\` for 64bit systems. Fiddler installs to the 32bit Program Files folder only because the installer technology is 32bit-- Fiddler itself will run in 64bit mode if the operating system supports it.

After a successful install, a web page will open providing key information about getting started with Fiddler. The tool itself can be launched using the Start Menu or the Fiddler icon in your browser toolbar or menu. Alternatively, you can type `fiddler2` in the **Windows+R** Run prompt.

Permissions and XCOPY Deployment

Fiddler requires Administrative permissions to install because it updates machine-wide folder and registry locations. If you don't have administrative permissions on a target machine, you can perform what is commonly called an **XCOPY Deployment**. Simply install Fiddler on a different computer, then copy the %ProgramFiles%\Fiddler2\ folder to the target machine or a USB key. While some Fiddler entry points will not be available (e.g. the Internet Explorer toolbar button and the FiddlerHook extension for Firefox), Fiddler itself will run successfully.

Updating Fiddler

On startup, Fiddler is configured to make a web-service request to determine if a new version of the tool is available. If a new version is found, you will be provided with an update notice.

If you choose **Yes**, Fiddler launches your browser to download the latest setup program; after closing Fiddler, you can run the setup program yourself. If you instead choose **Next Time**, the next time you start Fiddler, it will automatically download and install the latest version. If you choose **No**, the prompt closes and no new version is installed; the next time you start Fiddler, you will again be notified of the new version.

Installing Fiddler updates as they become available is strongly recommended, as each update typically adds features, improves performance, and removes bugs. At present, Fiddler Extensions do not participate in the auto-update feature, so you should periodically look for new versions of the Extensions you use on their developers' websites.

Administrators may prevent users from using the **Help** > **Check for Updates** command. To do so, use the Windows Registry Editor to create a new REG_STRING value named BlockUpdateCheck with value True inside the registry key HKLM\SOFTWARE\Microsoft\Fiddler2.

Uninstalling Fiddler

If you later wish to uninstall Fiddler, you can do so using the **Add/Remove Programs** applet in your Windows Control Panel. Uninstalling Fiddler leaves your settings intact and therefore is not a means to resolve any configuration problems you may encounter. Instead, see the **Troubleshooting** section in the appendix of this book for more help.

THE FIDDLER USER-INTERFACE

The Fiddler User-Interface can be overwhelming because it exposes a great deal of information about web traffic and it offers a significant degree of customizability.

On the left side of the Fiddler window is the **Web Sessions** list, and on the right a set of tabbed **Views** that display information about the Sessions which are selected in the Web Sessions list. Above these, the **Main Menu** and **Toolbar** offer quick access to common operations. At the bottom, the **Status Bar** shows key information and exposes important commands. Just below the Web Sessions list is a small command line box called **QuickExec** that permits rapid filtering and command invocation capabilities.

Tips:

- Many UI controls have context menus. Right-click early and often.

- If the mouse cursor turns into a pointing hand, the UI element can be clicked.

- Standard keyboard shortcuts are broadly supported (Use CTRL+C to copy, CTRL+A to select all, CTRL+G to go to a specific line number, F3 to perform a search).

- If a popup message box is shown, pressing CTRL+C will copy its text to the clipboard.

- Press the ESC key to dismiss dialog boxes or clear search boxes.

- To reset Fiddler's UI to its default layout, hold the SHIFT key while starting Fiddler.

- Remove a tab from the Views by middle-clicking the tab title.

- Double-click on a splitter to maximize the display area next to the splitter.

The Web Sessions List

The Web Sessions list is the most important feature of Fiddler—it displays a short summary of each Session that Fiddler has captured. Most operations in Fiddler begin by selecting one or more entries in the Web

Sessions list and then activating other features. To select more than one Session, hold the CTRL or SHIFT keys while clicking the desired rows. Double-click or press Enter to activate the default **Inspectors** for a single selected Session. When the Inspectors are activated, they will automatically decide which Inspector is best suited to display the selected Session's request and response.

Certain key information is displayed in the columns of the Web Sessions list, including:

- **#** – An identification number generated by Fiddler.
- **Result** – The status code from the response.
- **Protocol** – The protocol (HTTP/HTTPS/FTP) used by the Session.
- **Host** – The hostname and port of the server to which the request was sent.
- **URL** – The URL path, file, and query string from the request.
- **Body** – The number of bytes in the response body.
- **Caching** – Values from the Response's Expires and Cache-Control headers.
- **Content-Type** – The Content-Type header from the response.
- **Process** – The local Windows Process from which the traffic originated.
- **Custom** – Shows any ui-CustomColumn flag value set by FiddlerScript.
- **Comments** – Shows any comment set using the toolbar's Comment button.

You can resize and reorder the columns in the Web Sessions list by adjusting or dragging the column headers. To sort the entries in the Web Sessions list by the values in a specified column, click on that column's header. New columns may be added to the Web Sessions list using FiddlerScript, Extensions, or the QuickExec box.

Understanding Icons and Colors

The default text coloring of each row in the Web Sessions list derives from the HTTP Status (red for errors, yellow for authentication demands), traffic type (CONNECTs appear in grey), or response type (CSS in purple, HTML in blue; script in green, images in grey). You can override the font color by setting the Session's ui-color flag from FiddlerScript.

Each row is also marked with an icon for quick reference as to the Session's progress, Request type, or Response type:

⬆	The Request is being sent to the server.
⬇	The Response is being downloaded from the server.
📋	The Request is paused at a breakpoint to allow tampering.
📋	The Response is paused at a breakpoint to allow tampering.

	The Request used the HEAD or OPTIONS methods, or returned a HTTP/204 status code. The HEAD and OPTIONS methods allow the client to acquire information about the target URL or server without actually downloading the specified content. The HTTP/204 status code indicates that there is no response body for the specified URL.
	The Request used the POST method to send data to the server.
	The Response is HTML content.
	The Response is an image file.
	The Response is a script file.
	The Response is a Cascading Style Sheet (CSS) file.
	The Response is formatted as Extensible Markup Language (XML).
	The Response is formatted using JavaScript Object Notation (JSON).
	The Response is an audio file.
	The Response is a video file.
	The Response is a Silverlight applet.
	The Response is a Flash applet.
	The Response is a font file.
	The Response's Content-Type is not a type for which a more specific icon is available.
	The Request used the CONNECT method. This method is used to establish a tunnel through which encrypted HTTPS traffic flows.
	The Session wraps a HTML5 WebSocket connection.
	The Response is a HTTP/3xx class redirect.
	The Response is a HTTP/401 or HTTP/407 demand for client credentials, or a HTTP/403 error indicating that access was denied.
	The Response has a HTTP/4xx or HTTP/5xx error status code.
	The Session was aborted by the client application, Fiddler, or the Server. This commonly occurs when the client browser began downloading of a page, but the user then navigated to a different page. The client browser responds by cancelling all in-progress requests, leading to the Aborted Session state.
	The Response is a HTTP/206 partial response. Such responses are returned as a result of the client performing a Range request for only a portion of the file at the target URL.
	The Response is a HTTP/304 status to indicate that the client's cached copy is fresh.

The Web Session is unlocked, enabling modification after normal session processing has been completed.

Keyboard Reference

The following keyboard shortcuts are supported by the Web Sessions list:

Spacebar	Activate and scroll the currently-focused session into view.
CTRL+A	Select all sessions.
ESC	Unselect all sessions.
CTRL+I	Invert selection; selected sessions are unselected and vice versa.
CTRL+X	Remove all sessions (subject to the `fiddler.ui.CtrlX.KeepMarked` preference.)
Delete	Remove selected sessions.
Shift+Delete	Remove all unselected sessions.
R	Replay the current request
SHIFT+R	Replay the current request multiple times (specified in the subsequent prompt).
U	Unconditionally replay the current request, sending no `If-Modified-Since` and `If-None-Match` headers.
SHIFT+U	Unconditionally replay the current request multiple times (the count is specified in the subsequent prompt).
P	Attempt to select the "parent" request that triggered this request and set focus to it. This feature depends on the HTTP `Referer` header's value.
C	Attempt to select all "child" requests that were provoked by this response. This feature depends on the HTTP `Referer` header's value or the `Location` header on a redirect.
D	Select all "duplicate" requests that have the same request method and URL as the current session.
ALT+Enter	View the current Session's properties.
SHIFT+Enter	Launch Inspectors for this session in a new Fiddler window.
Backspace or "Back" mouse button	Activate the previously selected session.
Insert	Toggle marking of the selected sessions using a bold red font.
CTRL+1 CTRL+2 CTRL+3 CTRL+4 CTRL+5 CTRL+6	Mark the selected sessions in bold and one of the colors red, blue, gold, green, orange, or purple.
M	Add a comment to selected Sessions.

Web Sessions Context Menu

Right-clicking on the column headers at the top of the Web Sessions list offers a context menu with two options:

Ensure all columns are visible	Ensures that all columns are visible by resizing each to at least 30 pixels wide.
Learn about configuring columns...	Opens a help topic which explains how to add new columns to the Web Sessions list.

Right-clicking in the body of the Web Sessions list shows a large context menu. Many of the options are available only if one or more sessions are selected in the Web Sessions list. This menu can be extended by FiddlerScript, so it will often contain additional commands that are not listed here.

The **AutoScroll Session List** option controls whether or not Fiddler automatically scrolls to the bottom of the Web Sessions list as new sessions are added.

The **Copy** submenu enables you to copy the information of your choice from the sessions selected in the Web Sessions list:

Just Url	Copies the Urls of the selected Sessions to the clipboard, one per line. You may also invoke this command by pressing CTRL+U when focus is in the Web Sessions list.
This column	Copies the text in the column over which the context menu was opened. The text for each of the selected Sessions is added to the clipboard, one per line.
Terse summary	Copies a terse summary of the selected Sessions to the clipboard. This summary includes the Request Method and URL, and the responses' status codes and status text. If a response is a HTTP/3xx redirect, the text will include the target Location header. You may also invoke this command by pressing CTRL+SHIFT+T when focus is in the Web Sessions list.
Headers only	Copies Sessions' headers to the clipboard. The text is copied in both plaintext and HTML formats, so you will see different results if you paste into an editor that handles only plain text (e.g. notepad) versus one that handles rich text (e.g. Microsoft Word). As this is the "default" command, double clicking on the Copy submenu itself will invoke a header copy. You may also invoke this command by pressing CTRL+SHIFT+C when focus is in the Web Sessions list.
Session	Copies complete Sessions to the clipboard. The text is copied in both plaintext and HTML formats, so you will see different results if you paste into an editor that handles only plain text versus one that handles rich text. You may also invoke this command by pressing CTRL+SHIFT+S when focus is in the Web Sessions list.
Full Summary	Copies the information shown in the Web Sessions list to the clipboard. The columns are delimited by tabs which enables you to paste this information into Microsoft Excel or other programs neatly. You may also invoke this command by pressing CTRL+C when focus is in the Web Sessions list.

The **Save** submenu exposes options that allow you to save traffic to files:

All Sessions	Saves all sessions in the Web Sessions list to a SAZ file.

...and Open as Local File		Saves the selected sessions' response bodies to individual files, then opens each file in the registered handler for the response's file type. If you hold the CTRL key while invoking this option, Windows will prompt you to select which application to use to open the file.
Selected Sessions	In ArchiveZip	Saves Sessions selected in the Web Sessions list to a SAZ file.
	As Text	Saves selected Sessions to a single text file.
	As Text (Headers only)	Saves the selected Sessions' request and response headers to a single text file.
Request	Entire Request	Saves the selected Sessions' request headers and bodies to individual files.
	Request Body	Saves the selected Sessions' request bodies to individual files.
Response	Entire Response	Saves the selected sessions' response headers and bodies to individual files. This option is useful if you would like to create responses file that you can later play back using the AutoResponder.
	Response Body	Saves the selected sessions' request bodies to individual files. This option is useful if you would like to open the response body (say, an image) in another program that would be confused by the presence of HTTP response headers.

The **Remove Submenu** allows you to remove All, Selected, or Unselected Sessions from the Web Sessions list. The CTRL+X, Delete, or Shift+Delete keys may be used to activate these commands when focus is in the Web Sessions list.

The **Comment...** menu command allows you to add or update the Comment field for one or more selected Web Sessions.

The **Mark** submenu allows you to select a color to mark the Sessions selected in the Web Sessions list. The font of the Sessions will be bolded and colored according to your choice. The **Unmark** option will unbold the selected Sessions and revert their font color to the default.

The **Replay** submenu offers commands that replay the currently selected requests.

Reissue Requests	Reissues the selected requests as they were originally sent. If you hold SHIFT while invoking this command, Fiddler will prompt you for the number of times the requests should be repeated. You may invoke this command by pressing the R key in the Web Sessions list.
Reissue Unconditionally	Unconditionally replay the selected requests, sending no If-Modified-Since and If-None-Match headers to prevent the server from returning a HTTP/304 response. If you hold SHIFT while invoking this command, Fiddler will prompt you for the number of times the requests should be repeated. You may invoke this command by

	pressing the U key in the Web Sessions list.
Reissue and Edit	Reissues the selected requests as they were originally sent, setting a request break-point on each new Session to allow you to use Fiddler's Inspectors to modify the requests before they are sent to the server.
Revisit in IE	For each selected request, navigates to the request URL in Internet Explorer. Note that Internet Explorer will always navigate using a GET request and its own headers and cookies, regardless of what HTTP methods and headers were captured on the sessions you are replaying.

The **Select** submenu allows you to use your currently-selected session to select other sessions:

Parent Request	The Parent Request option will attempt to use this request's Referer header and request ID to determine what session, if any, was responsible for this request being sent. For instance, if you invoke this command on a JavaScript request, the Session selected will typically be the HTML page that caused this JavaScript file to be downloaded. Pressing the P key while focus is in the Web Sessions list will also invoke this command.
Child Requests	The Child Requests option will attempt to use this request's URL and request ID to select any requests sent as a result of this response. For instance, if you invoke this command on a HTML Session, the Sessions selected will typically be the CSS, JS, and image files mentioned in the HTML markup. Pressing the C key while focus is in the Web Sessions list will also invoke this command.
Duplicate Requests	Selects all sessions in the Web Sessions list which share the currently selected session's URL and HTTP method.

The **Compare** command is available only when two sessions are selected in the Web Sessions list. Selecting this command will save the sessions to two temporary files and then launch the configured comparison tool to allow you to compare the requests and responses.

The **COMETPeek** command will take a "snapshot" of an in-progress response, allowing you to inspect a partial response before it has been completed. This command is useful in cases where a web application is using the COMET pattern to return a never-ending stream of data to the client. Since the stream is, by-definition, without end, Fiddler wouldn't otherwise be able to show the response until the server terminates the connection.

The **Abort Session** command will terminate the client and server connections for an in-progress request.

The **Clone Response** command is only available when two sessions are selected in the Web Sessions list and one of the Sessions is currently paused at a breakpoint and the other Session is completed. The command will copy the response from the completed Session to the paused Session. This feature enables you to easily replicate a previously captured (or modified) response to satisfy a later request.

The **Unlock for Editing** menu command unlocks a single selected Session, allowing you to edit the completed Session's request and response using the Inspectors. You may invoke this command by pressing F2 when focus is in the Web Sessions list.

The **Inspect in New Window** command opens a Session Inspector window which allows you to view the session's request, response, and properties in a standalone window.

The **Properties...** command opens the Session Properties window which displays information about the currently selected Session, including its timers, session flags, and information about how the request was routed.

FIDDLER'S MAIN MENU

The main menu is designed to provide access to almost all of Fiddler's functionality. The menu system can be augmented by FiddlerScript or Extensions, but in this section, we'll discuss only Fiddler's default menu commands.

The File Menu

The File menu contains commands to start and stop Fiddler's capture of web traffic, as well as to load and store captured traffic.

The **Capture Traffic** toggle controls whether Fiddler is registered as the system proxy. When Fiddler is registered as the system proxy, applications that respect the WinINET proxy settings (e.g. Internet Explorer and many other browsers) will send their web requests to Fiddler. The FiddlerHook add-on for Firefox also respects this menu option. Even when it is not registered as the system proxy, Fiddler will continue to display and process any requests that are received.

The **Load Archive** item allows you to reload previously-captured traffic stored in a SAZ file.

The **Save** submenu exposes options that allow you to save traffic to files; the options on this menu are the same as those on the Web Sessions list's context menu.

The **Import Sessions...** menu command enables you to import previously-captured traffic from another tool or file format.

The **Export Sessions** menu allows you to export sessions captured by Fiddler to many different file formats. You may choose **All Sessions...** or **Selected Sessions...** from this submenu.

The **Exit** menu command will unregister Fiddler as the system proxy and close the tool.

The Edit Menu

Most of the commands on the Edit menu apply to the currently-selected Sessions in the Web Sessions menu, and thus most of the commands are disabled unless one or more Sessions are selected.

The **Copy Submenu** enables you to copy the information of your choice from the Sessions selected in the Web Sessions list. The commands on this menu are the same as those on the Web Sessions list's context menu.

The **Remove Submenu** allows you to remove All, Selected, or Unselected Sessions from the Web Sessions list. The CTRL+X, Delete, or Shift+Delete key combinations may be used to activate these commands when focus is in the Web Sessions list.

The **Select All** command selects all entries in the Web Sessions list. You may invoke this command by pressing CTRL+A when the focus is in the Web Sessions list.

The **Paste Files as Sessions** command will generate one or more mock Web Sessions based on the contents of the clipboard.

If the clipboard contains text and a DataURI can be found starting within the first 64 characters of the text, the DataURI will be parsed out of the markup and a new Session will be created and added to the Web Sessions list. This feature is very useful when you are using Fiddler to examine markup containing a DataURI-encoded image, and you want to see what the image looks like. Simply copy the DataURI from the markup and use the **Paste Files as Sessions** command to generate a new Session that you can then inspect using the ImageView Inspector.

If the clipboard contains a binary image (for instance, if you've used Alt+PrintScrn hotkey to take a screenshot of the active window) that image will be used to generate and add a mock Session to the Web Sessions list.

If the clipboard contains one or more files (e.g. copied from Windows Explorer) each file will be used to generate a mock Session that is added to the Web Sessions list. This feature is most useful when you are building a SAZ file to send to someone else and want to include a file that was not transmitted over the network. For instance, a web developer could use this option to include the source code behind a given ASPX page when sending a SAZ file of the output of that page as captured by Fiddler.

The **Mark** submenu allows you to choose a color to mark the selected Sessions in the Web Sessions list. The font of the Sessions will be bolded and colored according to your choice. The **Unmark** option will unbold the Sessions and reset their font color to the default.

The **Unlock for Editing** menu command unlocks a single selected Web Session, allowing you to edit the completed Session's request and response using the Inspectors. You may invoke this command by pressing F2 when focus is in the Web Sessions list.

The **Find Sessions...** command opens the Find Sessions window to begin a search of captured traffic. You may press CTRL+F to invoke this command.

The Rules Menu

The Rules menu is easily extensible, and most of its commands are generated from the FiddlerScript file.

The **Hide Image Requests** toggle controls whether Sessions that returned images are shown in the Web Sessions list.

The **Hide CONNECTs** toggle controls whether Sessions that use the CONNECT request method are shown in the Web Sessions list. The CONNECT method is used by a client to establish a "raw" connection to a server, to carry either HTTPS or WebSocket traffic.

The **Automatic Breakpoints** submenu allows you to control whether Fiddler automatically breaks **Before Requests** or **After Responses**. The **Ignore Image** toggle controls whether these breakpoints are applied to requests for images.

The **Customize Rules...** menu command will open your current FiddlerScript file using the configured script editor.

When checked, the **Require Proxy Authentication** menu item will respond to any request that doesn't submit a `Proxy-Authorization` header by returning a `HTTP/407` response demanding proxy credentials. This rule is useful for testing HTTP clients to ensure that they work properly in environments with authenticating proxy servers.

When checked, the **Apply GZIP Encoding** menu item will apply GZIP HTTP compression to all responses except images, so long as the request contained an `Accept-Encoding` header that included the `gzip` token. This rule is useful to test that clients that advertise GZIP support can actually decompress content. It also allows you to experiment with the performance and bytes-on-wire count for compressed traffic.

When checked, the **Remove All Encodings** toggle removes all HTTP Content-Encodings and Transfer-Encodings from requests and responses. This rule is also exposed by the **Decode** button on the Fiddler toolbar.

The remainder of the commands on this menu are provided by FiddlerScript, and thus your menu's commands may differ from the commands from those in the default FiddlerScript. You can examine the implementation of these commands (and add your own) by clicking the **Customize Rules...** option in the Rules menu.

The **Hide 304s** option hides all Sessions whose responses bear the `HTTP/304 Not Modified` status.

The **Request Japanese Content** option will set or replace all requests' `Accept-Encoding` header with the `ja` token, indicating that the client would like responses in the Japanese language.

The **User-Agents** submenu allows you to set or replace all requests' `User-Agent` header with a specified value. You can select among the values provided, or use the **Custom...** option at the bottom of the menu to specify any value you like.

Performance Submenu
The **Performance** submenu exposes simple options that impact web performance.

When enabled, the **Simulate Modem Speeds** option will set Flags on all subsequent sessions. The `request-trickle-delay` flag is set to 300 to delay all sends by 300ms per kilobyte uploaded. The `response-trickle-delay` flag is set to 150 to delay all sends by 150ms/kb downloaded.

When set, the **Disable Caching** option will remove all `If-None-Match` and `If-Modified-Since` request headers and add a `Pragma: no-cache` request header. It will also remove any `Expires` header on the response and set the `Cache-Control` response header to `no-cache`. This option cannot prevent a browser from reusing a previously cached response that was received *before* this option was enabled. Clear your browser's cache (`CTRL+SHIFT+DELETE`) after enabling this option for best results.

The **Show Time-to-Last-Byte** will display the number of milliseconds that it took to receive the entire response in the Web Sessions list's **Custom** column.

Similarly, **Show Response Timestamp** will show the timestamp at which the server's response was completely received by Fiddler in the Web Sessions list's **Custom** column.

The **Cache Always Fresh** option will automatically respond to any conditional HTTP request with a `HTTP/304` response indicating that the client's cache is up-to-date. This option can dramatically improve performance when visiting sites that fail to set cache expiration dates properly. Pressing `CTRL+F5` in the browser is usually enough to force a reload from the server in spite of this option, because browsers will omit the `If-Modified-Since` and `If-None-Match` headers on forced-refresh requests.

The Tools Menu

The **Fiddler Options…** item opens the Fiddler Options window.

The **WinINET Options…** item opens the Internet Explorer Internet Options window.

The **Clear WinINET Cache** item will clear all files in the WinINET cache that is used by Internet Explorer and many other applications.

The **Clear WinINET Cookies** item will clear all persistent WinINET cookies sent by Internet Explorer and many other applications. Session cookies will remain unaffected.

The **TextWizard…** item launches the TextWizard window to permit encoding and decoding of text.

The **Compare Sessions** item is enabled only if two sessions are selected in the Web Sessions list. When clicked, a differencing tool will be used to compare the two Sessions.

The **HOSTS…** item opens Fiddler's Host Remapping tool.

The View Menu

The **Squish Session List** toggle controls whether the Web Sessions list is collapsed horizontally, giving you more room to view Inspectors and other tabs. You can toggle this setting by pressing the F6 key.

The **Stacked Layout** list reorganizes the Fiddler user-interface such that the Web Sessions list appears atop the tabs. This can be useful when you have added a lot of custom columns and want more space to see those columns.

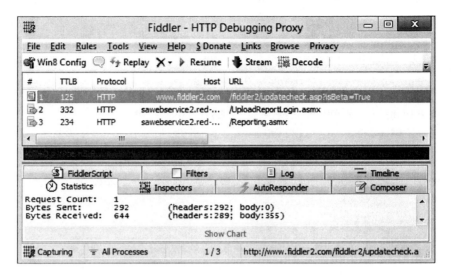

The **Show Toolbar** toggle controls whether the Fiddler toolbar is visible.

The **Statistics** item activates the Statistics tab; you can invoke this command by pressing F7.

The **Inspectors** item activates the Inspectors tab; you can invoke this command by pressing F8.

The **Composer** item activates the Composer tab; you can invoke this command by pressing F9.

The **Minimize to Tray** option or CTRL+M will minimize Fiddler to the system tray.

The **Stay on Top** option will force Fiddler on top of all other windows.

The **AutoScroll Session List** option controls whether or not Fiddler automatically scrolls to the bottom of the Web Sessions list as new sessions are added.

The **Refresh** option and the F5 key refresh the information for the currently selected Sessions in the Inspectors or Statistics tab.

The Help Menu

The **Fiddler Help** menu item will open your web browser and navigate to the help homepage for Fiddler. You can access this item by pressing the F1 key.

The **Fiddler Community Discussions** link opens your browser to the Fiddler discussion group, currently hosted by Google Groups.

The **HTTP References** item opens a page with links to various references, including RFC2616.

When you enable the **Troubleshoot Filters...** option, traffic that would otherwise be hidden is instead shown in a strikethrough font. The **Comments** column indicates which of Fiddler's filters was responsible for attempting to hide the traffic. If you ever find that traffic is "missing" from Fiddler's Web Sessions list, this command is your best bet for resolving the problem.

The **Check for Updates...** option contacts a web service to determine whether you're running the latest version of Fiddler. If you are not, you can install the newest version immediately or the next time Fiddler starts.

The **Send Feedback** option composes an email message to my email address.

The **About Fiddler** option opens a window showing the current Fiddler version.

Fiddler's About Box

At the top, the window shows information about the running version of Fiddler, including its version number, whether it's a beta version, and when it was compiled.

The next paragraph indicates whether Fiddler is running in 32bit or 64bit mode, and how much **Virtual Memory** and **Working Set** it is currently using. Below that, find the loaded version of the Microsoft .NET Framework, and the current Windows version information.

Next, you'll see a counter recording the number of times you've started Fiddler.

Below that, you'll see the hostname and port that Fiddler is currently using on your computer. The **Listening to** line shows the network connectoids on which Fiddler is registered. The **Gateway** line shows information about any upstream proxy server.

Lastly, you'll see my contact and copyright information.

You may press Escape or Spacebar to close the window. Hit CTRL+C to copy all of the text, or select a desired subset of the text with your mouse and press CTRL+C to copy only that text.

FIDDLER'S TOOLBAR

The Fiddler toolbar provides quick access to popular commands and settings.

◯ ✦ Replay ✕ ▾ ▷ Resume | ↓ Stream ⋇ Decode | Keep: All sessions ▾ ⊕ Any Process 🔍 Find

🖫 Save | 📷 🌐 Browse 🔷 Clear Cache ✂ TextWizard | 🗗 Tearoff | MSDN Search... ⊙ 🖥 Online ✕

The buttons and their functions are:

Comment	Click to add a Comment to all selected Sessions. The comment appears in a column of the Web Sessions list.
Replay	Click to reissue the selected requests to the server again. Hold the CTRL key while clicking to reissue the requests without any Conditional Request headers (e.g. If-Modified-Since and If-None-Match). Hold the SHIFT key while clicking to be prompted to specify the number of times each request should be reissued.
Remove	Shows a menu of options for removing Sessions from the Web Sessions list: • **Remove all** removes all Sessions from the list. • **Images** removes all Sessions that returned an image. • **CONNECTs** removes all CONNECT tunnels. • **Non-200s** removes all non-HTTP/200 responses. • **Non-Browser** removes all requests that were not issued by a web browser. • **Complete and Unmarked** removes Sessions which are in the Done or Aborted state and which are unmarked and have no Comment set. • **Duplicate response bodies** removes any Session which has no response body or has a response body which was received in an earlier Session in the list.
Resume	Resumes all sessions which are currently paused at a Request or Response breakpoint.
Stream	Enable the Stream toggle to disable response buffering for all responses except those for which a breakpoint was set.
Decode	Enable the Decode toggle to remove all HTTP Content and Transfer encodings from requests and responses.
Keep: *value*	The Keep dropdown controls how many Sessions are stored in the Web Sessions list. When the count is reached, Fiddler will begin removing older Sessions to attempt to limit the list to the desired value. Incomplete Sessions and those with comments, markers, or open Inspector windows are not removed.
Process Filter	Drag and drop the Process Filter icon to an application to create a Filter which hides all traffic except for that which originates from the selected process. Right-click the Process Filter icon to clear a previously set filter.
Find	Opens the Find Sessions window.
Save	Saves all Sessions to a SAZ file.
Camera	Adds a JPEG-formatted screenshot of the current desktop to the Web Sessions list.
Browse	If one session is selected, opens Internet Explorer to the target URL. If zero or multiple Sessions are selected, opens Internet Explorer to about:blank.
Clear Cache	Clears the WinINET caches. Hold CTRL while clicking to also purge persistent cookies stored by WinINET.

TextWizard	Opens the Text Encoding / Decoding Wizard which can be used to transform text between various encodings.
Tearoff	Creates a new window into which all Views are placed; the Web Sessions list expands to the full width of the main Fiddler window.
MSDN Search	Perform a search in the Web Content area of MSDN.
Help	Opens Fiddler's help.
Online Indicator	Indicates whether the system is currently online or offline. When online, hovering over the indicator will show a tooltip containing the local computer's hostname and IP addresses. Double-click the indicator to open the system's Network Connections control panel.
X	Removes the toolbar. To restore the toolbar later, click **View > Show Toolbar.**

You can hover over any element of the toolbar to show a tooltip that tersely explains the element's function. You can reorganize the toolbar by holding the ALT key and dragging individual toolbar elements to a new location. However, these changes are not currently saved and are reset when Fiddler restarts.

If you're using Fiddler on a small display, the shortened toolbar will overflow some of the commands into a dropdown menu on the far right. If you'd like, you may set the preference `fiddler.ui.toolbar` `.ShowLabels` to `false` to prevent the toolbar's text labels from showing, decreasing the toolbar's width.

Fiddler's Status Bar

The status bar along the bottom of Fiddler's main window shows a set of panels that display information about the current Fiddler configuration. Several of these panels can be clicked to quickly change the configuration. From the left, the panels are:

Capturing Indication	Indicates whether Fiddler is currently configured as the system proxy. Click the panel to toggle the capturing state.
Process-based Filter	Indicates whether Fiddler is currently configured to capture traffic from only one type of process. Click the panel to show a menu of process-type filtering options.
Breakpoint Indicator	Indicates whether Fiddler is configured to breakpoint all requests, all responses, or neither. Click the panel to quickly toggle breakpoint functionality.
Session Counter	Indicates the number of entries in the Web Sessions list. If one or more Sessions are selected, the indicator will show the number of Sessions selected and the total number of Sessions, e.g. "2 / 5".
Status Information	By default, shows the URL of the first selected Session. This panel is also used to show succinct information about the results of actions; for instance, when a SAZ file is loaded or saved, that fact is mentioned here.

QuickExec

The QuickExec box below the Web Sessions list provides quick keyboard access to common operations. Use the Alt+Q hotkey to set focus to the QuickExec box when Fiddler is active—if Fiddler isn't active, first press CTRL+ALT+F to activate the Fiddler window.

While QuickExec is focused, pressing CTRL+I will insert the URL of the first selected Session in the Web Sessions list. You can also drag/drop one or more Sessions from the Web Sessions list to insert their URLs in the QuickExec box, or you can drag/drop one or more files from your file system to insert their file paths.

QuickExec Selection Commands
The QuickExec allows you to quickly select traffic of interest based on search criteria you specify. After typing a selection command, hitting Enter will set focus to the Web Sessions list if the search returned any matches.

Command	Action	Example
?search	Selects Sessions whose URLs contain the specified search text. This is the only *find-as-you-type* search feature in the QuickExec box. For ?-prefixed searches, hitting Enter will set focus to the Web Sessions list. All other search types require that you press Enter to begin the search.	? example.com/pathchars
select type	Selects Sessions whose response Content-Type header contains the chosen *type*.	select css select image/jp
select header-or-flag value	Select Sessions where the named *Header* or *SessionFlag* case-insensitively contains the specified *value* string. Unless preceded by a slash, asterisk means *any value*. Use * to match a literal asterisk.	select ui-comments slow select ui-bold * select ui-backcolor red select ui-comments * select @Request.Accept html select @Response.Set-Cookie domain
>size	Select Sessions whose response size is greater than *size* bytes. Note: the character "k" is converted to "000", allowing you to easily write bytes in	>40000000 >4000k >4KK

	kilobytes or even megabytes.	
<size	Select Sessions whose response size is less than *size* bytes. Note: the character "k" is converted to "000".	<5k
@host	Select Sessions whose request Host header contains the specified *host*.	@example.com @.gov
=ResponseCode	Select sessions where the response's status code matches the provided value.	=200 =404
=Method	Select sessions where the request's HTTP Method matches the provided value.	=GET =POST

Beyond the ability to select traffic, QuickExec also includes support for other commands:

cols add *flagname*
 	
cols add *title flagname*
	Adds (for this instance only) a new column to the Web Sessions list. The title parameter is optional; if not present, the column will be titled with the flagname parameter. The flagname can either represent a Session Flag, or a request or response header name.
	
	After a column is added, it will be filled automatically for all subsequent sessions. To update the columns of already completed Sessions, select the Sessions and hit F5.
		cols add x-clientIP
		
		cols add Server
		  @Response.Server
		
		cols add Accept
		  @Request.Accept

!listen *port* [*SubjectCN*]	Starts a new proxy listener object on the specified *port*. This listener's Sessions will be added to the Web Sessions list. The listener instance is automatically configured to permit remote connections. If the CN parameter is present, all inbound connections on this listener will automatically invoke a HTTPS handshake; Fiddler will present a certificate containing the specified *SubjectCN*. This feature is primarily useful when Fiddler is being used as a reverse proxy for a HTTPS site.	!listen 8889 !listen 4443 secure.example.com
!dns *hostname* !nslookup *hostname*	Performs a DNS lookup (or consults Fiddler's DNS Cache) for the specified *hostname*, and shows the results in the Log tab.	!dns www.example.com

`prefs show` `[substring]`	Displays all of Fiddler's configured Preferences in a message box. If a *substring* is provided, only preferences containing that substring will be shown.	`prefs show` `prefs show composer`
`prefs remove` *name*	Deletes a Preference with the specified *name*. The next time the Preference is consulted, the default value will be used.	`prefs remove` `fiddler.ui.font.size`

`prefs set` *name* *value*	Updates or creates a Preference with the specified *name* and *value*.	`prefs set`
		  `fiddler.differ.UltraDiff`
		  `False`

`prefs log`	Writes all of Fiddler's configured Preferences to the Log tab, enabling you to easily copy them.	
`!spew`	Toggles "DebugSpew" mode, which is primarily used for debugging problems with Fiddler itself. In DebugSpew mode, Fiddler will log verbose logging information (including all raw traffic) to the system's debug port. You can monitor this information using SysInternals' DebugView tool. Fiddler will also log some additional information to Fiddler's Log tab when in this mode. Type `!spew` again or restart Fiddler to disable DebugSpew.	
`about:cache`	Adds information about Fiddler's listening port number and the contents of its connection-reuse cache and DNS caches to the Log tab.	
`about:config`	Displays Fiddler's Preference configuration tab, which lists all configured preferences and their values.	
`about:connectoids` `about:network`	Adds information about the WinINET-configured connections to the Log tab.	
`toolbar`	Shows the Fiddler Toolbar if it was hidden.	
`tearoff`	Removes the Inspectors from the main Fiddler window and shows them in a floating window instead.	

If the command entered in QuickExec does not match any of the above intrinsic commands, FiddlerScript and Fiddler Extensions will have the opportunity to respond to the command.

Default FiddlerScript Commands

The default FiddlerScript file used by Fiddler adds a number of useful commands which can be launched from the QuickExec box.

Command	Action	Example
`bold` *urltext*	Applies font bolding to any future Session whose URL contains the specified text. Type `bold` with no parameter to disable this formatting.	`bold uploaddata.asp`
`bps` *status*	Creates a response breakpoint for any Session whose response status code matches the specified value. Type `bps` with no	`bps 404`

	parameter to disable the breakpoint.	
bpm *method*	Creates a request breakpoint for any Session whose HTTP Method matches the specified value. Type bpm with no parameter to disable the breakpoint.	bpm POST bpm OPTIONS
bpu *urltext*	Creates a request breakpoint for any Session whose URL contains the specified text. Type bpu with no parameter to disable the breakpoint.	bpu uploaddata.asp
bpafter *urltext*	Creates a response breakpoint for any session whose URL contains the specified text. Type bpafter with no parameter to disable the breakpoint.	bpafter dodownload.cgi
nuke	Clears the WinINET cache and cookies.	nuke
tail ####	Trims the Web Sessions list so that it contains no more than the specified number of Sessions.	tail 200
log *string*	Sends the specified text or macro to the Log tab.	log "At this point, requests start failing" log @Log.Save
cls	Clears the Web Sessions list.	cls
dump	Stores all captured traffic to dump.saz in the \Captures\ folder.	dump
g	Immediately resumes all Sessions currently paused at breakpoints.	g
help	Shows online help for QuickExec.	help
urlreplace *oldtext newtext*	Replaces the specified substring in later requests' URLs with the provided string. Type urlreplace with no parameters to stop replacements.	urlreplace jQuery.min jQuery.dbg

overridehost *oldhost newhost*	Retargets requests so that they are sent to a different host. Type overridehost with no parameters to stop this retargeting.	overridehost
		  production.example.com
		  dev.internal.example.com

start	Enables capturing mode, registering Fiddler as the system proxy.	start
stop	Disables capturing mode, unregistering Fiddler as the system proxy.	stop
keeponly *MIMEtype*	Clears the Web Sessions list of all Sessions whose responses do not specify the supplied MIMEtype.	keeponly video/
quit	Exits Fiddler. This command exists to permit the ExecAction.exe automation utility to request that Fiddler cleanly shutdown.	quit

You can see the full list of FiddlerScript commands (and add your own) by editing your FiddlerScript. Simply click **Rules** > **Customize Rules**, and scroll to the OnExecAction method.

Extensions may add support for additional commands to the QuickExec box — check your extensions' documentation for more information.

Application Hotkeys

The QuickExec feature provides powerful keyboard support, but Fiddler offers additional hotkeys for keyboard lovers.

Fiddler registers a system-wide hotkey, CTRL+ALT+F to activate Fiddler regardless of what application is active. This hotkey may be changed to another using the **Tools > Fiddler Options > General** tab.

Beyond its global hotkey, Fiddler supports a number of hotkeys that should always be available when Fiddler is active:

ALT+Q	Set focus to the QuickExec box
CTRL+R	Open the FiddlerScript rules editor
CTRL+E	Open the TextWizard
CTRL+Down	Select the next session in the Web Sessions list
CTRL+Up	Select the previous session in the Web Sessions list
CTRL+T	Activate the TextView Inspectors
CTRL+H	Activate the HeaderView Inspectors
CTRL+0	Set the font size to 8.25pt (the default)
CTRL+Plus	Increase the font size by 1pt (up to 32pt)
CTRL+Minus	Decrease the font size by 1pt (down to 7pt)
CTRL+M	Minimize Fiddler
CTRL+SHIFT+DEL	Clear the WinINET cache
F12	Toggle registration as the system proxy

STATISTICS TAB

Fiddler's Statistics tab shows basic information about the currently selected Web Sessions. Textual information is shown at the top of the tab, while the bottom contains a pie chart showing a MIME-type breakdown of the traffic.

When multiple sessions are selected, the data shown includes:

Request Count	The number of Sessions selected.
Unique Hosts	The count of unique hosts to which this traffic was sent. This field will not be shown if all selected traffic was sent to the same server.
Bytes sent	Total number of outbound bytes in the HTTP Request headers and bodies. The number of bytes for each is shown parenthetically after the total count.
Bytes received	Total number of inbound bytes in the HTTP Request headers and bodies. The number of bytes for each is shown parenthetically after the total count.
Requests started at	The time that the first byte of the first request was received by Fiddler.
Responses completed at	The time that the last byte of the last response was sent by Fiddler to the client application.
Sequence (clock) duration	The "clock time" between the start of the first request and the end of the last response.
Aggregate session duration	The summation of each selected Session's overall time from request to response. Because sessions are usually running in parallel, this time can be longer than the amount of "clock time" taken. Similarly, because Sessions may be selected that were started and finished with idle time between them, this time can be much shorter than the amount of "clock time" between the first and last request.
DNS Lookup time	The total amount of time spent in DNS resolution for all selected Sessions. This field is not shown if no time was spent on DNS resolution because the DNS cache served all requests, or all connections had already been established.
TCP/IP Connect duration	The total amount of time spent in establishing TCP/IP connections for all selected Sessions. This field is not shown if no time was spent on TCP/IP connections because all requests occurred on reused connections.
HTTPS Handshake duration	The total amount of time spent in HTTPS handshaking for all selected Sessions. This field is not shown if no time was spent on HTTPS handshakes because all sessions were HTTP, decryption is disabled, or all requests occurred on already-secured connections.

Response Codes	The count of each unique HTTP response code among the selected Sessions.
Response Bytes by Content-Type	The count of bytes for each response Content-Type in the selected Sessions. This information is also presented in a pie chart at the bottom of the tab.
Estimated Performance	Very rough estimates of how long the selected traffic would spend on the network from different locales or when utilizing a variety of connection types. This data is simply calculated by looking at the number and size of the selected Sessions. There are many factors that impact real-world network performance, so the estimates shown here may be wildly inaccurate.

If only a single Session is selected, the Timers for that Session are shown. If the selected Session was recorded on a previous day, the date that the traffic was captured will also be listed-- this can be helpful when examining SAZ files captured by automated logging tools.

If a single CONNECT tunnel is selected, the number of bytes sent and received on that tunnel will be shown (unless the tunnel is configured for HTTPS decryption, in which case this information can be inferred from the decrypted HTTPS Sessions in the Web Sessions list.)

The bottom of the tab contains a pie chart which is hidden by default. Click the **Show Chart** link to show a chart of the selected Sessions. A slice is shown for the headers and each MIME type in the selected traffic; the size of the slice is based on the number of bytes of that type.

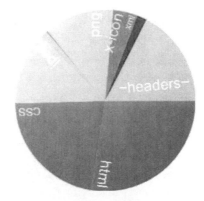

The **Copy this chart** link at the bottom-left copies the chart image to your clipboard as a bitmap, suitable for pasting into reports or presentations.

THE FILTERS TAB

The Filters tab provides a "point-and-click" means of applying simple filters against traffic as it is captured. Every setting on the tab can be mimicked in FiddlerScript (usually even more precisely or powerfully) but for simple jobs, the Filters tab will probably meet your filtering needs.

The **Use Filters** checkbox at the top-left of the tab enables the filters listed below to run against traffic as it is captured. When **Use Filters** is checked, the options below it can be adjusted to control whether a given session:

- Is hidden
- Is flagged in the Web Sessions list
- Is breakpointed for manual tampering
- Is blocked from being sent
- Has its headers modified automatically

Fiddler continues to proxy traffic from hidden Sessions, even though they aren't shown in the Web Sessions list.

The **Actions** button at the top-right of the tab allows you to save the currently selected filters as a Filterset, to load a previously saved Filterset, and to run the current Filters against previously-captured traffic. The Help option launches a help topic about the Filters tab.

Each group of filtering options is described below.

Hosts

The Hosts box provides filters that are based on the hostname of the request.

The **Zone Filter** dropdown allows you to show traffic only to your Intranet (e.g. dotless hostnames) or only to the Internet (e.g. dotted hostnames). This is a useful option when debugging a site in one zone while referencing web-based documentation from the other zone.

The **Host Filter** dropdown enables you to flag or hide traffic to domain names specified in the textbox under the dropdown.

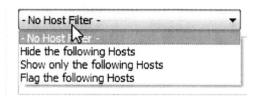

Note that textbox does not automatically wildcard subdomains. That means that if you have "Show only the following Hosts" set and only `fiddler2.com` is in the list, you will not see traffic to `www.fiddler2.com`. To see traffic to subdomains, add a wildcard like `*.fiddler2.com`. This wildcarded entry will include traffic to `test.fiddler2.com` and `sub.fiddler2.com`, and so on. If you want to see traffic to the root domain `fiddler2.com`, change the wildcard to `*fiddler2.com`— this will include traffic to any domain that ends with `fiddler2.com` without requiring a leading dot. List multiple hosts by using a semicolon between each.

Note: When the background of the text box is yellow, it means your changes have not yet been applied. Click anywhere outside the box to save your changes to the list.

Client Process

Process filters allow you to control which processes' traffic is shown within Fiddler. Fiddler can only determine which process issued a given request when the application process is running on the same computer as Fiddler itself.

The **Show only traffic from** dropdown contains a list of all currently-running processes on the system; select a process to show only traffic from that specific process.

The **Show only Internet Explorer** traffic option hides traffic unless the process' executable name begins with `IE` or the request bears a User-Agent header containing `compatible; MSIE`.

The **Hide traffic from Service Host** option will hide traffic from `svchost.exe`, a system process that synchronizes RSS Feeds and performs other background network activity.

Request Headers

Using these options, you can add or remove HTTP request headers, or flag requests that contain certain headers.

The **Show only if url contains** box allows you to hide requests based on the URL. You can demand case-sensitivity using the EXACT prefix:

```
EXACT:example.com/q=Case+Sensitive+String
```

...or you can use a regular expression:

```
REGEX:(?insx).*\.(gif|png|jpg)$ #only show image requests
```

The **Flag requests with header** option allows you to specify a HTTP header name, that if present, will cause the session to be bolded in the Web Sessions list.

The **Delete request header** option allows you to specify a HTTP header name, that if present, will be removed from the request headers.

The **Set request header** option allows you to create or update a HTTP Request header with a value of your choice.

Breakpoints

The breakpoints box enables you to break requests or responses that contain the specified attributes.

Break request on POST option will set a request breakpoint for any request whose method is POST. The **Break request on GET with QueryString** option will set a request breakpoint for any GET request whose URL contains a query string.

The **Break on XMLHttpRequest** option will set a request breakpoint for any request that can be determined to have been issued by the XMLHttpRequest object. Because requests issued by the XMLHttpRequest object are generally not distinguishable from other types of traffic, this feature looks for an X-Requested-With header (added by the jQuery framework). It will also check for an X-Download-Initiator header which Internet Explorer 10 and later can be configured to send.

The **Break response on Content-Type** option will set a response breakpoint for any response whose Content-Type response header contains the specified text.

Response Status Code

Using these options, you can filter display of Sessions based on the response's status code.

The **Hide success** option will hide any response whose status code is between 200 and 299 inclusive. These response codes are used to indicate a successful request. The **Hide non-2xx** option will hide any response whose status code is not between 200 and 299 inclusive.

The **Hide Authentication demands** option will hide responses with the 401 and 407 status code used to prompt the client for credentials.

The **Hide redirects** option will hide responses that redirect the request.

The **Hide Not Modified** option will hide responses with the 304 status code used in response to a conditional validation request to indicate that the client's cached entity remains fresh.

Response Type and Size

Using these options, you can control what types of responses appear within the Web Sessions list, and block responses matching certain criteria.

The **Type dropdown** list allows you to hide Sessions whose response does not match a specified type.

- **Show all Content-Types** performs no filtering.
- **Show only IMAGE/*** hides Sessions whose Content-Type header does not specify an image type.
- **Show only HTML** hides Sessions whose Content-Type does not specify an HTML type.
- **Show only TEXT/CSS** hides Sessions whose Content-Type does not specify the text/css type.
- **Show only SCRIPTS** hides Sessions whose Content-Type does not specify a script type.
- **Hide IMAGE/*** hides Sessions whose Content-Type specifies an image type.

The **Hide smaller than** option allows you to hide responses whose bodies are smaller than the specified number of kilobytes. The **Hide larger than** option allows you to hide responses whose bodies are larger than the size specified.

The **Time HeatMap** checkbox sets a background color for each Session based on how long the server took to return a given response completely (computed using the Timers object: ServerDoneResponse - FiddlerBeginRequest). Responses that take less than 50 milliseconds show in shades of green. Responses that take between 50 and 300 milliseconds are not colored. Responses that take between 300 and 500 milliseconds show in yellow. Responses that take more than 500 milliseconds show in shades of red.

The **Block script files** option will return a HTTP/404 response instead of the returned response if the response declared a script Content-Type. The **Block image files** option will return a 404 response if the response declared an image Content-Type. The **Block SWF files** option will return a 404 response if the response declared an Adobe Flash (application/x-shockwave-flash) Content-Type.

The **Block CSS files** option will return a 404 response if the response declared a CSS Content-Type.

Response Headers

Using these options, you can add or remove HTTP response headers, or flag responses that contain certain headers.

The **Flag responses that set cookies** option will mark in bold any response that contains a `Set-Cookie` header.

The **Flag responses with header** option allows you to specify a HTTP header name, that if present, will cause the Session to be bolded in the Web Sessions list.

The **Delete response header** option allows you to specify a HTTP header name, that if present, will be removed from the response headers.

The **Set response header** option allows you to create or update a HTTP response header with a value of your choice.

THE TIMELINE TAB

This tab allows you to view between 1 and 250 selected Sessions as a "waterfall" diagram, which is useful both for Performance analysis and to understand how requests relate to one another. The bulk of the tab is the view of the selected traffic. Across the top of the tab is the title which displays the mode ("Transfer Timeline", by default). The Help link at the top-right opens a help topic about the feature.

Right-click in the body of the tab to see the context menu. It exposes the following options:

AutoScale Chart	When enabled, the chart is scaled such that the entire chart fits in the horizontal width of the tab without a horizontal scrollbar.
Copy Chart	Clicking this option copies the chart to the clipboard in bitmap format, suitable for pasting into other documents.
Mode (dropdown)	The Mode dropdown controls how the chart is displayed: • **Timeline** – displays each Session on its own line, with a colored bar representing its duration. • **Client Pipe Map** – Displays each connection between a client program and Fiddler on its own line. Connections which were reused for multiple sessions will display multiple colored bars. • **Server Pipe Map** – Displays each connection between Fiddler and an upstream server on its own line. Connections which were reused for multiple sessions will display multiple colored bars. The Client Pipe Map and Server Pipe Map modes show how the client and server reuse connections, which can be useful in identifying performance bottlenecks.

The Timeline tab does not presently display any CONNECT tunnels because the traffic flowing through such tunnels is either opaque or tracked by one or more decrypted HTTPS Web Session entries.

Mode: Timeline

In this mode, Fiddler will show each selected Session on its own line, with filename extracted from the URL written to the left of the bar. Hovering over any entry will show more information about the entry in the status bar at the bottom of the tab. Double-clicking the entry will inspect that Session; holding SHIFT while double-clicking will inspect the Session in a new window.

The color of the bar is determined by the MIME type of the response; light-green for images, dark-green for JavaScript, purple for CSS, and blue otherwise.

TRANSFER TIMELINE

The start of the transfer bar is drawn at the time when the client sends the request to Fiddler (`Timers.ClientBeginRequest`). The end of the transfer bar is drawn at the time when the response to the client is completed (`Timers.ClientDoneResponse`). If the bar is "hatched" rather than smooth, this indicates that the HTTP response was buffered by Fiddler rather than being streamed to the client as it was read to the server. Buffering alters the waterfall diagram, as you can see in the Timeline below where none of the images begin to download until their containing page completes:

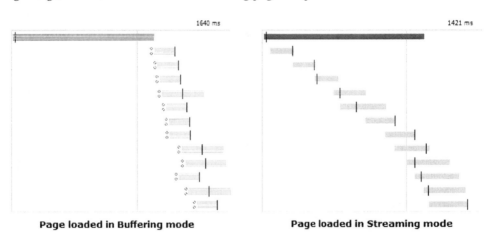

Page loaded in Buffering mode   Page loaded in Streaming mode

The black vertical line in the bar indicates the time to first byte of the server's response (`Timers.ServerBeginResponse`). The two small circles before the bar indicate whether the Session was transmitted on reused connections. A green circle shows that a connection was reused while a red circle means that the connection was newly created. The top circle represents the client's connection to Fiddler; the bottom circle represents Fiddler's connection to the server.

A red X icon [×] after the bar indicates that the server sent a `Connection: close` header (or failed to send a `Connection: Keep-Alive` header for a `HTTP/1.0` response), preventing subsequent reuse of the connection. The gray arrow icon ⬑ indicates that the server's response was a redirect (302). The red ! icon ⚠ indicates that the server returned an error code (4xx, 5xx).

Mode: Client Pipe Map

In this mode, the Timeline will show each inbound connection from a client on its own line. At the left edge of the chart is the connection identifier, which shows the process name, process ID, and client port number.

For instance, `iexplore:1364(p14421)` identifies that the client was Internet Explorer process number 1364, using port 14421 to connect to Fiddler. Connections which were reused for multiple sessions will display multiple horizontal bars:

Mode: Server Pipe Map

In this mode, the Timeline will show each outbound connection from Fiddler to a server on its own line. At the left edge of the chart is the connection identifier, which shows the outbound port number and the hostname of the target server. For instance `p14357->twimgs.com` indicates that Fiddler used port 14357 on your computer to establish a connection to port 80 on `twimgs.com`. Connections which were reused for multiple sessions will display multiple horizontal bars:

Using the Timeline for Performance Analysis

The Timeline tab provides an information-rich view of how your application is using the network. You can easily identify slow requests (long bars), bottlenecks where requests are blocked due to connection limits (stair-step groups of six requests), and cases where connections were unnecessarily closed (red X icons). Using this information, you may be able to adjust your application to better order requests to optimize network performance.

THE AUTORESPONDER TAB

This tab exposes some of the most powerful functionality in Fiddler. It permits you to create **rules** that will automatically trigger in response to requests, typically reacting by returning a previously-captured response without hitting the server.

Across the top of the tab are a set of options which control the AutoResponder's behavior, while most of the tab contains the **Rules List** that maps inbound URL **Match Conditions** to **Actions**.

The **Enable automatic responses** checkbox controls whether the AutoResponder is active. When this option is unchecked, the rest of the tab is disabled.

The **Unmatched requests passthrough** option controls what happens when a Session does not match any of the specified rules. When ticked, unmatched requests are sent to the server normally, as if the AutoResponder feature didn't exist. When unticked, Fiddler will generate a HTTP/404 Not Found response for any unconditional HTTP request that does not match any of the rules. If a client sends a conditional request containing If-None-Match or If-Modified-Since headers, the AutoResponder will return a HTTP/304 Not Modified response.

The **Enable Latency** option controls whether requests that match a rule are acted upon immediately, or if the action is delayed by the number of milliseconds specified in the rule's **Latency** column. The Latency column is hidden when latency is disabled. Enable the option to more accurately simulate a real-world server's response times, or disable the option for improved performance.

The **Import** button allows you to import a previously-captured SAZ file; each Session in the imported file will be used to generate a new rule in the Rules list. You can also import a FARX file which contains rules exported from the AutoResponder tab.

The center of the tab is a listview that contains the rules. The first column specifies the **Match Condition**, which is used to determine if an incoming request matches the rule. The checkbox preceding the Match Condition's text controls whether the rule is enabled. The second column contains the action to undertake if the rule is matched. The **Action Text** may specify a local filename to return, or may specify another type of action.

When a rule is selected, the **Rule Editor** box at the bottom of the tab enables you to adjust the rule's Match Condition and Action Text. The **Test** link allows you to test your Match Condition against the sample URL of your choice; this feature can be helpful if your regular expression skills have grown rusty over the years.

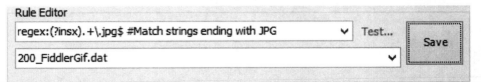

After making any changes to the Match Condition or Action Text, click the **Save** button to update the rule. If you select multiple rules, the Rule Editor will hide the Match Condition box and provide the option to update all selected rules' Action Text at once. This capability allows you to easily specify multiple rules that trigger the same response.

Specifying the Match Condition

By default, the Match Condition performs a case-insensitive match against the request URL. So, if you want a rule to match any request whose URL contains the word `fuzzle`, simply type `fuzzle` in the box. The rule will match any of the following URLs:

```
http://fuzzle.bunnies.com
http://bunnies.fuzzle.net
http://example.com/Fuzzle/
http://example.com/search?q=FuZzLe
```

A Match Condition of * will match all inbound requests.

By specifying the `NOT:` prefix, a rule will match any request whose URL does not case-insensitively contain the provided string. So, if you want a rule to match any request whose URL does not contain the word `fuzzle`, simply type `NOT:fuzzle` in the box. Unless the text `fuzzle` is found anywhere in the request's URL (case-insensitively), the rule will match.

By specifying the `EXACT:` prefix, you can require that the request's URL exactly match the target URL, case-sensitively. So, a rule of `EXACT:http://example.com/a/` will match:

```
http://example.com/a/
```

…but it will not match any of the following URLs:

```
https://example.com/a/
http://example.com/b/
http://example.com/a/otherstuff
```

By specifying the `REGEX:` prefix, you can provide a regular expression which will be evaluated against the request URL. Expressions are evaluated using the .NET regular expression engine.

There are many great books that explain how to develop powerful regular expressions; this book is not one of them. I recommend `http://fiddler2.com/r/?RegExHelp` to get started. A few sample regular-expression rules are:

Rule	Matches
`REGEX:.+`	Any URL of one or more characters
`REGEX:.+\.jpg.*`	Any URL that contains `.jpg` after at least one other character
`REGEX:.+\.jpg$`	Any URL that ends with `.jpg`
`REGEX:.+\.(jpg|gif|png)$`	Any URL that ends with `.jpg` or `.gif` or `.png`
`REGEX:^https.+$`	Any URL that begins with `https`
`REGEX:(?insx).*\.(jpg|gif|png)$`	Any URL that ends with `.jpg` or `.gif` or `.png`, case-insensitively

You can specify regular expression options (like case-sensitivity) by leading the expression with an appropriate declaration. The option string (?insx) works well; it turns on case-insensitivity, requires explicit capture groups, enables single-line syntax, and enables comments after the # character. Comments are useful to combat regular expressions' "write once, read never" nature. Without an informative comment, you may quickly forget what your carefully-crafted regular expression was meant to match.

Matching Against Request Bodies

In some cases, a site may use the same request URL for many unrelated operations, specifying the operation desired in the request's body instead of the URL. You may extend your Match Condition to examine a POST or PUT request's body by specifying the URLWithBody: prefix for your Match Condition. When this prefix is used, the portion of the string up to the first space character is used as the Match Condition for the request's URL, while the remainder of the string is used as a Match Condition for the string-representation of the request's body. You should make the URL portion of the Match Condition as specific as possible to minimize the number of request bodies that the AutoResponder is forced to evaluate. If a request has no body, it will not match any URLWithBody rule.

Your Match Condition may specify the EXACT:, NOT:, and REGEX: prefixes for both the URL and the body. For example:

```
URLWithBody:upload.php TextToFindInBody
URLWithBody:login.php EXACT:Action=Login
URLWithBody:ping.php NOT:POST Data I Do Not Care About
URLWithBody:EXACT:https://example.com/upload.php REGEX:^.+TextToFind.*$
URLWithBody:REGEX:^.+/upload.php.*$ REGEX:^.+TailOfPOST$
```

Keep in mind that most POSTs from Web Forms encode the body text, so you should ensure that your Match Condition accounts for such encoding. For instance, to match the following POST:

```
POST http://www.enhanceie.com/sandbox/FileForm.asp HTTP/1.1
Content-Type: application/x-www-form-urlencoded
Content-Length: 54

2=This+is+some+text&fileentry2=&_charset_=windows-1252
```

Your Match Condition should look like this:

```
URLWithBody:/sandbox/FileForm.asp This+is+some+text
```

Specifying the Action Text

The Action Text instructs the AutoResponder how to react when a Match Condition is hit. The Action may involve returning content, redirecting the request, or performing some other action.

Any Action may be either **Final** or **Non-Final**. Non-Final Actions allow the request to match multiple rules. As soon a rule specifying a Final action is reached, the matching process exits and no further rules are processed for that Session. Rules are evaluated in the order that they appear, so you should adjust the order of the rules to match your needs.

Action Text	Explanation	Final?
`filename`	Return contents of `filename` as the response.	yes
`http://targetURL`	Return the contents of the `targetURL` as the response. This action effectively retargets the request to a different URL without informing the client application.	yes
`*redir:http://targetURL`	Return a `HTTP/307` Redirect to the target URL. Unlike a plain URL, using the `*redir` prefix ensures that the client knows where its request is going, so it can send the correct cookies, etc.	yes
`*bpu`	Set a request breakpoint.	no
`*bpafter`	Set a response breakpoint.	no
`*delay:####`	Delay sending request to the server by the specified number of milliseconds.	no
`*flag:flagname=value`	Set a Session Flag to a specified value. For instance, use `*flag:ui-bold=1` to bold the item in the Web Sessions list. Leave the `value` blank to delete the specified Session Flag.	no
`*drop`	Close the client connection immediately without sending a response. The closure is graceful at the TCP/IP level, returning a `FIN` to the client.	yes
`*reset`	Close the client connection immediately without sending a response. The closure is abrupt at the TCP/IP level, returning a `RST` to the client.	yes
`*exit`	Stop processing rules.	yes

The AutoResponder is most commonly used to return a local file from disk. When that file is loaded, Fiddler will scan it for a set of HTTP headers at the start of the file. If present, those headers will be returned on the response, with the rest of the file as the body. If no headers are found, Fiddler will automatically generate a set of default headers, and return the entire contents of the file as the body. When the local file is returned, the session is shown with a Lavender background in the Web Sessions list.

Using RegEx Replacements in Action Text

Fiddler's AutoResponder permits you to use regular expression group replacements to map text from the Match Condition into the Action Text. For instance, the rule:

Match Text	Action Text
`REGEX:.+/assets/(.*)`	`http://example.com/mockup/$1`

...will map a request for `http://example.com/assets/Test1.gif` to `http://example.com/mockup/Test1.gif`.

The following rule:

Match Text	Action Text
`REGEX:.+example\.com.*`	`http://proxy.webdbg.com/p.cgi?url=$0`

...will rewrite the inbound URL so that all URLs containing `example.com` are passed as a URL parameter to a page on `proxy.webdbg.com`.

Many sites serve up "crunched" or "minified" versions of their scripts on production servers, but also keep the original version of the script available for debugging purposes. For instance, the crunched version of a script will be at the URL:

    http://example.com/main/js/main_c.js

...and the uncrunched version will be available at:

    http://example.com/main/js/main.js

You can write a RegEx replacement rule that maps requests for the crunched version to the original version like so:

Match Text	Action Text
`REGEX:(?insx)^http://example.com(?'path'.+)_c\.js$`	`http://example.com${path}.js`

This rule captures the path to the file in the variable named `path` and that variable is later used to replace the `${path}` token in the Action Text. Beyond changing the URL's host or path, you can create similar rules that modify, add, or remove query string parameters.

The replacement functionality is smart enough to swap forward-slashes for backslashes when mapping URLs to files, so the rule:

Match Text	Action Text
`REGEX:(?insx).+/assets/(?'fname'[^?]*).*`	`C:\users\ericlaw\desktop\${fname}`

...will map a request for `http://example.com/assets/img/1.png?bunnies` to `C:\users\ericlaw\desktop\img\1.png`.

Drag-and-Drop support

The AutoResponder allows you to easily create new AutoResponder rules using drag-and-drop. You can drag-and-drop files or folders full of files from Windows Explorer to automatically generate rules for those files. Alternatively, you can drag-drop sessions from the Web Sessions list to reuse responses captured previously. You may edit a rule's stored response by selecting the rule and hitting `Enter` or by selecting the **Edit Response** item on the rule's context menu.

The context menu on the Rules listview exposes the following commands:

Remove	Deletes the selected rules. Alternatively, select one or more rules and press `Delete`.
Promote Rule	Moves the rule one slot earlier in the list. Alternatively, select one rule and press the `Plus` key.
Demote Rule	Moves the rule one slot later in the list. Alternatively, select one rule and press the `Minus` key.
Set Latency...	Prompts you for a number of milliseconds to use as a latency value when the rule is matched. For instance, if you specify 50 and a filename, Fiddler will wait 50 milliseconds before returning the selected file as the response. You may specify a leading + or - indicator if you wish to adjust the current latency value rather than setting it to an absolute value.
Clone Rule	Makes a copy of the current rule and appends it to the list.
Edit Response	For a rule that is backed by a file, opens that file for editing. For a rule that is backed by a previously-captured response, opens a standalone Inspectors window to enable editing the response.
Generate File	For a rule that is backed by a previously-captured response, saves that response to a file and adjusts the rule to point to that file. Use this when you need to edit a response using a standalone editor like Expression Web or Visual Studio.
Edit File With...	Prompts you to select an application to use to edit the specified response. Use this to edit a response using a standalone editor which is not the default program for handling the saved response's file type.
Open URL	Opens the URL specified in the Match Condition using the default web browser.
Export All...	Prompts you to save the current set of rules as a FARX file. This file can be later imported to reload the rules.

FARX Files

Fiddler AutoResponder XML (FARX) files contain a set of AutoResponder rules. Your current set of AutoResponder rules is automatically saved on exit and reloaded when you restart Fiddler. This automatically saved file is named `AutoResponder.xml`, but if you use the Export command to save a separate file, it will have a `.farx` file extension.

FARX files contain the full set of rules, including any previously captured responses used for playback. Binary responses are base64 encoded and compressed to help reduce the size of the file, but a large set of AutoResponder rules (or a small set of rules with large responses) can cause a FARX file to grow very large.

Because your default set of AutoResponder rules is automatically reloaded when Fiddler starts up, a large default FARX file can make Fiddler slow to start. To avoid problems with slow startup, export large Rule sets to a FARX file of your choosing and remove those rules from your default list before closing Fiddler.

THE TEXTWIZARD

When interacting with web content, text is often encoded using one or more formats. The TextWizard allows you to quickly transform text to and from popular formats.

The TextWizard can be opened by clicking **Tools > TextWizard** or by pressing CTRL+E. You may open multiple copies of the TextWizard at the same time.

At the top of the TextWizard is the **Input box** into which you can type or paste the input text. Along the bottom left is a set of **Transformations** you can apply to generate the output text, which is shown in the read-only **Output box** at the bottom right.

The list of available transformations is hardcoded, and only one transformation can be applied at one time. If you'd like to "chain" multiple transformations, use the **Send output to input** button to copy the last operation's Output into the Input box, then select the next transformation to apply.

As the tool opens, if text (32kb or less) is present on the system clipboard, it is automatically pasted into the Input box. The selected transformation is applied immediately as the text in the Input box is updated. The title bar indicates the number of characters in the input and the number of characters of output generated.

If any transformation results in creation of a null character (which would terminate the string prematurely), the TextWizard will replace the null character with the Unicode Replacement Character (0xFFFD, �).

The **View bytes** checkbox allows you to view the output in hexadecimal, which can be useful when decoding binary content that is not easily represented as text.

The **Send output to input** button allows you to replace the input text with the output text, used when chaining a series of transformations.

Available transformations include:

To Base64	Converts the Input string into UTF-8 and then encodes the result down to a 7-bit ASCII string using Base64 encoding.
From Base64	Decodes the Input string from 7-bit ASCII to a byte array, then interprets the result as a UTF-8 string.
URLEncode	Applies the URL Encoding Rules to the Input string.
URLDecode	Decodes escape sequences from the Input String.
HexEncode	Converts each character of the input string into its hexadecimal equivalent preceded by a % character.
To JS string	Replaces \ with \\, Carriage Returns with \r, Line Feeds with \n, " with \", and any character over ASCII 127 with \u*XXXX* where *XXXX* is the Unicode code point.
From JS string	Reverses the **To JS string** operation.
HTML Encode	Encodes the Input string using HTML Entities; for instance < becomes <.
HTML Decode	Reverses the **HTML Encode** operation.
To UTF-7	Converts the Input string into a UTF-7 string preceded by a byte-order marker.
From UTF-7	Converts the Input string from a UTF-7 string.
To Deflated-SAML	Converts the text to UTF-8 bytes, then uses the DEFLATE compression algorithm on them, converts the resulting string into Base64, and URLEncodes the final result.
From Deflated-SAML	URLDecodes the string into Base64, converts to a byte array, decompresses the array, and converts the resultant array into a UTF-8 string.

Character Encodings

By default, the TextWizard uses UTF-8 to convert between characters and bytes and back. Most applications use UTF-8 as their standard text encoding, but if you are working with a site that uses another encoding, you can set a Preference to select the required text encoding.

Set the preference `fiddler.textwizard.InputEncoding` to specify a character set from which percent-encoded characters will be decoded. Set the preference `fiddler.textwizard.OutputEncoding` to specify a character set using which characters will be percent-encoded. The string value provided must be an `Encoding` name recognized by the .NET Framework; valid values can be found at `http://fiddler2.com/r/?EncodingNames`.

THE COMPOSER TAB

This tab enables you to manually build and send HTTP, HTTPS, and FTP requests. Alternatively, you can drag a Session from the Web Sessions list to the Composer tab to copy the request from that Session into the interface. Clicking the **Execute** button sends the request to the server.

The bulk of the Composer tab is a set of three sub-tabs: **Parsed**, **Raw**, and **Options**. I'll explain each tab in turn, although starting from the right for simplicity.

Request Options

The **Options** tab provides the following choices:

Inspect Session	After the request is executed, the Inspectors tab will activate to enable you to view the results of the request.
Fix Content-Length header*	This option controls whether the Composer will automatically add or update the Content-Length request header to reflect the size of the request body. In many cases, requests that lack a proper Content-Length header will hang or result in a HTTP error response.
Follow Redirects*	This option controls whether the Composer will automatically follow a HTTP/3xx redirection using the response's Location header. When this option is enabled, the Composer will follow a maximum of 10 redirects before failing.
Automatically Authenticate*	This option controls whether the Composer will automatically respond to a server's HTTP/401 or HTTP/407 authentication demands. When this option is enabled, the Windows credentials of the account that Fiddler is running under will be used to automatically respond to such challenges. To supply a different set of credentials, set the fiddler.composer.AutoAuthCreds preference. If the server requires credentials that are different than those provided, the request will fail, typically with a HTTP/403 response.
Tear off button	This button removes the Composer from the main Fiddler window and opens it as a separate floating window. This option is especially useful when you have the **Inspect Session** option enabled, as it permits you to see both the Composer and Inspectors tabs at the same time.

The options marked with * above only apply to requests sent using the Parsed tab; requests from the Raw tab do not support these options.

Raw Requests

The **Raw** tab provides a simple text box into which you must enter a properly formed HTTP request. If your request is not well-formed (say, because you forgot the trailing CRLF after the request headers) then clicking the Execute button will not issue a request.

This tab is rarely useful—most requests should be composed using the Parsed tab instead.

Parsed Requests

The **Parsed** tab allows you to construct the request using separate boxes for each component of the request.

Across the top of the tab are three boxes: The first allows you to specify the HTTP Method (e.g. POST). The second allows you to specify the full URL of the request (it must begin with http://, https://, or ftp://). The third box allows you to specify the HTTP Version (typically HTTP/1.1).

Below the top line are two large text areas: the top box allows you to edit the request headers. The bottom box allows you to edit the request body. If the currently selected HTTP Method is one that typically does not allow a body (e.g. GET) the body box will turn red if any text is entered into it.

Issuing Sequential Requests

In some scenarios, it is useful to issue multiple requests that are identical except for a single number. For instance, when trying to download a series of sequentially-named images, each download request only differs by the name of the file. The Composer can generate a series of sequentially-numbered requests – simply include a # symbol in the URL where the number should appear.

When the request is executed, Fiddler will prompt you for the first number. You can enter a simple number (e.g. 8) or if the all numbers must be the same number of digits, pad the number with leading zeros. For instance, to ensure that all URLs' numbers contain two digits, use 08:

Next, you'll be prompted for the number at which you would like Fiddler to stop issuing requests:

After providing the Start and End numbers, Fiddler will then issue the sequential requests for the range you specified:

#	Result	Protocol	Host	URL	Body
2	200	HTTP	www.example.com	/08.jpg	308
3	200	HTTP	www.example.com	/09.jpg	308
4	200	HTTP	www.example.com	/10.jpg	308
5	200	HTTP	www.example.com	/11.jpg	308
6	200	HTTP	www.example.com	/12.jpg	308
7	200	HTTP	www.example.com	/13.jpg	308

Some servers will not return responses unless an expected `Referer` header is present. Placing a # in your request's `Referer` header will instruct Fiddler to replace that character with the current request number.

The Sequential Requests feature is only available when using the **Parsed** tab; the # is treated as a plain character if the request is written using the **Raw** tab.

File Upload Requests
You can construct a file upload by clicking the **Upload File** link near the top-right of the tab. A **Select File for Upload** file picker window will appear. You may only choose one file if your request's Method is `PUT`, or you may choose multiple files if the Method is `POST`.

After you select the files for upload, the Composer will construct a request with the proper format; all `@INCLUDE` references in the body will be replaced with the contents of the specified files when the request is executed.

In HTTP, file uploads are typically conducted using either the `PUT` or `POST` methods. When uploading a file using the `PUT` method, the Request Body typically contains the raw content of the file.

In contrast, uploads using the POST method usually format the Request Body using Content-Type: multipart/form-data.

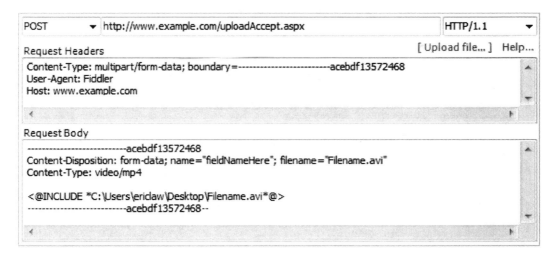

For POST uploads, you may need to edit the Name attribute to ensure that it matches the form field name expected by the server.

Automatic Request Breakpoints

In some cases, Fiddler's Request Inspectors can provide a better request editing experience than using the Composer tab. By holding the Shift key while clicking the Execute button, you can set a breakpoint on the new request. The new Session will be immediately paused at a breakpoint and the Request Inspectors will become active. This allows you to modify the new request using Fiddler's Inspectors before it is sent to the server.

THE LOG TAB

The Log tab collects logged message strings that are generated by extensions, FiddlerScript, or Fiddler itself. Fiddler logs a notification in response to application events (e.g. when a SAZ file is saved or loaded) as well as system events (e.g. when the system's network connectivity is lost or restored).

In current versions of Fiddler, WebSocket traffic is also displayed in the Log tab.

Right-clicking on the Log textbox displays a context menu offering a few basic commands for interacting with the log:

Copy	Copies selected text to the clipboard.
Save...	Saves the current Log to a file on disk. You may save in plaintext (.txt) or formatted RichText format (.rtf).
Clear	Clears all text in the Log.

The Log tab also supports simple macro commands which you can invoke from the QuickExec box. Type log @Log.Clear to clear the log. Type log @Log.Save to generate a new Session in the Web Sessions list whose response body contains the Log tab's text. Type log "@Log.Export \"filename\"" to save the Log tab's text to the specified file. Use a filename ending in .rtf to save in Rich Text Format, preserving font size and weight, or ending in .txt to save as plaintext.

THE FIND SESSIONS WINDOW

Fiddler's Find Sessions window enables you to search through captured requests and responses and select those that contain text of interest. Open the Find Sessions window using the option on the Edit menu, or press the CTRL+F hotkey anywhere in Fiddler.

The **Find** box at the top enables you to specify the text for which a search will be conducted. Previously searched terms will appear in a drop-down and autocomplete as you type.

The **Options** box controls how the search is conducted. The **Search** dropdown allows you to select what gets searched; choices are **Requests and responses** (the default), **Requests only**, **Responses only**, and **URLs only**. Unless you choose **URLS only**, the **Examine** dropdown enables you specify whether you wish to search the session's **Headers**, **Bodies**, or both (the default).

Below the dropdowns are a set of checkboxes. When ticked, the **Match case** box makes the search case-sensitive. The **Regular Expression** box causes Fiddler to treat the search text as a regular expression. The **Search binaries** option instructs Fiddler to perform the search even inside Sessions with a Content-Type header that suggests that body is of a binary type like audio, video, images, Flash objects, etc. The **Decode compressed content** option instructs Fiddler to remove HTTP content- and transfer-encodings from requests and responses as it searches. This option can significantly slow the search and will permanently remove the encoding from the affected bodies. The **Search only selected sessions** box is enabled (and ticked by default) if multiple Sessions are selected in the Web Sessions list when the Find Sessions window is opened. This option restricts the search to only those Sessions that were selected when the search began. The **Select matches** option causes Fiddler to automatically select any Sessions which contain the search text. The **Unmark old results** option will remove the highlight color from any Sessions highlighted as a result of a prior search. The **Result Highlight** dropdown allows you to select the background color which should be set for all Sessions that contain the search text. If the **Unmark old results** option is disabled, this color is automatically cycled every time the Find Sessions operation is performed-- that way, when performing multiple searches, the results of each search will be highlighted in a different color.

After configuring the search, press the **Find Sessions** button to perform the search. The Find Sessions window will close and matching search results will be highlighted (and selected, if that option was chosen) in the Web Sessions list. Fiddler's status bar will indicate the number of matches found.

Press Cancel or hit Escape to close the window without performing a search.

THE HOST REMAPPING TOOL

The **Hosts Remapping** tool allows you to easily reroute requests from one host to another, overriding the normal DNS association between a hostname and its IP address list. To enable the feature, click the **HOSTS...** item on Fiddler's **Tools** menu. The **Host Remapping** window will appear.

Use the **Enable remapping** checkbox to enable or disable the feature. In the textbox, enter a list of overrides, one per line. Type the new host or IP address in the first column, one or more whitespace characters, and finally the corresponding hostname to override. Any line may be preceded by a pound character (#) to indicate that the line represents a comment.

You may import the system's HOSTS file (%SYSTEMROOT%\System32\drivers\etc\hosts) using the link at the bottom of the window.

Unlike the Windows HOSTS file, this feature does not require that you specify the IP address of the new target; you may specify a host instead. If needed, you can even specify a target port.

The following rule:

```
127.0.0.1:8088    meddler
```

...will send all requests for http://meddler/ to http://127.0.0.1:8088/.

Sessions rerouted from one hostname to another using the Host Remapping tool are rendered with a light blue background in the Web Sessions list. HTTPS Sessions that have been rerouted have the X-IgnoreCertCNMismatch and X-OverrideCertCN Session Flags set to avoid raising "Certificate Name Mismatch" errors.

Techniques and Concepts

RETARGETING TRAFFIC WITH FIDDLER

Fiddler offers three different mechanisms you can use to change the target of a request. These mechanisms all have different implications for the client and server, and understanding the differences will allow you to choose the proper mechanism for your needs.

Method #1 - Rewriting

A *rewrite* occurs when you use Fiddler to change the request's headers (either the target URL or the Host header) such that a request targeted to Server A is instead sent to a Server B.

The client will be unaware that the request it sent has been changed underneath it, so any cookies sent with the request will belong to the original URL instead of the new one. Similarly, if you look at the resource's URL in the browser's address bar or in the DOM, you will see the original URL and not the rewritten one.

Since the URL and HOST header of request itself are updated, rewritten requests can safely flow through an upstream proxy server without problems. The target server will see its own Host header in the inbound request.

If the request uses HTTPS and decryption is enabled, you may want to control the certificate the client computer receives to avoid seeing "Certificate Name Mismatch" errors. To do so, use the Session's X-OverrideCertCN flag to supply the Subject CN Fiddler will send to the client.

Method #2 - Rerouting

A *reroute* sends a request meant for Server A to Server B without changing the request itself. Instead, before Fiddler connects to the server to send the request, it notices that the request is marked to be rerouted. Rather than connecting to the host specified by the request's Host header, Fiddler instead connects to the new target hostname specified in the Session's X-OverrideHost flag.

Because the client is unaware that the target has been changed underneath it, the Host header, URL, and Cookies of the request will be those intended for the original host, not the new target host. Request rerouting only works when Fiddler itself determines the target IP address to which the request will be sent. If an upstream gateway proxy is in use, it will be unaware of Fiddler's desire to reroute the request and will instead use the request's original Host header for routing. Therefore, the Host Remapping tool sets the X-OverrideHost flag *and* the bypassGateway boolean to ensure that rerouted requests bypass any upstream gateway proxy.

When the web server receives the request, it will find the original server's hostname in the Host request header because rerouted requests are sent unmodified. Depending on its configuration, the server may reject the request with a HTTP/400 error message complaining that "No such host is known."

When HTTPS requests are rerouted to a different server, either the client or Fiddler is likely to complain about a "Certificate Name Mismatch." For instance, when using the following remapping FiddlerScript:

```
if (oSession.HTTPMethodIs("CONNECT") && oSession.HostnameIs("example.com"))
{
  oSession["X-OverrideHost"] ="www.fiddler2.com";
}
```

...loading `https://example.com/` will show a certificate warning complaining that the server presented a certificate for `www.fiddler2.com` instead of the expected `example.com` certificate:

You can avoid the Certificate Error message by setting the `X-IgnoreCertCNMismatch` flag:

```
if (oSession.HTTPMethodIs("CONNECT") &&
  oSession.HostnameIs("example.com"))
{
  oSession["X-OverrideHost"] ="www.fiddler2.com";

  // Set flag to suppress Fiddler's HTTPS Name Mismatch errors
  oSession["X-IgnoreCertCNMismatch"] = "no worries mate";
}
```

If you would prefer that Fiddler ignore *all* certificate errors for a Session, because the target site is using an expired or self-signed test certificate, set the `X-IgnoreCertErrors` flag instead.

The Host Remapping tool sets the `X-IgnoreCertCNMismatch` flag automatically. When the Certificate Name Mismatch error is ignored, you will see the `https://www.fiddler2.com/` page while the browser's address bar shows `https://example.com/`.

Method #3 - Redirecting

A *redirect* occurs when you use Fiddler to return a `HTTP/307` redirection response to the client so that it will resend its request using a new URL. Because the client is responsible for resending the request, it is aware that the request target has changed, and the new request will be sent with an updated `Host` header and URL. The client will send the proper cookies for the target URL, and if the request is over HTTPS, the client will expect the target server to use the correct certificate for the new target URL. Since the new request is sent with the new target URL and matching `Host` header, the request will safely flow through an upstream gateway proxy to the desired server.

Features to Retarget Requests

Fiddler allows use of any of these three basic techniques via several independent features:

1. Use the **HOSTS...** command on the **Tools** menu to <u>reroute</u> traffic from one IP address to another.

2. Using FiddlerScript or an extension, you can set the X-OverrideHost flag on the Session object to <u>reroute</u> traffic from one IP address to another.

3. Using FiddlerScript or an extension, you can set the Session object's host property or fullUrl property to <u>rewrite</u> a request from one URL to another.

4. You can use the utilCreateResponseAndBypassServer method from FiddlerScript or an extension to generate a <u>redirect</u> from one URL to another.

5. You can also use the AutoResponder to <u>rewrite</u> a request from one URL to another by supplying the new URL as the Action text.

6. You can use the AutoResponder to <u>redirect</u> a request from one URL to another using the *redir: prefix on the Action text.

7. You can use the AutoResponder to reroute a request from one host to another by using *flag: X-OverrideHost=targethost as the Action text.

COMPARING SESSIONS

One of the most common debugging tasks is to determine why one request was successful while another failed in some way. The ability to compare one Session to another is a powerful tool for accomplishing this task.

To compare two Sessions, simply select both in the Web Sessions list and choose **Compare** from the context menu (or hit CTRL+W). When you invoke the comparison command, the two selected Sessions will be saved to temporary files and then the file comparison tool will be launched and passed the path to the two files.

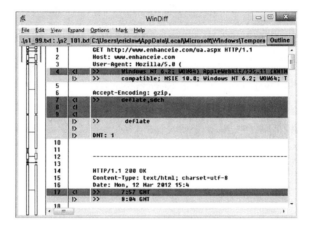

Fiddler does not itself install a file comparison tool, although most developers already have WinDiff, Odd, Beyond Compare, WinMerge or a similar utility installed. If you have WinDiff, copy it to the \Program Files\Fiddler2 folder, or put it somewhere within your system's PATH (e.g. C:\Windows\System32) in order for Fiddler to find it. If you *don't* already have a comparison tool, grab WinMerge from http://WinMerge.org.

To instruct that Fiddler should launch a tool other than WinDiff, you need to set three Preferences using the QuickExec box or the **about:config** tab. First, provide the path to the tool:

```
PREFS SET fiddler.config.path.differ "C:\Program Files (x86)
    \Microsoft Visual Studio 11.0\Common7\IDE\devenv.exe"
```

Then, configure the command line arguments to match what the tool expects:

```
PREFS SET fiddler.differ.Params "/diff \"{0}\" \"{1}\""
```

You can also set an "alternate" command line that will be invoked if you hold SHIFT while invoking the comparison:

```
PREFS SET fiddler.differ.ParamsAlt "/diff \"{0}\" \"{1}\""
```

The alternate command-line feature works with file comparison utilities that support multiple modes. For example, WinDiff offers the -p command line flag to break each line of the comparison at the first instance of punctuation. When you hold SHIFT while clicking the "Compare" option, Fiddler will pass the -p flag to WinDiff and a new line will appear after each character of punctuation. This is useful to observe deltas within long lines of text (e.g. a URL's query string).

UltraDiff

By default, Fiddler reformats the temporary files for easier viewing in line-based comparison tools like WinDiff. Called UltraDiff, this feature reorders the headers of both files such that headers that are exactly the same in both Sessions are listed first, then headers with different values are listed, then headers that are entirely different are listed last. UltraDiff reformats request URLs to ensure that if the URLs are only slightly different (e.g. a single character differs in the middle of a 512-character URL) then that difference is made obvious.

You can set the fiddler.differ.ultradiff preference to false if you don't want Fiddler to modify the headers and URL when saving the temporary files.

Comparing Multiple Sessions at Once

If you want to compare multiple sessions (or even entire SAZ files) at one time, you should use the **Traffic Differ** extension, described in the Extensions chapter. That extension allows you to compare lists of Web Sessions and then perform text-comparisons of individual sessions within those lists.

DEBUGGING WITH BREAKPOINTS

In a traditional debugger, you can select instructions in your program at which you would like execution to pause; these are called **breakpoints**. While paused at a breakpoint, you can examine the state of the program and modify memory or the flow of execution to change the behavior of the program.

Fiddler offers similar breakpoint-based debugging functionality for web requests. Sessions may be paused at two points during their execution:

1. After the request is read from the client, before it's sent to the server
2. After the response is received from the server, before it's returned to the client

These are known as **request breakpoints** and **response breakpoints**.

When paused at a request breakpoint, you can change any aspect of the request, including the URL, headers, or body. You may prevent the request from being sent to the server at all, returning a response of your choosing. With rare exceptions, the client application will never know that Fiddler has modified its request.

Similarly, when paused at a response breakpoint, you can change any aspect of the response, including the headers or body. You may also generate a new response and substitute it in place of the response received from the server. At a response breakpoint, you *can* change any aspect of the request, but since the request has already been sent, the change is only reflected in Fiddler — the server will never see your changes.

Setting Breakpoints

There are many different ways to set breakpoints; under the covers, all of them set the Session's X-BreakRequest or X-BreakResponse flag.

You can easily break on all requests or responses using the **Rules** > **Automatic Breakpoints** menu, or by clicking into the 3rd panel from the left on Fiddler's status bar. The problem with setting such broad breakpoints is that you will likely find it tedious to unpause each request that you are not interested in debugging.

Instead, consider using the Filters or AutoResponder tabs to more precisely target your breakpoints. The Filters tab allows you to set breakpoints on Sessions that use the POST method, those sent with a Query String, those sent by XMLHttpRequest, or those that returned a particular Content-Type. The AutoResponder tab allows you to set a request or response breakpoint for any request whose URL matches the text or regular expression you provide. Set the rule's Action text to *bpu to create a request breakpoint, or *bpafter to create a response breakpoint.

If you need to define more elaborate breakpoint conditions, use **Rules** > **Customize Rules** to set the
X-BreakRequest or X-BreakResponse flags within your FiddlerScript's OnBeforeRequest,
OnPeekAtResponseHeaders, or OnBeforeResponse methods.

The default FiddlerScript file allows you to easily set a single request breakpoint and a single response
breakpoint using the QuickExec box. Simply type:

```
bpu TextFromURL
```

…to set a request breakpoint for any session whose URL contains the specified text. Similarly, type:

```
bpafter TextFromURL
```

…to set a response breakpoint for any session whose URL contains the specified text.

You can also set a request breakpoint for any request using a specified HTTP Method:

```
bpm POST
```

… and you can set a response breakpoint for any response returning a specified HTTP Status code:

```
bps 307
```

Typing any of the breakpoint commands (bpu, bpafter, bpm or bps) with no parameter following will
clear the specified breakpoint.

Recompiling your FiddlerScript (or restarting Fiddler) will also clear breakpoints set using QuickExec.

Tampering Using Inspectors
When paused at a breakpoint, you can use Inspectors to edit the request or response. As discussed in the
Inspectors chapter, many Inspectors support Read/Write functionality that you can use to change the
request and response headers or body. Changes you make while paused at a breakpoint are committed
automatically by the Inspector.

In addition to using the Inspectors, you can clone a previously-captured response into a Session paused at a
breakpoint. The **Clone Response** command is available from the context menu when two Sessions are
selected in the Web Sessions list and one of the Sessions is currently paused at a breakpoint and the other is
completed. The command will copy the response from the completed Session to the paused Session. This
feature enables you to easily replicate a previously captured (or modified) response to satisfy a later
request.

The Breakpoint Bar
A red Breakpoint Bar will appear between the Request and Response Inspectors when a Session is paused.
This bar includes two buttons and one dropdown.

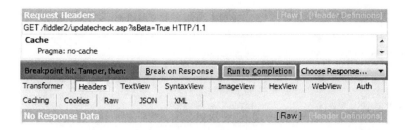

The yellow **Break on Response** button is enabled only when paused at a request breakpoint. When pressed, it will set a response breakpoint for the current Session and then unpause its execution, sending the (potentially modified) request to the server. The green **Run to Completion** button will unpause the request and allow it to run freely without breaking on the response.

The dropdown at the right side of the Breakpoint Bar allows you to select a template response or the file of your choosing to return as the response to a request.

When you select a file from the dropdown, it will be immediately loaded into the response Inspectors so that you may further modify the response (without changing the file on disk) before it is returned to the client. If you use the dropdown to select a response while paused at a request breakpoint, the request will never be sent to the server, because Fiddler will provide the response.

Resuming Multiple Sessions

If your breakpoints are not targeted specifically enough, you may have many requests paused at break-points that you wish to resume quickly.

Simply click the **Resume** button on the Fiddler toolbar, or type g in the QuickExec box to immediately resume all paused Sessions.

Configuring Fiddler and Clients

FIDDLER OPTIONS

The Fiddler Options window, shown by clicking **Tools > Fiddler Options**, exposes many of the basic settings that control Fiddler's behavior. Many of the settings in the Fiddler Options window require that Fiddler be restarted to take effect, although some changes will take effect immediately or when Fiddler's **Capture Traffic** option is toggled. After adjusting options, click the **Ok** button at the bottom of the window to save the changes or **Cancel** to abandon your updates. Click the **Help** link at the bottom left to learn more about the options available on this dialog.

General Options

The General tab allows you to adjust settings related to Fiddler's general operation.

The **Check for updates on startup** option controls whether Fiddler will consult a web service on startup to determine whether a new version of Fiddler is available. If you disable this option, you may manually check for new versions by clicking **Check for Updates...** on Fiddler's Help menu.

The **Participate in the Fiddler Improvement Program** option is available only in certain versions of Fiddler (currently, the beta versions). When enabled, Fiddler will upload anonymous usage data to a web service. This data includes non-personally identifiable information about your system and your use of Fiddler; this information is used in the design of improved versions of Fiddler.

The **Show a message when HTTP protocol violations are encountered** option controls whether Fiddler will show a popup message when malformed web traffic is encountered. Protocol violations can cause problems for clients and servers, so this option should be left enabled when you are debugging your own clients and sites. Malformed traffic will be shown in the Web Sessions list with a yellow background and the Session's Properties will contain a copy of the protocol violation message.

The **Enable IPv6 (if available)** option controls whether Fiddler will listen on and attempt to connect to IPv6 endpoints. Even if this option is disabled, Fiddler will still attempt to connect to an IPv6 server endpoint if DNS did not return any IPv4 addresses.

The **Map requests to originating application** option controls whether Fiddler will attempt to determine which locally-running process issued each request. The process information is shown in the **Process** column in the Web Sessions list, and is stored in the Session's X-Process-Info flag. This feature works by querying Windows for the list of open network connections and checking each inbound connection against that list. Some requests may not be successfully mapped back to their original process; in particular, process information is not available for requests from devices or remote client computers.

The **Automatically stream audio & video** option controls whether responses with audio/* and video/* MIME types are automatically streamed to the client without buffering the entire response within Fiddler. When this option is set, you cannot use Fiddler's Inspectors or FiddlerScript to modify audio or video responses. The advantage in setting this option is that streamed responses are available to begin playback immediately in the client browser or application. To stream *all* responses in Fiddler, click the **Stream** button in the Fiddler toolbar.

The **Systemwide Hotkey** setting enables you to select a hotkey which will restore and activate Fiddler when it is minimized or inactive.

HTTPS Options

The HTTPS tab controls settings related to Fiddler's interception of secure traffic.

The **Capture HTTPS CONNECTs** option controls whether Fiddler will register as the system proxy for HTTPS requests. If this option is disabled, none of the other HTTPS options are available.

The **Decrypt HTTPS traffic** option controls whether Fiddler will decrypt HTTPS requests and responses sent using CONNECT tunnels. The **Learn more...** link adjacent to the checkbox launches a help page that explains how traffic decryption works. When you first enable the decryption option, Fiddler will generate a new self-signed certificate and ask whether you would like to configure Windows to trust that root certificate.

When decryption is enabled, a dropdown box is shown to enable you to select which processes will have their traffic decrypted by default. You can select between:

- **All processes** – Attempt decryption regardless of where the traffic originates.
- **Browsers only** – Attempt decryption only when the process name is a web browser.
- **Non-Browsers** – Attempt decryption only when the process name is not a web browser.
- **Remote clients** – Attempt decryption only when the process name is not known (suggesting that the request is from a remote computer or device).

The Decryption Process Filter can be very useful to avoid decrypting traffic that you do not care about — for instance, you may not care about the background HTTPS requests made from a file-synchronization program like Dropbox, and thus you can exclude such traffic easily using this option.

The **Ignore server certificate errors** checkbox controls whether Fiddler will warn you when a server presents an invalid security certificate. When this option is enabled, Fiddler will ignore any certificate errors encountered when handshaking with a HTTPS server. When this option is disabled, Fiddler will warn you if it encounters a certificate error when connecting to a HTTPS site. Such errors are always "hidden" from the client application because Fiddler always generates valid security certificates. In general, you should leave this option disabled unless you use Fiddler exclusively in a trusted network environment where you expect invalid server certificates (e.g. self-signed development servers).

The **Skip decryption for the following hosts** box allows you to specify that traffic bound to selected servers should not be decrypted. This feature allows you to avoid decrypting traffic that you do not care about. For instance, you may not care about the HTTPS requests made to Exchange RPC-over-HTTPS endpoints and this filter allows you to easily exclude such traffic. Use semicolons to delimit the list, and use * as a wildcard. For instance, to skip decryption of traffic to example.com and any of its subdomains, as well as traffic to fiddler2.com, specify the filter fiddler2.com;*example.com.

The **Export Root Certificate to Desktop** button will copy Fiddler's root certificate from the Windows Certificate store to the file FiddlerRoot.cer on your desktop. This certificate file can then be easily copied to another device or placed in Firefox's or Opera's Trusted Certificates store.

The **Remove Interception Certificates** button is enabled only when the **Decrypt HTTPS traffic** box is unchecked. Clicking the button will remove from your Windows Certificate store the Fiddler Root certificate and the server certificates that chain to it. If you later re-enable HTTPS decryption, Fiddler will generate a new root certificate and prompt you to trust that new root certificate.

Extensions Options

The Extensions tab exposes options to control FiddlerScript and lists loaded Extensions.

The **Automatically reload script when changed** option controls whether Fiddler will automatically reload the FiddlerScript CustomRules.js file when it detects that the file has been changed.

The **Editor** box allows you to control which text editor is used to edit the FiddlerScript. The "..." button launches a file picker to allow selection of the editor.

The **References** box allows you to specify any additional .NET assemblies that your FiddlerScript depends upon. Learn more about this option in the chapter on FiddlerScript.

The **Extensions** box shows all loaded Extensions except Inspectors and Transcoders. You can copy the information from this textbox to include in bug reports or support queries.

The **Find more extensions** link opens the Fiddler Add-ons directory webpage.

Connections Options

The Connections tab exposes options to control Fiddler's proxy settings.

The **Fiddler listens on port** box controls the port number that Fiddler uses to listen for web traffic. Using the default port (8888) is recommended unless that port is already in use on your system.

The **Copy Browser Proxy Configuration URL** link copies a Proxy Configuration Script link that you can paste into a client's proxy configuration screen. This feature is rarely used.

The **Capture FTP requests** checkbox controls whether Fiddler registers as the system proxy for FTP requests. This option is off-by-default.

Allow remote computers to connect controls whether or not Fiddler will accept HTTP requests from other computers or devices. This option may also need to be set in order to allow Windows 8 Metro-style applications to connect to Fiddler. After enabling this option, you must restart Fiddler. Upon restarting, you may see a prompt from your Firewall software confirming that Fiddler should be allowed to receive inbound connections.

 Warning: You should not enable this option on a hostile network, as an attacker who knows you are running Fiddler could send traffic from his computer through your Fiddler instance, making it appear that the traffic was coming from you.

The **Reuse client connections** option controls whether Fiddler will reuse client connections (client keep-alive). Similarly, the **Reuse connections to servers** box controls whether Fiddler will reuse server connections (server keep-alive). The connection reuse options should be left enabled for performance reasons; only disable them for troubleshooting purposes.

The **Chain to upstream gateway proxy** option controls whether or not Fiddler will use the proxy configured inside Internet Explorer as Fiddler starts as an upstream gateway proxy. By unchecking this box, you're telling Fiddler "ignore the system's default proxy settings, and just send requests directly to web servers."

The **Show Gateway Info** link shows information about any known upstream gateway proxy.

The **Act as system proxy on startup** option controls whether or not Fiddler registers as the system's proxy on startup. Internet Explorer and many other applications use the system proxy by default and are notified when it changes.

The **Monitor all connections** checkbox controls whether Fiddler will register as the proxy for all WinINET Connections. This option should be enabled if you are connected to a VPN, RAS, or dialup connection because WinINET will always use the proxy settings for any such connections if they are active.

The **Use PAC Script** checkbox controls how Fiddler registers as the system proxy; specifically, when this box is ticked, Fiddler will tell the browser to use the proxy configuration script (which can be found by clicking the Copy Browser Proxy Configuration URL link) instead of using the default fixed proxy configuration of 127.0.0.1:8888. This option is rarely useful except on IE8 and below when attempting to capture loopback traffic (e.g. http://localhost or http://127.0.0.1); such traffic is not sent to Fiddler when configured as a fixed proxy, but is sent if a PAC Script is used instead.

The **WinINET Connections** list shows what network connections are configured for this machine. This may be useful if you are connected to the Internet via dialup or VPN and want Fiddler to automatically hook a connection other than your LAN connection.

The **IE should bypass Fiddler** list controls which requests should not be sent through Fiddler at all when it is registered as the system proxy. Note that this list is generally only respected by WinINET clients like Internet Explorer. The default <-loopback> token tells IE9 and later that loopback requests *should* be sent to Fiddler; when this token is not present (and on IE8 and lower) WinINET will automatically bypass the system proxy server for loopback traffic. This box accepts a semicolon delimited list of hostnames, and supports * as a wildcard. For instance, to specify that you would like all traffic (including loopback traffic) to go to Fiddler except for secure traffic bound for `example.com`, and any traffic bound for `fiddler2.com`, use the string:

```
<-loopback>;https://example.com;*.fiddler2.com
```

Appearance Options

The Appearance tab exposes options that control how Fiddler is displayed.

The **Font Size** box allows you to select the size of text in Fiddler. A restart is required to fully complete the change.

The **Set Readonly Color** button allows you to select the background color for textboxes that are in a readonly state. This setting exists because gray is the default readonly color for Windows but the lack of contrast between grey and black can be hard on the eyes. A restart is required to complete this change.

The **Hide Fiddler when minimized** checkbox will show the Fiddler icon in your system tray rather than the taskbar when Fiddler is minimized.

When the **Always show tray icon** checkbox is checked, Fiddler's tray icon will always be visible in the system tray.

The **Use SmartScroll in Session List** option controls Fiddler's behavior when new Sessions are added to the Web Sessions list. When this option is disabled, Fiddler will automatically scroll to show the newest sessions added to the list as they appear (if **View** > **AutoScroll Session List** is enabled).

When this option is disabled, Fiddler will only scroll to show the newest Sessions *if* the Web Sessions list is already scrolled to the bottom. Leave this option enabled to help avoid losing your place when inspecting and capturing traffic simultaneously.

Enabling the **Reset Session ID counter on CTRL+X** option causes the session ID numbering to restart from 1 when the Web Sessions list is cleared via the CTRL+X hotkey or the **Remove** > **All Sessions** menu command. When this option is not set, the session IDs will start at 1 and continually increment until Fiddler is restarted.

HEADERENCODING SETTING

When transmitting text over the network, both the client and the server must agree on how to convert between text strings and the raw bytes that are transmitted over the wire. The HTTP specification uses the charset attribute of the Content-Type header to convey the character set used within the request and response bodies.

Unfortunately, HTTP does not provide a broadly-respected mechanism for representing non-ASCII characters within the HTTP headers themselves. Instead, the HTTP specification indicates that only ASCII characters may be used. Some clients and servers respect this directive (usually by percent-encoding non-ASCII characters) but others will emit and accept non-ASCII characters. There are some instances where bytes-to-characters conversion discrepancies will exist between the client application (e.g. a browser), an intermediary (e.g. a proxy like Fiddler) and the server (e.g. Apache or IIS).

To support the broadest range of clients and servers, Fiddler assumes that HTTP headers are transmitted in UTF-8 encoding. There are some locales (particularly in Asia) where, by convention, a different encoding is used (e.g. EUC-CN). You can manually configure Fiddler to utilize a different default encoding for headers by creating a new registry string named HeaderEncoding inside HKCU\Software\Microsoft\Fiddler2. The string value provided must be an Encoding name recognized by the .NET Framework; valid values can be found at http://fiddler2.com/r/?EncodingNames.

You must restart Fiddler for any change to HeaderEncoding to take effect.

PREFERENCES

Fiddler supports an extensible list of Name/Value-paired settings called Preferences that are used by extensions and other components of Fiddler. Many Preferences can be adjusted using menus or checkboxes in the Fiddler user-interface, but some Preferences are not exposed and can *only* be viewed or changed using the Preferences system.

Using the QuickExec box below the Web Sessions list, you can use the PREFS command to interact with Preferences. Typing prefs log will log all Preferences to Fiddler's Log tab. You can type prefs set [prefname] [prefvalue] to create or update a Preference's value; wrap the value in quotation marks if it contains any spaces. Type prefs remove [prefname] to delete a Preference; the next time Fiddler queries the value of the Preference, its absence will be noted and the default value for that Preference will be used. Type prefs show [partialname] to show the list of Preferences whose name contains the provided string (Preference names are case-insensitive).

You can see all of the configured Preferences by typing about:config in the QuickExec box; this will create or activate the **about:config** tab in the Fiddler UI that lists all Preferences sorted alphabetically by name.

You can remove a Preference by selecting its row and tapping the Delete key. Press CTRL+C on a cell to copy its value, or select a row and press CTRL+C to copy both the name and value. You may modify a Preference's value by clicking into the Value column and entering a new value. You can add a new Preference by clicking into the last row (marked with an asterisk in the left margin) and typing a new Name and Value.

A complete list of Preferences supported by Fiddler and the Fiddler Extensions I've created may be found in Appendix D.

Configuring Clients

As a proxy server, Fiddler is only able to observe traffic that is sent to it. By default, web traffic from most applications will automatically flow through Fiddler because it registers itself with Windows as the default proxy when running. Most client programs will use the registered system proxy when sending network traffic. In the few cases where this doesn't happen automatically, configuration changes can be made to either the client or to Fiddler to capture traffic. As a proxy, Fiddler is also able to capture traffic from remote computers and network devices that support proxy servers (e.g. tablet computers and phones that support Wi-Fi).

In this chapter, I'll explain the myriad ways in which Fiddler can be configured to capture traffic.

Capturing Traffic from Browsers

Internet Explorer, Chrome, and Safari for Windows automatically send traffic to the default proxy server, meaning that Fiddler will capture their traffic automatically.

Both Firefox and Opera can be easily reconfigured to send traffic to Fiddler.

Firefox

Current versions of Fiddler install **FiddlerHook**, a Firefox add-on to simplify use of Fiddler with Firefox. You may need to enable the add-on using **Firefox's Tools > Add-ons > Extensions** screen. When enabled, FiddlerHook adds a **Monitor with Fiddler** command to Firefox's **Tools** menu.

The menu offers the ability to change whether Fiddler is used as Firefox's proxy, and permits you to launch Fiddler directly.

If the **Show StatusBar item** in the Monitor with Fiddler menu is ticked, and Firefox's **View > Toolbars > Add-on Bar** option is also ticked, Firefox's status bar will show the current state of FiddlerHook at the bottom right:

Fiddler: ON (auto)

If you click on this status bar panel, a popup menu enables you to change your FiddlerHook settings, as well as providing one-click entry points to clear the Firefox cache and cookies:

When FiddlerHook is enabled, you can also add a button to Firefox's toolbar that launches Fiddler. Right-click the Firefox toolbar and choose **Customize**. Drag the **Fiddler** button to the desired location:

Even if you disable or cannot use the FiddlerHook plugin, it is simple to reconfigure Firefox to use Fiddler. In Firefox 4 and later, click **Tools** > **Options** to open Firefox's Options window. Click the **Advanced** icon at the top, and click the **Network** tab. On that tab, click the **Settings** button in the **Connections** box. Select the **Use system proxy settings** option from the list. After this change is made, Firefox will respect the system proxy settings that are controlled by Fiddler.

Opera

Click the Opera button at the top-left, click **Settings**, and then click **Preferences**. Click the **Advanced** tab, and click **Network** in the list at the left. Click the **Proxy Servers** button, and set the **HTTP** and **HTTPS** proxy server fields to 127.0.0.1 and the Port for each to 8888.

Other Browsers

Of the dozens of minor browsers that run on Windows, most will pick up the default proxy settings automatically. For the few that do not, you can usually follow configuration steps similar to those used for

Opera—use whatever UI the browser provides to set the HTTP and HTTPS proxy to point at Fiddler's proxy endpoint, which runs on `127.0.0.1:8888`.

Alternatively, you can also configure many browsers to use a Proxy Configuration script. Fiddler automatically generates such a script and updates its contents as the Capture Traffic setting is toggled. Use the **Copy Browser Proxy Configuration URL** link in the **Tools** > **Fiddler Options** > **Connections** tab to copy the proxy configuration script URL to your clipboard for easy pasting into the browser's configuration settings.

Capturing Traffic from Other Applications

The most-commonly used HTTP/HTTPS/FTP network stack in Windows is called WinINET, and it is used by Internet Explorer and tens of thousands of other client applications. These applications generally work seamlessly with Fiddler because Fiddler sets the WinINET proxy settings directly when capturing is started.

However, Windows includes several other networking stacks that are not based on WinINET, and some other applications, like Firefox, ship with their own networking components. In some cases, those components will automatically adopt the WinINET proxy settings when their applications start up, while in other cases, you will need to manually configure the component or application to point at Fiddler.

WinHTTP

WinHTTP is similar to WinINET except that it is designed for silent operation in Windows Services and other contexts. It is used by Windows components like BITS (background intelligent transfer service) and by features like Windows Update and the CryptoAPI certificate validation code. Depending on how it is being used, WinHTTP may automatically chain to Fiddler if Fiddler is running *before* the WinHTTP-based application is started. If your application is calling into WinHTTP, you may use the `WinHttpOpen` or `WinHttpSetOption` APIs to direct requests through Fiddler. If you cannot change the application's code, you can change the default WinHTTP proxy settings using command line tools.

On Windows XP & Windows 2003 or earlier:

```
proxycfg -p http=127.0.0.1:8888;https=127.0.0.1:8888
```

On Windows Vista and later, use:

```
netsh winhttp set proxy 127.0.0.1:8888
```

If you follow these configuration steps, you should manually change the proxy settings back when you close Fiddler, otherwise WinHTTP-based applications may subsequently fail to connect to the network.

.NET Framework

The Microsoft .NET Framework provides implementations of the HTTP/HTTPS and FTP protocols using the `System.Net` assembly. In some cases, .NET-based applications will automatically adopt the WinINET proxy when the application starts, so starting Fiddler before the application can ensure that its traffic is captured.

If that doesn't happen, the application's code can be temporarily modified to point at Fiddler by setting the proxy configuration as follows:

```
GlobalProxySelection.Select = new WebProxy("127.0.0.1", 8888);
```

Alternatively, you can manually specify the proxy on an individual `WebRequest` object like so:

```
objRequest = (HttpWebRequest)WebRequest.Create(url);
objRequest.Proxy= new WebProxy("127.0.0.1", 8888);
```

If you don't have access to the application's source, you can specify the proxy inside the application's configuration manifest. Edit (or create) the `yourappname.exe.config` file in the application's folder, adding or updating the following section:

```
<configuration>
  <system.net>
    <defaultProxy>
      <proxy
        usesystemdefault="true"
        bypassonlocal="false"
        proxyaddress="http://127.0.0.1:8888"
      />
    </defaultProxy>
  </system.net>
</configuration>
```

Instead of modifying an individual application's manifest, you might also adjust the machine-wide settings in the `machine.config` file's `configuration` section. The advantage of updating `machine.config` is that the change will apply to .NET code running in *any* application in *any* user-account, including the service accounts used by ASP.NET applications running atop IIS.

Regardless of how you specify your proxy settings, .NET will always bypass the Fiddler proxy for URLs that point to the current machine (also known as "loopback"). Debugging of loopback traffic requires additional configuration, as described later in this chapter.

Java

Some Java Runtime Environments (JREs) will automatically adopt the WinINET proxy settings automatically. Otherwise, the mechanism to set the default proxy server may depend on which JRE you use; one JRE includes an applet in the Windows Control Panel that enables proxy selection.

If neither of the following two command lines works for your JRE:

```
jre -DproxySet=true -DproxyHost=127.0.0.1 -DproxyPort=8888 MyApp
```

```
jre -DproxySet=true -Dhttp.proxyHost=127.0.0.1 -Dhttp.proxyPort=8888
```

...please consult the documentation for the JRE to learn how to configure its proxy.

PHP / CURL

To proxy traffic from CURL running inside PHP, add the following line of code before you send your web requests, where $ch is the handle returned by `curl_init()`:

```
curl_setopt($ch, CURLOPT_PROXY, '127.0.0.1:8888');
```

Capturing Traffic from Services

Fiddler only registers as the system proxy for the current user running Fiddler. That means that system services running in different accounts, including ASP.NET and IIS Worker Processes, will not send their traffic to Fiddler by default.

Unfortunately, the configuration steps to proxy traffic from system accounts are generally scenario-specific. For instance, to capture Web Service calls from ASP.NET pages, edit the `web.config` or `machine.config` files for the ASP.NET installation, or modify the code to manually specify a web proxy using the steps in the .NET Framework configuration section.

For Windows Services that utilize other networking stacks (e.g. Java or WinHTTP), you will need to find the configuration settings for those services and configure their proxy manually.

Capturing Traffic to Loopback

You may need to take special configuration steps to capture traffic that is sent to a server running on the same computer as the client application and Fiddler are both running on. Such traffic is called "loopback" traffic because it never leaves the machine; loopback traffic typically includes traffic sent to the loopback addresses of 127.0.0.1, [::1], the hostname `localhost`, and sometimes to any of the current computer's TCP/IP addresses.

There are three scenarios that can cause problems with loopback traffic:

1. Many client applications and frameworks are hardcoded to bypass the proxy server for loopback traffic.

2. On Windows Vista and later, HTTP authentication behaves different when the client and server are on the same computer.

3. On Windows 8, Metro-style applications are not able to connect to loopback listeners (like Fiddler) running outside of the app package.

Let's explore each of these in turn.

Loopback Bypasses

Many clients automatically bypass the proxy for loopback traffic with the expectation that a remote proxy server wouldn't know what to do with traffic bound for "127.0.0.1", since the proxy's definition of that address is different than the client's. However, these clients failed to consider the case where the proxy server is running on the same computer as the client (like Fiddler), in which case both the client and the proxy have the same definition for such addresses.

Prior to Internet Explorer 9, all traffic sent via the WinINET networking stack (used by IE, Office, etc.) would bypass the proxy server if it was sent to addresses of 127.0.0.1, [::1], or the hostname localhost. Current versions of Opera do the same, and Firefox's **No Proxy For** setting is set to localhost, 127.0.0.1 by default. Microsoft .NET Framework versions 1 to 4 also bypass the proxy for loopback requests.

If you attempt to use one of these clients to connect to a server running on your local computer, the client ignores the proxy setting and sends traffic directly to the server.

The simplest way to capture such traffic in Fiddler is to change the hostname requested by the client so that the client doesn't recognize it as bound for a loopback address. One option is to simply use the current computer's DNS hostname (e.g. http://mymachinename) instead, but this requires that you know the current computer's hostname and can make it complicated to build test cases that work across multiple machines.

To help mitigate that shortcoming, Fiddler supports several "virtual hostnames" that alias the loopback addresses:

Rather than:	Instead use:
127.0.0.1	ipv4.fiddler
[::1]	ipv6.fiddler
localhost	localhost.fiddler

By using these virtual hostnames, the client will send the traffic to Fiddler, and Fiddler will automatically substitute the correct hostname in the request URL and Host header.

In Internet Explorer 9, WinINET was enhanced with a new feature that allows the client to configure WinINET to proxy loopback traffic. To opt-in to this behavior, the Proxy Bypass List is configured with the special token <-loopback>; Fiddler sets this token automatically by default, ensuring that you can easily see traffic sent to the local computer. Starting in Windows 8, the WinHTTP stack also respects the <-loopback> token. Hopefully, Opera and the .NET Framework will permit loopback proxying in future versions.

Loopback Authentication
Windows Vista and later attempt to protect the user against "loopback authentication" attacks, in which a client thinks it is authenticating with a remote server but is actually authenticating back to the local computer. Such attacks are usually attempting to elevate privilege against the local computer. When Windows encounters an unexpected attempt to authenticate to the local machine, the authentication request will be blocked.

To disable loopback protection, set `DisableLoopbackCheck=1` as described here: `http://support`
`.microsoft.com/kb/926642`.

Loopback Blocked from Metro-style Windows 8 Apps

Windows 8 introduced a new application-isolation technology known as AppContainer. This technology is
used by new "Metro-style apps" including the Metro-style mode of Internet Explorer, as well as all
applications you download from the Windows Store. In order to prevent inter-process communication
between the isolated AppContainer processes and other processes (most of which run at higher privilege)
Metro-style applications are prevented (by the firewall) from making network connections to servers
running on the local computer. This blockage occurs no matter what hostname is used-- attempts to
connect to `http://localhost`, `http://127.0.0.1`, and `http://machinename` will all fail. Using the
`CheckNetIsolation.exe` tool, an end-user may exempt a single process from this restriction for debugging or development purposes only. Debugging an application with the upcoming version of Visual Studio
will also temporarily allow it to connect to loopback.

By default, if you run Fiddler on Windows 8 and launch the Metro-style browser or any Metro-style
application, you will find that the app is unable to connect to any site, including Internet sites. That's
because Fiddler is running on the local computer and the firewall will block the application from proxying
its traffic to Fiddler. Because Fiddler is the configured proxy server, the app will conclude that the network
is unavailable and abort the request.

To resolve this problem, I've created a graphical utility called **EnableLoopback** which allows you to
exempt one or more AppContainers from Loopback restrictions. Users of the v4 builds of Fiddler will find
the `EnableLoopback.exe` utility installed by default; it can be launched using the **Win8 Config** toolbar
button at the left edge of the Fiddler toolbar:

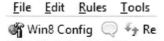

Users of the v2 builds of Fiddler can download the utility from `http://fiddler2.com/r/?Win8EL`. The
tool requires Administrative privileges to adjust the Loopback Exemptions list, and will prompt for
permission to run as an Administrator when launched.

As the utility starts, it will enumerate all of the AppContainers on the local computer and display them in a
listview. A checkbox before each entry indicates whether the AppContainer is exempted from loopback
restrictions. You can individually change the setting on a per-AppContainer basis, or you may use the
buttons at the top of the tool to adjust all AppContainers' exemptions together. After making changes, click
the **Save Changes** button to commit the list back to Windows.

After exempting an app's AppContainer from loopback restrictions, you will find that Fiddler can successfully debug its traffic, just like any other desktop application.

Running Fiddler on Mac OSX

As a Windows Application, Fiddler cannot run on Mac OSX natively. However, virtualization products like **VMWare Fusion** or **Parallels Desktop** permit you to run Windows applications like Fiddler in a virtual machine on your Mac.

To run Fiddler under Parallels, only minor configuration changes are needed. Install Parallels and reconfigure the Windows Virtual Machine's **Hardware** > **Network 1** Type setting to use **Bridged Network** mode:

This configuration will enable your Mac to send network traffic into the Virtual Machine. Restart the Virtual Machine and install Fiddler. To configure Fiddler, click **Tools > Fiddler Options > Connections** and check the box labeled **Allow remote computers to connect**. You will need to restart Fiddler for the change to take effect, and you may need to reconfigure your firewall to allow incoming connections to the Fiddler process. These steps allow Fiddler to accept connections from the Mac environment. Now, you must manually configure your Mac to direct its web traffic through Fiddler running in your Virtual Machine.

First, you must learn the IP address of the virtual machine. To do so, hover over the **Online** indicator at the far right of the Fiddler toolbar. A tooltip will show you the IP addresses assigned to the virtual machine:

Next, click the Apple Menu and click **System Preferences**. Click the **Network** icon and click the **Advanced** button. Click the **Proxies** tab. Enable the **Web Proxy (HTTP)** and **Secure Web Proxy (HTTPS)** options to point to the IPv4 address of the virtual machine; also specify that the proxy runs on port 8888.

After configuring the Mac's proxy, Fiddler will begin capturing traffic from Safari and other applications. When you're done using Fiddler, return to the OSX System Preferences and disable the proxy settings.

Capturing Traffic from Other Computers

You can use Fiddler to capture traffic from any application running on another computer if that application supports a proxy server; after all, that's how proxy servers normally work. To capture traffic in this configuration, you must first configure Fiddler, then configure the other computer.

To configure Fiddler, click **Tools** > **Fiddler Options** > **Connections** and check the box labeled **Allow remote computers to connect**. You will need to restart Fiddler for the change to take effect, and you may need to reconfigure your firewall to allow incoming connections to the Fiddler process.

You should verify the client computer can successfully reach Fiddler without problems caused by the firewall or routing by opening the browser and visiting `http://FiddlerMachineIP:8888`. If you see the "Fiddler Echo Service" webpage, then you know that the client and Fiddler are able to communicate.

After verifying connectivity, your next step is to configure the proxy settings on the other computer, using the techniques described in the Capturing Traffic from Other Applications section above. The one difference is that instead of using `127.0.0.1:8888` as the proxy address, you must instead use `IPOfTheFiddlerPC:8888`. So, for instance, the other computer's **Internet Explorer** > **Tools** > **Internet Options** > **Connections** > **LAN Settings** screen might look like this:

A few tips:

- When traffic is from another computer, Fiddler filters that rely upon the process name (e.g. "Show only Web Browser traffic") will not work, as the process name cannot be determined for remote traffic.

- If you plan to decrypt HTTPS traffic from a client not running on the same computer as Fiddler, see the HTTPS Configuration chapter for configuration steps.

- When you stop debugging by closing Fiddler, you will need to clear the other computer's proxy settings. Otherwise, all of its subsequent requests will fail because the proxy server is not running.

Capturing Traffic from Devices

Most computing devices that support Wi-Fi or Ethernet can be configured to send their traffic to Fiddler; this includes iOS devices like the iPhone, iPad, and iPod Touch, many Android devices, and all Windows Phone and Windows RT devices.

Begin by following the steps in the previous section to configure Fiddler to allow traffic from remote computers. Next, it's best to test the connection between the device and the computer running Fiddler—use the device's browser to visit http://FiddlerMachineIP:8888 and verify that the device's traffic appears in the Web Sessions list. You may need to disable the device's cellular (3G) connection in order to ensure that traffic is sent only over Wi-Fi. If you don't see traffic from the device and it shows a connection error, you may need to configure your Wi-Fi network. Two common configuration issues occur:

1. Wi-Fi Isolation

2. IPSEC

Many home routers offer a **Wi-Fi Isolation** feature, in which Wi-Fi-connected devices may not connect to devices that are attached directly to the router's Ethernet ports. Some routers even offer the ability to block one Wi-Fi client from connecting to another Wi-Fi client. If your router offers such features, you will need to disable them to allow your device to reach Fiddler.

Some corporate networks use **IPSEC** for security; IPSEC prevents connections from non-IPSEC clients to IPSEC clients. Most devices do not support IPSEC, so when you need to send traffic from such a device, you must configure the machine running Fiddler with an "IPSEC Boundary Exception" to permit inbound traffic not protected with IPSEC. On many networks, such exceptions can only be created by a Network Administrator.

After you've successfully connected your device to Fiddler, you will need to configure it to proxy its HTTP and HTTPS traffic.

Apple iOS Proxy Settings

To access the proxy settings on an iPhone, iPad, or iPod, click the **Settings** icon on the home screen. In the Settings list, pick **General** and then choose **Network** from the list. Click **WiFi** and push the small blue arrow at the right of the Wi-Fi network's name to configure its settings. Click the **Manual** option in the **HTTP Proxy** section. In the **Server** box, enter the IP address or hostname of your Fiddler instance. In the **Port** box, provide the port Fiddler is listening on. You should leave the **Authentication** slider set to Off.

Windows Phone Proxy Settings

To access the proxy settings on your Windows Phone, open the **Settings** app and click the **Wi-Fi** entry. Tap and hold the Wi-Fi network's name and click **Edit**. Set the **Proxy** slider to On. In the **Server/URL** box, enter the IP address or hostname of your Fiddler instance. In the **Port** box, provide the port Fiddler is listening on. Leave the **Proxy authentication** slider set to Off.

Windows RT Proxy Settings

The new Windows 8 on ARM operating system, recently renamed to Windows RT, only runs Metro-style applications. This blocks Fiddler from running directly on your device. However, you can configure your Windows RT device to send its traffic to a traditional Windows 8 desktop or laptop computer. From the Windows 8 Start screen, type **proxy** and click the **Settings** option to show the **Configure Proxy Server** tile. Click the tile to launch the **Internet Properties** dialog box on the desktop. Click the **LAN Settings** button and adjust the settings as in the following screenshot, placing the IPv4 address of the Fiddler PC in the **Address** box:

Other Devices

Most other devices that support Wi-Fi offer a way to configure a proxy using a Settings applet. However, a small number of devices, like the current version of Amazon's Kindle Fire, do not provide a supported mechanism to configure the proxy server. To use Fiddler with these devices, you may need to "jailbreak" the device to get access to non-public configuration settings, or utilize Fiddler in reverse-proxy mode, described later in this chapter.

Tips:

- If you don't see all traffic, ensure that you've disabled the device's cellular features to force all traffic to use the Wi-Fi network.

- Most devices will require special configuration to allow Fiddler to decrypt their HTTPS traffic. Configuration details can be found in the chapter on HTTPS decryption.

Using Fiddler as a Reverse Proxy

Sometimes, you may want to use Fiddler to trap traffic but cannot configure the client to use a proxy server. To address this need, Fiddler can operate as a "reverse proxy." In the reverse proxy configuration, Fiddler runs on a server and forwards inbound requests to a different port or even a different computer.

For instance, say you're running a website on port 80 of a machine named WEBSERVER. You're connecting to the website using a Kindle Fire, for which you cannot configure the web proxy. You want to capture the traffic from the tablet, and the server's response.

1. Start Fiddler on the WEBSERVER machine, running on the default port of 8888.

2. Click **Tools** > **Fiddler Options**, and ensure the **Allow remote computers to connect** checkbox is checked. Restart if needed.

3. Choose **Rules** > **Customize Rules**.

4. Inside the OnBeforeRequest handler, add a new line of code:

```
if (oSession.HostnameIs("webserver") oSession.host = "webserver:80";
```

5.   On the Kindle, navigate to `http://webserver:8888`

Requests from the tablet will appear in Fiddler. The requests are forwarded from port 8888 to port 80 where your webserver is running. The responses are sent back through Fiddler to the device, which has no idea that the content originally came from port 80.

If you'd like, you can use Fiddler as a reverse proxy without changing the port that the client application targets. To do so, you must reconfigure both your web server software and Fiddler. First, reconfigure your web server to listen on a new port. For instance, if your web server runs on port 80, you must reconfigure it to run on port 81. Then, configure Fiddler to listen on port 80, using the box on the **Tools** > **Fiddler Options** > **Connections** tab.

Acting as a Reverse Proxy for HTTPS
One problem with running as a reverse proxy is that the client never knows that its traffic is really flowing through a proxy server. That means that if the client makes a HTTPS request to Fiddler, it does not establish a CONNECT tunnel first, it instead attempts to begin a HTTPS handshake immediately. Fiddler, expecting a HTTP request, will consider the binary HTTPS handshake as malformed traffic and will abort the connection.

This problem can be solved by creating an additional network listener for Fiddler to receive HTTPS connections. In the QuickExec box below the session list, type

```
!listen 444 WebServer
```

This will create a new network listener on port 444 which will expect all inbound connections to start with a HTTPS handshake. Fiddler will act as the server, returning a certificate for whatever hostname was specified in the second parameter to the listen command. In the example above, the certificate would match any request to `https://WebServer`.

After the secure connection is established, your `OnBeforeRequest` handler may route the inbound secure requests to the actual server.

Chaining to Upstream Proxy Servers
By default, Fiddler will adopt the current system's proxy settings and use those settings as the default upstream gateway proxy for all outbound requests:

Fiddler supports all types of proxy settings, including manually specified proxies, proxy scripts, and automatically detected (WPAD) proxies. Any proxy bypass list will also be respected.

Your system's default proxy settings (see Internet Explorer's **Tools** > **Internet Options** > **Connections** > **LAN Settings** screen) are used as the upstream gateway by default. That's true even if you don't normally use Internet Explorer for anything else, or you rely upon a dialup modem or VPN connection that has a different default proxy. If you wish to prevent Fiddler from automatically chaining to your system's default proxy, untick the **Chain to upstream gateway proxy** option inside **Tools** > **Fiddler Options** > **Connections**.

If required, you may use FiddlerScript to override the default gateway proxy for any Session. To do so, set the X-OverrideGateway flag. If you set the flag's value to DIRECT then Fiddler will bypass the gateway and send the request directly to the target server. If you set the value to an *address:port* combination like myproxyserver:80, Fiddler will instead use the specified proxy for that Session.

Chaining to SOCKS / TOR

By default, Fiddler expects a proxy specified by the X-OverrideGateway flag to use the CERN proxy protocol used by nearly all proxies. However, one less popular proxy standard exists, called SOCKS. In the SOCKS protocol, the client sends the proxy a binary preface which specifies the target address to which a TCP/IP connection should be made. After the SOCKS proxy confirms that the requested connection tunnel has been generated, the client sends its web traffic through the tunnel.

The SOCKS protocol is occasionally used by corporate Virtual Private Networking (VPN) software, but it is also used to make connections into the TOR Project. The TOR Project can be thought of a global proxy network designed to provide anonymity for users of the project. TOR network requests are bounced between worldwide endpoints in an attempt to prevent network monitors from determining the origin of any given request. SOCKS protocol version 4a also allows the proxy server to perform DNS lookups, enhancing privacy. When connected to TOR using SOCKS v4a, DNS resolution happens privately in the cloud rather than from your local computer.

Beyond enhancing privacy, one other interesting aspect of the TOR network is that it allows you to experience your site as if you were coming from a different location. For instance, when using TOR I visited a page with advertising. The ads were in Dutch because my request exited the TOR network in Amsterdam.

When setting the X-OverrideGateway flag, use the socks= prefix to indicate that Fiddler should use the SOCKS v4a protocol when speaking to the upstream server. For instance, the TOR installer sets up an entry point to the TOR network using a SOCKS proxy on port 8118 called **Polipo**. You can add the following inside your FiddlerScript's OnBeforeRequest method to route any request to test.example.com through the TOR network:

```
if (oSession.HostnameIs("test.example.com")) {
  oSession["x-OverrideGateway"] = "127.0.0.1:8111";
}
```

If you'd instead prefer to send *all* of your web traffic via TOR, you can simply set the X-OverrideGateway flag unconditionally for each Session.

VPNs, Modems, and Tethering

When you establish a VPN, 3G tethering, or dial-up modem connection in Windows, WinINET will use that connection's proxy settings for all requests. To ensure that such traffic is captured by Fiddler, ensure that the **Monitor all connections** box is checked inside **Tools** > **Fiddler Options** > **Connections**.

Some uncommon network software products operate outside of the WinINET layer. When connected using such software, your web traffic may not be visible to Fiddler because it is being captured and routed using mechanisms beyond WinINET's control.

DirectAccess

Recent versions of Windows support a technology known as DirectAccess (`http://technet.microsoft.com/en-us/network/dd420463`) that permits remote access to a corporate network without establishing a VPN. DirectAccess is integrated into WinINET so that requests which flow over DirectAccess are never sent to the system default proxy.

Unfortunately, this behavior means that Fiddler cannot observe traffic when DirectAccess is in use.

It appears that individual DirectAccess configuration entries can be updated in the registry to specify a per-target proxy server, but debugging via this mechanism would prove very cumbersome. Instead, when using Fiddler in such an environment, engineers typically use Remote Desktop to access a desktop PC running inside the corporate network, then run Fiddler and the client application on that PC.

Memory Usage and Fiddler's Bitness

Fiddler stores the entire request and response in memory; this means that Fiddler can use large amounts of memory (RAM) while it is running. The Operating System's memory manager is designed to manage the use of memory by applications and ensures that even if Fiddler is using a large amount of memory, rarely-accessed objects are swapped out of system RAM into the disk-based pagefile.

However, even with lots of RAM and disk space, Fiddler may occasionally show a warning message:

```
Exception of type 'System.OutOfMemoryException' was thrown.
    at System.IO.MemoryStream.set_Capacity(Int32 value)
    at System.IO.MemoryStream.EnsureCapacity(Int32 value)
    at System.IO.MemoryStream.Write(Byte[] buffer, Int32 offset, Int32 count)
    at Fiddler.Session.Execute(Object objThreadstate)
```

This message is somewhat misleading because the system isn't really *out of memory*—instead, this means that the memory manager could not find a *contiguous* block of address space large enough to store the request or response. This problem most often occurs when downloading large files (e.g. a video over a hundred megabytes in size). No matter how much RAM you have, a 32bit process is limited to an address space of 2 gigabytes in size. Each object in that address space can cause "fragmentation" that could prevent storage of large objects by splitting available memory into chunks that are too small to store an entire response within one contiguous block.

On a 32bit computer, if you have thousands of sessions in Fiddler's Web Sessions list, fragmentation can prevent a response as small as a few megabytes from being stored. You can reduce the incidence of this problem by clearing Fiddler's Web Sessions list periodically. Alternatively, use the **Keep Only** box on the toolbar to automatically trim the Web Sessions list to a fixed number of sessions to free up space.

Out-of-memory errors are rarely encountered when Fiddler runs on a 64bit version of Windows because the 64bit address space is so large that you cannot possibly fill it or fragment it enough to prevent storage of even giant sessions. However, even on 64bit computers, each individual request and response is limited to 2 gigabytes due to an underlying limit within the .NET Framework.

On a 32-bit machine, you can help avoid out-of-memory errors when downloading huge files by adding the following code to your FiddlerScript inside the `OnPeekAtResponseHeaders` function. This snippet will cause files larger than 5 megabytes to stream to the client and Fiddler will not keep a copy:

```
// This block enables streaming for files larger than 5mb
if (oSession.oResponse.headers.Exists("Content-Length"))
{
  var sLen = oSession.oResponse["Content-Length"];
  if (!isNaN(sLen)) {
    var iLen = parseInt(sLen);
    if (iLen > 5000000) {
      oSession.bBufferResponse = false;
      oSession["ui-color"] = "yellow";
      oSession["log-drop-response-body"] = "save memory";
    }
  }
}
```

If you're building on FiddlerCore or writing a Fiddler Extension, you can use similar logic:

```
FiddlerApplication.ResponseHeadersAvailable += delegate(Fiddler.Session oS)
  {
    // This block enables streaming for files larger than 5mb
    if (oS.oResponse.headers.Exists("Content-Length"))
    {
      int iLen = 0;
      if (int.TryParse(oS.oResponse["Content-Length"], out iLen))
      {
        // File larger than 5mb? Don't save its content
        if (iLen > 5000000)
        {
          oS.bBufferResponse = false;
          oS["log-drop-response-body"] = "save memory";
        }
      }
    }
  };
```

By default, Fiddler will always run in 64bit mode when running on a 64bit version of Windows. In rare instances, you may prefer to run Fiddler in 32bit mode. For instance, you must run in 32bit mode when you're using an extension that requires native binaries that are only available as 32bit modules (e.g. Silverlight 4) or your FiddlerScript depends upon other modules unavailable in 64bit. For example, the `Microsoft.Jet.OLEDB.4.0` database provider used to write to Microsoft Access `.MDB` database files is not available in 64bit mode. To force Fiddler to run in 32bit mode on 64bit Windows, use the `ForceCPU.exe` tool located in the Fiddler installation folder.

BUFFERING VS. STREAMING TRAFFIC

In order to enable modification of requests and responses, Fiddler is configured to completely buffer request and response messages before passing them along to their destinations.

Request Buffering

When a client connects to Fiddler, Fiddler reads the entire HTTP request from the client. If a breakpoint is set, the request is then paused to allow tampering using the Inspectors. After the request is resumed, the server connection is established and Fiddler transmits the entire request to the server.

Fiddler does not expose any mechanism to "stream" a HTTP request to the server as it is read from the client—requests are *always* buffered completely before sending. HTML5 WebSockets are the one exception to this rule—WebSocket messages stream bi-directionally.

Response Buffering

After sending the request to the server, Fiddler begins reading its response. Some common web scenarios (particularly streaming audio and video) are impacted negatively by response buffering, so Fiddler permits *streaming* of responses. Streamed responses cannot be modified using Fiddler's Inspectors. By default, only audio and video responses are configured to stream. You can configure all responses to stream using the toggle on the Fiddler toolbar, or you may stream selectively on a per-response basis by setting the Session's bBufferResponse property to false using FiddlerScript.

When streaming is enabled for a response, each block of data read from the server is immediately passed to the client application. By default, if the client application closes its connection to Fiddler, Fiddler will continue to read the response from the server to permit collection of the entire response. If you'd prefer Fiddler to abort the download if the client disconnects, set the fiddler.network.streaming .AbortIfClientAborts preference to true.

When buffering is disabled for a response, FiddlerScript's OnBeforeResponse method runs *after* the response is fully returned to the client. This (perhaps surprising) behavior allows operations that don't modify the response (e.g. logging the response body to a database) to work properly for all Sessions. If your code needs to determine whether a given response was streamed, it can test the Session's BitFlags:

```
bool bWasStreamed = oSession.isFlagSet(SessionFlags.ResponseStreamed));
```

If you need to modify the response body before it is sent to the client, you must disable streaming by setting oSession.bBufferResponse=true in either the OnBeforeRequest or OnPeekAtResponseHeaders handlers.

COMET

Fiddler's Inspectors will only show the response's body after the response data has been completely read from the server. But what happens if the server's response never ends? Such responses occur with streaming radio stations and on sites that use a web programming technique called COMET.

With COMET, a server uses a "hanging frame" or other mechanism to push data to the client using a long-held HTTP connection that trickles data to the client as needed. HTML5 introduces a similar mechanism called "Server Sent Events" which works using the same general mechanism. Because a server's COMET response never really "finishes," the data returned on that connection is not normally visible to Fiddler's Inspectors until the connection closes.

To enable such data to be inspected, Fiddler offers the **COMETPeek** command on the Web Session's context menu. When you invoke the command, Fiddler will take a "snapshot" of the in-progress response, allowing you to inspect the partial response read from the server.

Fiddler's default behavior of buffering responses wreaks havoc with sites that depend on COMET. That's because the server's response never ends and therefore Fiddler's buffering of a COMET stream will usually cause the web application to stall. Unfortunately, COMET responses aren't marked in any way, so you will need to manually exempt such responses from buffering if you do not wish to enable the Streaming option globally.

HTML5 WEBSOCKETS

The HTML5 specification introduces WebSockets, a technology that enables real-time socket communication between a client and server. To create a WebSocket, the client first establishes a HTTP(S) connection to the server. Next, the client and server handshake and agree to use the WebSocket protocol for subsequent traffic on the connection. The ws:// and wss:// URI schemes are used for plaintext and secure WebSockets respectively, even though the initial handshakes take place over HTTP or HTTPS.

To help ensure that WebSocket traffic flows unimpeded through an proxy (like Fiddler), clients will first establish a CONNECT to the proxy, requesting a tunnel to the destination server. If the WebSocket URI uses the wss:// scheme, a HTTPS handshake then occurs. If the unsecure ws:// scheme was used, then the HTTPS handshake is skipped.

The client then uses the newly-established connection to send a HTTP GET request with an Upgrade header proposing a switch to the WebSocket protocol. If the server agrees to change protocols, it sends a HTTP/101 Switching Protocols response. You can easily observe this process using the Web Sessions list and Inspectors:

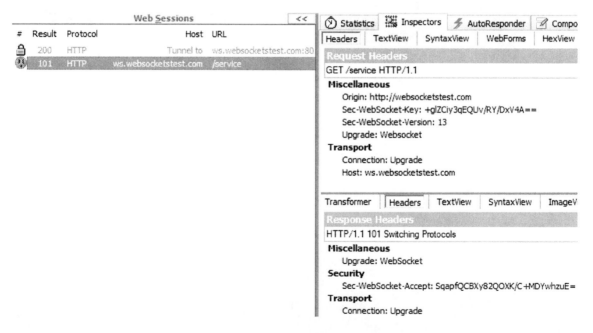

After the handshake, the client and server may send each other WebSocket messages in any order. Unlike HTTP's request-response pattern, the server may send WebSocket messages to the client without the client first sending a WebSocket message to the server. Because HTTP messages are no longer exchanged on a connection which has been upgraded to the WebSocket protocol, you will not see the WebSocket messages in the Web Sessions list or the request or response Inspectors.

However, Fiddler *does* have the ability to parse WebSocket messages, and in future versions of Fiddler, a new type of Inspector will be introduced to enable display and modification of WebSocket traffic. For now, WebSocket messages from the client and server are shown in the **Log** tab. The bytes of these messages are parsed and displayed in plaintext:

```
Upgrading Session #47 to websocket

[WebSocket #47] Server->Client (12 bytes)
TYPE: TEXT.
MESSAGE: connected,
FLAGS: 10000001 DATA: 10 bytes.
-----------------------------

[WebSocket #47] Client->Server (14 bytes)
TYPE: TEXT.
MESSAGE: timer,
FLAGS: 10000001 DATA: 6 bytes, masked using KEY: BD-36-84-D5.
-----------------------------

[WebSocket #47] Server->Client (23 bytes)
TYPE: TEXT.
MESSAGE: time,2012/4/30 14:50:38
FLAGS: 10000001 DATA: 23 bytes.
-----------------------------

[WebSocket #47] Client->Server (8 bytes)
TYPE: CLOSE.
CLOSE REASON: 1001
FLAGS: 10001000 DATA: 2 bytes, masked using KEY: 25-A2-56-AE.
-----------------------------
```

To help prevent attacks against transparent proxies or other buggy but well-meaning intermediaries, a client's WebSocket messages are typically "masked" by XOR'ing the message text against a masking key that is not visible to JavaScript running on the client. When logging the client's WebSockets messages, Fiddler automatically unmasks the text for ease of reading.

As the standard finalizes and browsers implement the specification, more websites will begin building upon WebSockets. As that happens, Fiddler will be updated to better support this exciting new protocol.

FIDDLER AND HTTPS

When visiting a HTTPS site in Fiddler, there's not a lot to see by default. Instead of the expected list of requests and responses, you'll only see one or more CONNECT tunnels:

#	Result	Protocol	Host	URL	Body
🔒 1	200	HTTP	Tunnel to	www.fiddler2.com:443	0
🔒 2	200	HTTP	Tunnel to	ssl.google-analytics.com:443	0

The HTTPS protocol sandwiches an encrypted (SSL or TLS) connection between HTTP requests and the underlying TCP/IP network connection upon which those requests are sent. Network intermediaries or observers are thus prevented from viewing or modifying the HTTP traffic thanks to the use of the cryptographic protocols.

You might then be surprised to learn that Fiddler can both view and modify HTTPS traffic if configured appropriately. Fiddler achieves this by using a "man-in-the-middle" approach to HTTPS, which means that when talking to the client, it pretends to be the server, and when talking to the server, it pretends to be the client.

The HTTPS protocol is explicitly designed to block this attack by using digital certificates to authenticate the identity of a HTTPS server (and optionally the client). When a client receives a certificate from the server, it validates that the certificate itself is trustworthy by determining whether it is chained to a **Root Certification Authority** that is trusted by the client or the operating system. Since you are typically running Fiddler on your own computer, you can reconfigure your browser or operating system to trust Fiddler's root certificate. After you do so, the client application will not complain when it detects that traffic is being protected by Fiddler-generated certificates.

To enable HTTPS traffic decryption in Fiddler, click **Tools** > **Fiddler Options**. On the **HTTPS** tab, tick the box labeled **Decrypt HTTPS traffic**.

When you enable HTTPS decryption, Fiddler will generate a self-signed root certificate and a matching Private Key. Fiddler will use this root certificate to generate HTTPS server certificates (also called "End Entity" certificates) for each secure site that you visit.

Trusting the Fiddler Root Certificate

After generating the root certificate, Fiddler gives you the opportunity to add it to Windows' Trusted Root Certificate Authorities store. Adding the root to the Trusted Store will allow the HTTPS server certificates Fiddler later generates to be deemed valid by browsers and other applications. This will help stop browsers from showing warning screens and prevent applications from failing to connect due to "trust errors."

Fiddler and Windows show prompts to warn off users who might not understand the implications of trusting a certificate:

If you click **Yes**, Windows will then prompt you to confirm the change:

These warnings are deliberately verbose and scary, but the actual level of risk is minimal. Each Fiddler root certificate is generated uniquely per-computer, which improves security by ensuring that no other Fiddler user has the same root certificate. As such, the root certificate could only really be abused by malware running on the local computer, and if your computer is already infected by malware, you have bigger problems to worry about.

Machine-wide Trust on Windows 8

On Windows 8, Metro-style applications will not trust Fiddler's root certificate unless it is in the per-Machine Trusted Root certificate store. Therefore, after the prior steps add the certificate to your per-User Trusted Root certificate store, Fiddler will then launch an administrative program to add the certificate to the Machine store:

If you click **Yes** to launch the utility, it will confirm the operation:

After you click through this flurry of prompts, Fiddler's root certificate will be installed and applications that rely on the Windows certificate store will no longer present security errors when Fiddler is decrypting their traffic.

To later remove all Fiddler-generated certificates, untick the **Decrypt HTTPS traffic** checkbox and then press the **Remove Interception Certificates** button.

Manually Trusting the Fiddler Root

If you'd prefer to manually trust the FiddlerRoot, launch certmgr.msc and drag the DO_NOT_TRUST_ FIDDLERROOT certificate from the **Personal** folder to the **Trusted Root Certification Authorities** folder. If you wish to make this change on a machine-wide basis:

1. Right-click the DO_NOT_TRUST_FIDDLERROOT certificate from the **Personal** folder and choose **All Tasks > Export.**
2. Export the certificate as DER Encoded X509 Binary to FiddlerRoot.cer on your desktop.
3. Launch mmc.exe.

4. Click **File > Add/Remove Snap-In.**
5. Select the **Certificates** snap-in and press **Add.**
6. When prompted **This snap-in will always manage certificates for:** choose **Computer Account**
7. Click **Local Computer**, then **Finish**, then **OK.**
8. Open the **Certificates (Local Computer)** node.
9. Right-click the **Trusted Root Certificate Authorities** folder and choose **All Tasks > Import**.
10. Choose the file you exported in step #2 and import it.

Additional HTTPS Options

Before closing the Fiddler Options window, consider using the dropdown to configure which processes should have their traffic decrypted:

If you only plan to decrypt browser traffic, choose that option to avoid decrypting traffic from other applications that aren't of interest to you. Beyond saving CPU cycles and memory, doing so can prevent problems with applications that are not using HTTPS in standard ways (e.g. Outlook uses RPC-over-HTTPS tunnels to connect to Exchange Server) or that will not respect the Fiddler root certificates' presence in the Windows Trusted store (e.g. Dropbox).

You may also use the textbox to list servers for which HTTPS traffic should not be decrypted. For instance, I use the following settings to prevent decryption of Outlook Web Access and Dropbox traffic:

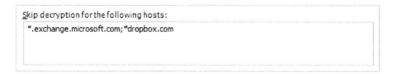

Use semicolons to delimit the hostnames in the list, and use * as a wildcard character.

CONFIGURING CLIENTS FOR HTTPS DECRYPTION

While most applications (Internet Explorer, Microsoft Office, Chrome, Safari, etc.) use the Windows Certificate Store to validate certificate chains, some applications maintain their own certificate stores. For instance, Java Runtime Environments often have their own certificate stores, and the Firefox and Opera browsers also maintain their own certificate lists.

To configure such clients to trust Fiddler-generated certificates, you must first obtain Fiddler's root certificate as a .CER file. You have two options to do so:

1> Click the **Export Root Certificate to Desktop** button on the **Fiddler Options** window's **HTTPS** tab.

2> Visit http://127.0.0.1:8888/ in the browser and click the **FiddlerRoot Certificate** link to download the certificate as a .CER file.

After you have the root certificate file, you can add it to the client application's Trusted certificates list.

Browsers

Firefox
In Firefox, click **Tools** > **Options**. Click the **Advanced** button, and switch to the **Encryption** tab. Click **View Certificates** to open the **Certificate Manager**. Click the **Authorities** tab and click the **Import** button. Select the FiddlerRoot.cer file and click **Open**. Tick the **Trust this CA to identify websites** checkbox and press **Ok**. Firefox will now trust HTTPS server certificates generated by Fiddler.

Opera
In Opera, click **Opera** > **Settings** > **Preferences**. Click the **Advanced** tab, and click **Security** in the list. Click **Manage Certificates**. Click the **Authorities** tab and click the **Import...** button. Select the FiddlerRoot.cer file and click **Open**. Click the **Install** button and click the **Ok** button to confirm that you want to trust the certificate. Opera will now trust HTTPS server certificates generated by Fiddler.

Cross-machine scenarios

If you have configured Fiddler to proxy HTTPS traffic from other computers, those other computers must be manually configured to trust the root certificate from the Fiddler server machine. You can enable this trust by downloading the root certificate from the http://FiddlerMachineName:8888/ page, then using the manual certmgr.msc steps to trust that root certificate.

One important reminder: Each Fiddler root certificate is generated uniquely *per-machine*. If a client PC has previously generated a Fiddler root certificate, that root certificate will interfere when proxying traffic through Fiddler running on a different machine. That's because the root certificates will not match (they'll have the same Subject CN but different public keys). This mismatch will cause fatal errors when establishing HTTPS connections-- even if the client has been configured to trust both root certificates. To avoid this problem, you must first remove all existing Fiddler root certificates from the client before trusting the new root certificate downloaded from the Fiddler server machine.

HTTPS and Devices

Windows Phone

In order for a Windows Phone device to trust the FiddlerRoot certificate, you must install the certificate onto the phone. To do so, open `http://FiddlerMachineName:8888/` from the device, and download the root certificate. Tap to open the `FiddlerRoot.cer` file, and when prompted by the **Install certificate?** screen, click the **Install** button.

Android and iOS

Fiddler's default Certificate Maker is based on the `makecert.exe` command-line tool. The certificates it generates are accepted by virtually all Windows clients and most other platforms as well. However, Apple iOS devices including the iPad, iPhone, and iPod require that the root and server certificates contain additional metadata not included in `makecert.exe`-generated certificates. Some Android distributions have similar requirements.

To enable Fiddler to generate certificates compatible with these devices, download the **Certificate Maker** plugin for Fiddler from:

```
http://fiddler2.com/r/?FiddlerCertMaker
```

This plugin requires Windows Vista or later. It replaces the default certificate generation code in Fiddler with a version based on the open-source Bouncy Castle cryptography library. The plugin generates iOS-compatible certificates by default, and respects several Preferences to enable compatibility with a wide-variety of platforms.

For instance, at least one Android platform requires that server certificates must not have the `Critical` constraint applied to their `EKU`. You can configure the Certificate Maker plugin to remove that constraint by using QuickExec to set the preference:

```
prefs set fiddler.certmaker.bc.ee.criticaleku false
```

The server certificates that generated by this plugin are not placed in the Windows Certificate store and are instead kept only in memory only. Every time Fiddler restarts, new server certificates will be generated. In contrast, `makecert.exe`-generated certificates are individually added to the Personal certificates store as they are generated, and are only removed when you push the **Remove Interception Certificates** button.

After configuring Fiddler to generate certificates that are compatible with your device, you must configure the device to trust Fiddler's root certificate. To do so, configure your device to use Fiddler as its proxy as described earlier in this book. Then open `http://ipv4.fiddler:8888/` from your device, and download the root certificate. Open the `FiddlerRoot.cer` file:

Tap the **Install** button. You'll then see a warning, which you may acknowledge by pressing the **Install** button:

After Fiddler's root certificate is installed, your device's browser and applications should no longer complain about certificate errors when Fiddler is decrypting their traffic.

If you later decide to uninstall the root certificate from the device, open the **Settings** app, click **General**, and scroll down to **Profiles** at the bottom. Select the `DO_NOT_TRUST_FiddlerRoot` profile, and tap **Remove**.

Buggy HTTPS Servers

A small number of HTTPS servers implement the TLS protocol handshake incorrectly and will fail when Fiddler handshakes with them. The same connection failure will occur when a web browser connects to the server, but that failure may be silently handled by the browser automatically falling back to use an older version of the handshake protocol.

Fiddler can be configured to offer only specific protocol versions to the server in order to accommodate buggy implementations. From FiddlerScript, you can add the following code in the `Main()` function to limit Fiddler to offering only SSLv3 when making HTTPS connections:

```
CONFIG.oAcceptedServerHTTPSProtocols =
    System.Security.Authentication.SslProtocols.Ssl3;
```

Alternatively, you can limit the protocols on a per-request basis. Inside the OnBeforeRequest function, add code like so:

```
if (oSession.HTTPMethodIs("CONNECT") &&
    oSession.HostnameIs("buggy.example.com"))
{
  oSession["x-OverrideSslProtocols"] = "ssl3.0";
}
```

By offering only SSLv3, you can accommodate servers that do not properly support extensions or other features of the TLS protocol.

Certificate Validation

When Fiddler connects to a HTTPS server, it will validate the server's certificate to ensure that the certificate is valid and contains the target site's hostname. By default, any certificate errors are presented for you to decide how to proceed:

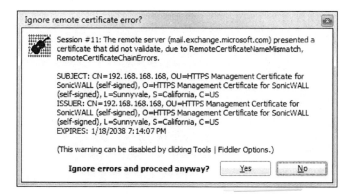

If you choose **No**, the connection will be dropped. If you choose **Yes**, the certificate error will be ignored and the connection will be used normally. Fiddler will cache your decision until restarted. Because Fiddler generates its own certificate to secure the connection from the client, the client application will be unaware that the server's certificate was invalid.

Certificate Pinning

A very small number of HTTPS client applications support a feature known as "Certificate Pinning" whereby the client application is hardcoded to accept only one *specific* certificate. Even if the connection uses a certificate that chains to a root that is otherwise fully-trusted by the operating system, such applications will refuse to accept an unexpected certificate.

To date, some Twitter and Dropbox apps include this feature, and Windows 8 Metro apps *may* opt-in to requiring specific certificates rather than relying upon the system's Trusted Root store.

When a Certificate-Pinned application performs a HTTPS handshake through a CONNECT tunnel to Fiddler, it will examine the response's certificate and refuse to send any further requests when it discovers the Fiddler-generated certificate.

Unfortunately, there is no general-purpose workaround to resolve this; the best you can do is to exempt that application's traffic from decryption by setting the x-no-decrypt Session flag on the CONNECT tunnel. This flag will prevent Fiddler from decrypting the traffic in the tunnel and it will flow through Fiddler uninterrupted.

FIDDLER AND FTP

Like HTTP, the File Transfer Protocol (FTP) is a TCP/IP-based protocol used for transferring files, but it predates and is not compatible with HTTP. However, the protocol remains the one exception to the rule that Fiddler can only view HTTP-based protocols. That's because when a client browser or application is configured to proxy FTP traffic using a CERN-style proxy (like Fiddler), the client will convert FTP download requests into HTTP GET requests before sending them to the proxy.

The client's expectation is that the proxy will then act as a *gateway*, converting each FTP-over-HTTP request into a FTP request that will be sent to the origin server using the FTP protocol. Only the HTTP request's URL and Authorization header are used in the FTP request; all other request headers are ignored.

Fiddler can deal with FTP traffic in three ways:

1. By acting as a HTTP-to-FTP gateway.

2. By chaining to an upstream CERN-style proxy server (e.g. Microsoft ISA) which will act as the HTTP-to-FTP gateway.

3. By responding to requests using the Fiddler AutoResponder (or other features).

To configure Fiddler to register as the system's FTP proxy, click **Tools > Fiddler Options**. On the **Connections** tab, tick the **Capture FTP requests** option and restart Fiddler.

If Fiddler receives a FTP request which is not sent to an upstream gateway proxy and which is not handled by an AutoResponder rule, it will attempt to connect to the server using the FTP protocol. Fiddler will reformat the FTP server's response as an HTTP response and return it to the client. There are several limitations when acting as a HTTP-to-FTP gateway; for instance, some of the Session's Timers will not be set. Streaming of FTP responses is not supported-- the complete FTP response will be buffered before being converted and returned to the client.

Fiddler and Web Authentication

Most public websites use HTML Forms for authentication—they prompt the client for a username and password. If the credentials supplied are valid, the client gets a login cookie that is sent for all subsequent requests. Fiddler can easily view and submit such cookies.

However, HTTP and HTTPS offer two native mechanisms for authenticating a client:

- HTTP Authentication
- HTTPS Client Certificates

Fiddler can be used with servers using either form of authentication.

HTTP Authentication

With HTTP Authentication, the client makes a HTTP request and the server responds with a `HTTP/401` or `HTTP/407` response demanding credentials. `HTTP/401`s are sent by servers that require authentication, while `HTTP/407`s are sent by proxy servers.

There are four common authentication schemes in use in HTTP:

- Basic
- Digest
- NTLM
- Negotiate

In **Basic** authentication (RFC 2617) the client supplies the username and password in the `Authorization` request header. The client's credentials are simply base64-encoded and can be trivially decoded using the Auth Inspector. The Basic authentication scheme is primitive and obviously unsafe to use over unencrypted HTTP connections.

In **Digest** authentication, also described in RFC 2617, the server presents a challenge to the client using the `WWW-Authenticate` response header. The client combines the challenge data and its knowledge of the user's password to compute a message digest that proves to the server that it knows the password. This authentication scheme is stronger than Basic but is rather uncommon, owing to limited server support and various client bugs.

The **NTLM** authentication scheme is rarely used on the public Internet but is commonly used on Windows-based Intranets. When the server presents a `HTTP/401` to the client, the client reissues the request indicating that it supports NTLM, then the server provides a challenge. The client uses the challenge and the credentials to generate the reply to the challenge, and the server returns the resource if the challenge was answered successfully. This pattern means that when NTLM authentication occurs, the client receives two `HTTP/401` challenges before the resource is finally returned with a `HTTP/200`.

Unlike Basic and Digest, the NTLM scheme is not generally per-request. Instead NTLM is *per-connection*, meaning that a single authentication proof will be used to authorize all subsequent requests on the same connection. That's why you'll often see a flurry of HTTP/401s when first loading an Intranet site, then don't see any subsequent authentication challenges on later page loads.

The **Negotiate** authentication scheme (sometimes called Integrated Windows Authentication) is a "wrapper" protocol that uses either the NTLM or Kerberos protocol under the covers. At the HTTP layer, Negotiate generally behaves very much like NTLM, requiring between one and three roundtrips per request.

When NTLM or Negotiate is used through a proxy server, client applications require that the proxy add a `Proxy-Support: Session-Based-Authentication` response header. This header indicates that the proxy understands that authenticated connections must not be shared between different clients. Fiddler adds this header automatically.

Automatic Authentication in Fiddler

Fiddler is able to automatically authenticate to servers that use the `Digest`, `NTLM` and `Negotiate` protocols. When Fiddler automatically authenticates, the client that issued the request will not see the interim `HTTP/401` or `HTTP/407` responses. That's because Fiddler itself consumes these responses, answers the server's challenges, and returns data to the client only after authentication is complete.

To have Fiddler automatically respond to a server or gateway proxy's authentication challenges, set the `X-AutoAuth` property on the Session to a plaintext credential string. If you use a value of `(default)`, then Fiddler will use the credentials of the Windows logon user account in which Fiddler is running:

```
static function OnBeforeRequest(oSession: Session)
{
  // To use the current Fiddler user's credentials:
  if (oSession.HostnameIs("ServerThatDemandsCreds")) {
    oSession["x-AutoAuth"] = "(default)";
  }

  // or, to use explicit credentials...
  if (oSession.HostnameIs("ServerUsingChannelBinding")) {
    oSession["x-AutoAuth"] = "redmond\\ericlaw:MyP@$$w0rd";
  }

  //...
```

 Warning: If Fiddler is configured to accept requests from other devices or user-accounts, using `(default)` creates a security vulnerability. That's because those requests will be authenticated using the credentials of the account in which Fiddler is running.

If the **Automatically Authenticate** box is ticked on the **Options** subtab, requests from the Composer tab automatically set the `x-AutoAuth` flag to the value of the `fiddler.composer.AutoAuthCreds` Preference.

For scenarios that require HTTP Basic authentication, you can simply generate the required `username:password` string, base64-encoding it using the TextWizard. Take the base64-encoded credential string and add it as the value of an `Authorization` or `Proxy-Authorization` request header. That header can be added to outbound requests using the Filters tab, FiddlerScript, or the Composer tab's **Request Headers** box.

Authentication Problems

Because Fiddler acts as a proxy and offers powerful capabilities like HTTPS decryption, sometimes authentication scenarios are impacted when Fiddler is running. Three common Authentication issues relate to Channel-Binding Tokens, WinHTTP credential release, and Loopback authentication protections. Each will be described in turn.

Channel-Binding

One shortcoming of the NTLM authentication scheme is that it can fall victim to "pass-through" attacks. In such an attack, the client is lured to a malicious site which presents an authentication challenge that was originally generated by a victim server. The client dutifully responds to the authentication challenge, and the malicious site uses that client's challenge-response to authenticate to the victim server. This attack permits the attacker to steal data from the victim server using the unwitting client's credentials.

To address this problem, the concept of Channel-Binding was introduced. Channel-Binding binds the authentication challenge-response to the underlying connection so that it cannot be reused on another connection. Typically this works by binding the credentials to the current HTTPS connection. Channel-Binding is enabled via the **Extended Protection** option in IIS.

Channel-Binding presents a problem for Fiddler because the client binds its credentials to its connection *to Fiddler*, such that when Fiddler forwards those credentials to the actual server, the server rejects them. To resolve this problem, you can configure Fiddler to *itself* authenticate to the server, taking the client out of the loop. Because Fiddler itself generates the challenge-response, using the Channel-Binding information matching its own connection to the server, the credentials will be accepted. To configure Fiddler to authenticate on the client's behalf, use the `X-AutoAuth` flag described in the "Automatic Authentication in Fiddler" section above.

WinHTTP Credential Release Policy

The WinHTTP network stack does not support the concept of security zones, which means that it sometimes will refuse to respond to authentication challenges when a proxy like Fiddler is involved. This problem sometimes appears when attempting to download documents from SharePoint sites using the Microsoft Office client applications. You can resolve this problem by configuring Fiddler to authenticate on the client's behalf using the `X-AutoAuth` flag. Alternatively, see `http://support.microsoft.com /kb/956943` to learn how to modify the `AuthForwardServerList` in the registry.

Loopback Protection

Windows also attempts to protect the user against "loopback authentication" attacks. In these attacks, a client thinks that it is authenticating with a remote server but it is really authenticating back to the local computer. Such attacks usually attempt to elevate privilege from a low-privilege process to a higher-privilege local process. When Windows encounters an unexpected attempt to authenticate to the local machine, the authentication request will be blocked.

To disable loopback protection, set the flag DisableLoopbackCheck=1 as described at: http://support.microsoft.com/kb/926642.

HTTPS Client Certificates

In addition to the HTML Forms-based and HTTP Authentication protocols, a third authentication type is used for high-security sites. HTTPS Client Certificates are a very strong form of authentication used in some high-stakes scenarios like banking and document-signing. When using Client Certificate authentication, the client supplies a client certificate to the server that cryptographically proves the identity of the user.

One of the key design goals of Client Certificate authentication is to prevent network intermediaries (like Fiddler) from abusing the client's credentials. Even if the client application sent its certificate to Fiddler, Fiddler cannot successfully reuse that certificate to respond to the server's demand, because the client never provides Fiddler with its private key.

To resolve this limitation, you can supply any necessary client certificates and private keys directly for Fiddler to use when handshaking with the server. By default, if a server prompts the client for a certificate, Fiddler will look inside the %USERPROFILE%\Documents\Fiddler2\ folder for a file named ClientCertificate.cer and will use that certificate when responding to the server's certificate demand.

In some cases, you may want to use a different client certificate for each secure connection. To do so, specify the location of the certificate using the https-Client-Certificate property on the CONNECT tunnel to the secure server. For instance, you can write code like this:

```
static function OnBeforeRequest(oSession: Session)
{
  if (oSession.HTTPMethodIs("CONNECT") {
    if (oSession.HostnameIs("exampleA")) {
      oSession["https-Client-Certificate"] = "C:\\certs\\CertA.cer";
    }
    else
    if (oSession.HostnameIs("exampleB")) {
      oSession["https-Client-Certificate"] = "C:\\test\\CertB.cer";
    }
  }

  //...
```

A `.CER` file does not contain the private key associated with the certificate's public key. Instead, the `.CER` file merely acts as reference to Windows' Personal certificates store (`certmgr.msc`). The Windows certificate store holds the private key associated with the certificate and releases it only as needed. Client certificates stored on a Smartcard will automatically appear within the Personal store when the Smartcard is inserted:

When the Smartcard is inserted, you may export a `.CER` file from `certmgr.msc` and use it just like any other client certificate. Note that your Smartcard must remain inserted for Fiddler to use its private key.

If the desired certificate isn't yet installed Windows' Personal certificates store (e.g. you only have a .pfx file) you must first import it into the certificate store, then export a `.CER` file. After your certificate is installed, simply right-click the certificate and choose **All Tasks > Export...**. Save the `.CER` file to either the default `ClientCertificate.cer` location or the location you will specify via the `https-Client-Certificate` flag.

Inspectors

Fiddler's Inspectors are used to display the request and response for the selected Session in the Web Sessions list. Inspectors appear in two places: On the **Inspectors tab** in the main Fiddler window, and in the standalone **Inspect Session** windows. The latter are opened using the command on the Web Sessions context menu.

On the Inspectors tab, the Request Inspectors are shown in a panel at the top, and the Response Inspectors are shown at the bottom. You can switch between Inspectors by clicking on the desired Inspector's name (e.g. HexView).

When you first double-click or press the Enter key on a session in the Web Sessions list, the Inspectors tab will become active. Each request or response inspector will be polled to ask it how applicable it is to inspecting the selected request and response. For instance, the ImageView Inspector returns a high "score" for image/* types while returning a low score for textual types. In contrast, the TextView Inspector returns a high score for textual types and a low score for binary formats.

Whichever inspectors return the highest score for the Session will become active. To force Fiddler to always activate a particular Request Inspector, set the `fiddler.ui.inspectors.request.alwaysuse` preference to the title of the Inspector's tab. To force Fiddler to always activate a specific Response Inspector, set the `fiddler.ui.inspectors.response.alwaysuse` preference to the title of the Inspector's tab.

A thin blue line splits the top and bottom panels; you can use the mouse to move the line and resize the panels. Double-clicking the line will maximize the Response Inspectors panel, as this is the panel most users use most of the time.

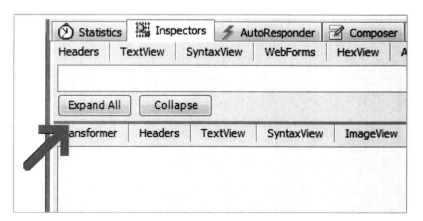

To get even more display area, the Inspectors tab can be extracted from the main window, either by clicking the Tearoff button in the toolbar or by typing the command `tearoff` in the QuickExec box. Closing the Inspectors window will return them to their default position on the main window.

Right-clicking on an individual request or response inspector's tab will show a menu containing two options: **Inspector Properties** and **Hide Inspector**. The first shows information provided by the Inspector about itself, while the second will remove the inspector from the Inspectors tab. To restore a hidden Inspector later, edit the `fiddler.inspectors.hidelist` Preference and restart, or hold the SHIFT key while starting Fiddler.

By default, the Inspectors are ReadOnly when inspecting a session, unless the session is currently paused at a breakpoint. Additionally, the Inspectors will permit editing if the session is in an Unlocked state, which can be achieved by using the command on the Edit menu. Most Inspectors will display with a specific background color while in ReadOnly mode, and a different color (typically white) when editing is permitted. The default ReadOnly color is light-blue, and can be changed using the **Tools** > **Fiddler Options** > **Appearance** tab.

The remainder of this chapter will describe each of the Inspectors included with Fiddler.

AUTH

Type	Request & Response
Allows Editing	No

Fiddler's Auth Inspector interprets the contents of the Authorization- and Authentication- related headers on requests and responses. Typically, these headers can be found on HTTP/401 and HTTP/407 responses that demand credentials, and the subsequent requests that provide the requested credentials.

For instance, if you enable the "Require Proxy Authentication" rule in the Rules menu, Fiddler will return a HTTP/407 response demanding that the user supply credentials for each request. This demand is made by the Proxy-Authenticate header, which the Auth Response Inspector displays:

```
Auth

Proxy-Authenticate Header is present: Basic realm="FiddlerProxy"
No WWW-Authenticate Header is present.
```

After the user enters the name *UserName* and the password *SecretKey* in the browser's Authentication dialog, the browser's subsequent requests supply a Proxy-Authorization header with the user's credentials. Since the authentication scheme in use in this scenario is HTTP Basic, the credentials are encoded using base64 encoding. The Auth Request Inspector decodes the string automatically and displays it in plaintext:

```
Auth

Proxy-Authorization Header is present: Basic VXNlck5hbWU6U2VjcmV0S2V5
Decoded Username:Password= UserName:SecretKey

No Authorization Header is present.
```

Of course, most websites will use a stronger form of authentication, either HTTP Digest or the Windows NTLM or Negotatiate schemes. The latter are especially popular on Windows networks.

Fiddler' Auth inspector knows how to parse NTLM blobs and will show you the information contained within those blobs, like so:

```
-[NTLM Type3: Authentication]------------------------------
Provider: NTLMSSP
Type: 3
OS Version: 6.2:8329
Flags:    0xa2888205
    Unicode supported in security buffer.
    Request server's authentication realm included in Type2 reply.
    NTLM authentication. Negotiate Always Sign. Negotiate NTLM2 Key.
```

```
    Target Information block provided for use in calculation of the
      NTLMv2 response.
    Supports 56-bit encryption. Supports 128-bit encryption.
lmresp_Offset: 134; lmresp_Length: 24; lmresp_Length2: 24
ntresp_Offset: 158; ntresp_Length: 396; ntresp_Length2: 396
Domain_Offset: 88; Domain_Length: 14; Domain_Length2: 14
User_Offset: 102; User_Length: 14; User_Length2: 14
Host_Offset: 116; Host_Length: 18; Host_Length2: 18
msg_len: 554
Domain: REDMOND
User: ericlaw
Host: ERICLAWT8
lm_resp: 00 00 00 00 00 00 00 00 00 00 00 00 00 00 00 00 00 00 00 00 00 00 00 00
nt_resp: 42 40 AE AB 3E D7 7F 02 B5 F9 76 D7 C9 5E 6B 82 01 01 00 00 00 00 00 00
         05 96 B2 D4 01 23 CD C1 D3 D9 8A 33 47 87 40 3D 00 00 00 00 02 00 52 ...
```

The Auth Inspector cannot currently parse Kerberos authentication messages, but will show the decoded bytes of the challenge and response.

CACHING

Type	Response only
Allows Editing	No

The Caching Response Inspector examines the HTTP response headers to determine whether the selected response is cacheable under the rules of HTTP, and if so, for how long. It consults the response headers `Cache-Control`, `Expires`, `Pragma`, `Vary`, `ETag`, `Age`, and `Last-Modified` in its evaluation of the response.

Some browsers (including Internet Explorer) support the specification of caching information in HTML documents using `META HTTP-EQUIV` tags. The Caching Inspector scans responses that have a HTML `Content-Type` and will display any `HTTP-EQUIV` or `PRAGMA` directives found in the markup.

For responses which do not explicitly specify their cacheability or freshness lifetime, the Caching Inspector will compute the "heuristic freshness lifetime" using the `Last-Modified` header and the algorithm suggested in RFC2616.

Auth	Caching	Cookies	Raw	JSON	XML

This response does not specify an explicit expiration time and does not specify a Last-Modified date. Heuristic expiration is typically based on Last-Modified date. Lacking Last-Modified, this response may be revalidated on every use or once per browsing session, depending on the browser configuration.

This response contains neither an ETAG nor a Last-Modified time. This will prevent a Conditional Revalidation of this response.

You can learn more about how browsers utilize caches at `http://fiddler2.com/r/?httpperf`.

Cookies

Type	Request & Response
Allows Editing	No

The Cookies Inspector displays the contents of any outbound `Cookie` and `Cookie2` request headers and any inbound `Set-Cookie`, `Set-Cookie2`, and `P3P` response headers. Note that the `Cookie2` and `Set-Cookie2` headers are uncommonly used and not supported by Internet Explorer and some other browsers.

The display of the cookies is basic (you can see the same information in the Headers inspector). This Inspector's value primarily consists of examining the `P3P` response header, if present, to determine whether the cookie is likely to be stored. P3P (Platform for Privacy Preferences) is a standard whereby the server can communicate to the client how it will be using the cookies that accompany the `P3P` header.

```
Set-Cookie: ASPSESSIONIDCCBTDCRD=CIFKIKJDFMJFFODAJPFMFKGN; path=/
P3P: CP="ALL IND DSP COR ADM CONo CUR CUSo IVAo IVDo PSA PSD TAI TELo
        OUR SAMo CNT COM INT NAV ONL PHY PRE PUR UNI"
```

The tokens in the `P3P` header's `CP` (Compact Policy) string are interpreted by the Inspector and their meaning is listed:

The Inspector will further evaluate the string to determine whether the cookie is deemed "acceptable" by the default privacy policy used by Internet Explorer. It's worth mentioning that some sites (Facebook and Google, as of this writing) send invalid `P3P` statements to circumvent the browser's privacy features. Under the rules of P3P, unknown tokens (like those sent by such sites) are deliberately ignored.

The Cookies Request Inspector displays the size of the outbound `Cookie` header, helping identify over-sized cookies to eliminate or shrink to improve the network performance.

The Cookies Response Inspector flags common problems. For instance, Internet Explorer will refuse to set a cookie for any server whose hostname containing an underscore character, and the Inspector will warn you if it encounters this condition.

Headers

Type	Request & Response
Allows Editing	Yes

Every HTTP request begins with plaintext headers that describe what resource or operation is sought by the client. The first line (the "Request Line") of the request contains three values, the HTTP Method (e.g. "GET" or "POST"), the URL path which is being requested (e.g. "/index.htm"), and the HTTP version (e.g. "HTTP/1.1"). Following the Request Line are one or more lines containing name-value pairs of metadata about the request and the client, such as the User-Agent and Accept-Language.

Similarly, every HTTP response begins with plaintext headers that describe the result of the request. The first line of the response (the "Status Line") contains the HTTP version (e.g. "HTTP/1.1"), the response status code (e.g. "200") and the response status text (e.g. "OK"). Following the Status Line are one or more lines containing name-value pairs of metadata about the response and the server, such as the length of the response file, its Content-Type, and information about how the response may be cached.

The Headers Inspector allows you to view the HTTP headers of the request and the response, showing the name-value pairs in a treeview below the Request Line or Status Line. The name-value pairs of headers are grouped based on their function and then sorted alphabetically by name. Groupings are simply for your ease of reading, and are not sent on the network. For Request headers, the groups include [Cache, Client, Entity, Transport, Cookies/Login, Miscellaneous]. For Response headers, the groups include [Entity, Transport, Cookies/Login, Security, Miscellaneous].

By default, the contents of the Headers Inspector are read-only and cannot be edited. While in ReadOnly mode, the background color of the treeview and the Raw Headers box will display using the ReadOnly appearance color (light-blue). When you select a Web Session paused at a breakpoint, or when you select the **Unlock for Editing** option on the Edit menu, the Headers Inspector is shown in Edit mode. While in Edit mode, the background color is the default window color (white), and the contents of the headers may be edited.

Click the **Raw** hyperlink at the top-right of the Inspector to display the plaintext of the headers as they are sent on the network. Click the **Header Definitions** link to view a help topic describing common HTTP headers and their use.

Due to limitations in the Windows treeview control, only the first 260 characters of the header's name and value are shown. To view headers which exceed this length, select the header and press Enter or F2, or right-click the header and choose **View Header**. The Header Viewer window will open in read-only mode and allow you to inspect the full name and value. The length (in characters) of the value will be displayed in the title bar of the window.

While the Inspector is in ReadOnly mode, any `Cookie` request headers are broken out into name-value pairs for easier reading. While in Edit mode, any `Cookie` header is shown as a single line as it is actually sent to the server.

Context Menu

Right-clicking on the list of Headers will show a menu with the following options:

View Header	Open the Header Viewer window for the selected header.
Edit Header	(Only shown in Edit mode) Open the Header Editor window for the selected header.
Copy Header	Copy the entire selected header to the clipboard.
Copy Value only	Copy the selected header's Value to the clipboard.
Send to TextWizard	Send the selected header's Value to the TextWizard to permit decoding of encoded text.
Add Header	When in Edit mode, create a new blank header.
Remove Header	When in Edit mode, remove the selected header.
Paste Headers	When in Edit mode, attempt to add new headers based on the information on the clipboard.
Lookup Header	Open a web page with information about the selected HTTP header.

Keyboard Shortcuts

After selecting a session in the Web Sessions list, you can press CTRL+H to activate the Request and Response Header Inspectors. Within the Inspector, the following hotkeys are available:

CTRL+C	Copy the selected header to the clipboard.
CTRL+SHIFT+C	Copy the selected header's value to the clipboard.
F2 or Enter	Open the Header Viewer or Header Editor window for the selected header.
CTRL+V	When in Editing mode, attempt to add one or more new headers based on the text on the clipboard.
Insert	When in Editing mode, create a new blank header.
Delete	When in Editing mode, remove the selected header.

Editing

When the Inspector is in Edit mode, you can make changes to the headers before they are sent to the server or the client. If you would like to edit the entire set of headers at once, click the **Raw** link at the top-right of the Inspector. The Raw Headers window will appear and enable you to save the new set of headers.

Alternatively, you can directly change the contents of the Request or Status Line by editing the text in the box at the top of the Inspector. To edit an individual name-value header, select it and press F2 or hit Enter and the Header Editor window will appear. To add a new Header, press the Insert key; a new header will appear and the Header Editor will automatically open.

You may update the name and value of the new header using the boxes, or you may click the **Header Templates** button at the bottom of the window to choose from commonly-used headers.

HEXVIEW

Type	Request & Response
Allows Editing	Yes

The HexView Inspector allows you to view the request and response headers and body using a hexadecimal edit box. This capability is most useful when inspecting binary content.

The Inspector contains a HexEdit control organized into three vertical columns. In the left column, in light grey, is the hexadecimal address for the adjacent line of bytes. In the center column are the hexadecimal representations of the individual bytes. The right column redisplays those bytes, interpreted as ASCII text. If the HexView is configured to show the headers, the request headers will be shown using in blue text and response headers will be shown in green. The body bytes are shown in black.

At the bottom of the Inspector is a status bar containing three panels. The first panel shows the current cursor position within the bytes in decimal form and hexadecimal form. If the Inspector is configured to show the header bytes, the offset will automatically reset to zero when the cursor enters the body bytes.

If one or more bytes are selected in the control, the middle panel displays the length of the current byte selection.

The right panel indicates the current mode: **Read only**, **Overwrite**, or **Insert**. The Inspector is in Read only mode except when the Session is paused at a breakpoint or is Unlocked for Editing. In Edit mode, you may press the Insert key to toggle between overwriting bytes and inserting new bytes.

The HexView Inspector's context menu offers the following items:

Insert File Here...	In Edit mode, inserts the bytes of a selected file at the current cursor position.
Select Bytes...	Prompts you for a number of bytes to select, then selects that number of bytes starting at the current cursor position. Enter a leading $ character if you wish to specify the number of bytes in Hexadecimal format. Tip: This feature can be useful if you wish to examine HTTP Chunked Encoding blocks, as the length of each block is specified as a hexadecimal number.
Save Selected Bytes...	When one or more bytes are selected, this item enables saving the selected bytes to a file of your choosing.
Goto Offset...	Enables you to move the cursor to a selected byte of the content. Enter a leading + or – character to specify the offset from the current cursor position instead of the start of the content. Enter a leading $ character if you wish to specify the number of bytes in Hexadecimal format.
Find Bytes...	Enables you to specify a sequence of hexadecimal characters to search for. The search begins at the current cursor position. Press F3 to continue the search after each match.

Find String…	Enables you to specify a sequence of characters to search for (the bytes will be interpreted as UTF-8 characters). The search begins at the current cursor position. Press F3 to continue the search after each match.
Show Headers	This checkbox controls whether the header bytes will be displayed within the control. When unticked, only the body bytes will be shown. Note: In current versions of Fiddler, this option is automatically unticked when the HexView Inspector enters Edit mode, as the Inspector currently does not support editing of headers.
Set Bytes per Line…	Enables you to specify how many bytes to show on each line of the display. Enter 0 to instruct the HexView to automatically select the number of bytes based on the available width (a minimum of four bytes per line will be shown).

IMAGEVIEW

Type	Response
Allows Editing	No

The ImageView Inspector allows you to view the response as an image. The Inspector can display most common web image formats, including JPEGs, PNGs, and GIFs, as well as less common formats including cursors, images, bitmaps, EMF/WMF, and TIFF. The Inspector does not support display of SVG graphics; if IE9 or later is installed, SVG responses can be viewed using the WebView Inspector.

The grey panel at left shows information about the currently selected image, including its size in bytes, pixel dimensions, and file format. At the bottom of the grey panel is a dropdown that allows you to control how the image is scaled:

- **No scaling** – Images are shown at their native dimensions.

- **Autoshrink** – Images that are larger than the display area are scaled down.

- **Scale to fit** – Images that are larger than the display area are scaled down, and images that are smaller than the display area are scaled up to fill the area.

The Inspector's context menu allows you to copy the image to the clipboard as a bitmap, or quickly save the image file to your Windows desktop using the current time as the basis for the filename. Also available is an option to copy the image as a DataURI, a text format which can be embedded in HTML or stylesheets and displayed in modern browsers (IE8+). If the resulting URI is over 32kb in length, Fiddler will warn you that that IE8 does not support 32kb+ URIs; IE9 or later will be required to render the image. The final option on the menu allows you to change the background color (normally light blue) which can provide useful contrast when examining small or transparent images.

Middle-clicking on the image will silently copy the image to your Desktop folder. Double-clicking on the image will open a full-screen view. In full-screen view, the following functions are available:

Key or Mouse action	Function
Enter or Z	Toggle Zoom between Full-Screen and Actual Size
H	Flip the image horizontally
V	Flip the image vertically
R	Rotate the image clockwise by 90 degrees.
Mousewheel up	Zoom to Full-Screen
Mousewheel down	Show Actual Size
Escape	Exit the full-screen viewer

To more rapidly view a large number of image responses, use the GalleryView extension.

JSON

Type	Request & Response
Allows Editing	No

The JSON Inspector interprets the selected request or response body as a JavaScript Object Notation (JSON) formatted string, showing a treeview of the JSON object's nodes. If the body cannot be interpreted as JSON, the treeview will remain empty. Unlike most inspectors, the JSON Inspector is able to render the data even if the request or response is compressed or has HTTP Chunked Encoding applied; you do not need to remove the encoding to display the content.

Many responses delivered with the JSON Content-Type are not really JSON. Instead, they're JSONP, a JavaScript file consisting of a single function call with a string argument containing JSON. The JSON Inspector is able to handle many types of JSONP by ignoring the leading function call and trailing parenthesis and semicolon. However, some JSONP is malformed such that the name component of the name/value pairs is unquoted: the JSON Inspector cannot handle this type of malformedness and will refuse to parse the content.

The context menu offers two options: **Copy**, to copy the selected node to the clipboard (or press CTRL+C), and **Send to TextWizard**, to send the selected node's content to the TextWizard window for encoding or decoding.

The **Expand All** button in the footer will expand all nodes of the tree, while the **Collapse** button will collapse all nodes of the tree. The JSON tree will be automatically expanded if the body contains less than 2000 nodes; for performance reasons, you must manually expand the tree for larger documents.

RAW

Type	Request & Response
Allows Editing	Yes

The Raw Inspector allows you to view the complete request and response, including headers and bodies, as text. The term "raw" is a bit of a misnomer, because Fiddler is still interpreting the bytes of the request and response; if you need a purely "raw" view of network traffic, use a packet sniffer like Microsoft Network Monitor (NetMon) or Wireshark.

Most of the Inspector is a large text area that displays headers and the body interpreted as text using the character set detected using the headers, the byte-order-marker, or an embedded META tag declaration. Pressing CTRL+G in the text area allows you to move the cursor to a specific line number. When right-clicking, the text area's context menu offers standard Cut, Copy and Paste options. The menu also offers an option to send the currently selected text to the TextWizard tool. There are two checkboxes on the menu: one controls whether Word Wrap is enabled and the other controls whether the AutoTruncate feature is enabled.

Along the bottom of the Inspector is a bar that offers additional features. First is a search box that allows you to select matching text within the content. The search text is case-insensitive and does not support regular expressions. Pressing the Up or Down arrow keys in the search box will scroll the text area above (to allow you to view search results in context). Matches are selected as you type, and the box will turn green if a match was found or red if no further matches were found. Pressing Enter or F3 will select the next match. Pressing CTRL+Enter will highlight all matches in the content.

The **View in Notepad** button saves the text content to a temporary file and opens a text editor to view the file. The text editor launched is controlled by the `fiddler.config.path.texteditor` preference; `notepad.exe` is the default.

The Inspector replaces any null bytes with the Unicode replacement character (�) and as such can be used to view binary response bodies, although the HexView remains more suitable for that task. Because displaying large binary bodies in the textbox can require large amounts of CPU time and memory, the Inspector is configured to automatically truncate the display of large responses. The threshold at which truncation occurs is controlled by the Content-Type and four preferences:

- `fiddler.inspectors.request.raw.truncatebinaryat`
- `fiddler.inspectors.request.raw.truncatetextat`
- `fiddler.inspectors.response.raw.truncatebinaryat`
- `fiddler.inspectors.response.raw.truncatetextat`

By default, binary Content-Types are truncated at 128 bytes, and text types are truncated at 262144 bytes. Truncation can be disabled using the context menu.

SYNTAXVIEW

Type	Request & Response
Allows Editing	Yes

The SyntaxView Inspector allows you to view request and response body text highlighted according to type-specific rules. This is a very useful feature when reading HTML, XML, CSS, and JavaScript. The Inspector uses the Content-Type header when deciding which highlighting rules to apply.

The SyntaxView Inspector is one of the most useful Inspectors available for Fiddler, but it is not included in the default install package for size reasons. Fiddler's installer is currently around 750kb, and including the Syntax Highlighting extensions would nearly double that size. To ensure that Fiddler updates are as compact as possible, the SyntaxView extension is available as a separate download from http://fiddler2.com/r/?SYNTAXVIEWINSTALL.

Along the bottom of the Inspector is a bar which exposes additional features and functionality. First is text which displays the current caret position in **Line:Column** format. Next is the QuickFind box which enables inline search. Next is a button which launches advanced Find and Replace functionality. At the far right of the bar is text indicating whether the Inspector is in **Read Only** or **Edit** mode.

The QuickFind box supports the use of Regular Expressions; simply prefix your search string with the text REGEX: and the remainder of the string will be interpreted as a regular expression.

In addition to the standard Cut, Copy, Paste, Undo, and Redo commands, the SyntaxView's Context Menu offers the following features:

Send to TextWizard	Sends the currently-selected text to the TextWizard window for encoding or decoding.
Format XML	Attempts to parse the document as XML. If successful, the text is

	reformatted as an indented XML treeview. This option remains available even when the Inspector is in Read Only mode, but the reformatting is only permanently applied in Edit mode.
Format Script/JSON	Attempts to parse the document as JavaScript/JSON. The text will be reformatted using standard JavaScript indentation styles. This option remains available even when the Inspector is in Read Only mode, but the reformatting is only permanently applied in Edit mode.
Find…	Opens a Find and Replace dialog which offers a variety of search and replacement options.
Word Wrap	This checkbox toggles whether text is word-wrapped.
Editor Options…	Opens an options window containing dozens of advanced text display options.

TextView

Type	Request & Response
Allows Editing	Yes

The TextView Inspector allows you to view the request and response bodies as text. The Inspector truncates its display at the first null byte it finds, and as such is unsuitable for displaying binary content.

Most of the Inspector is a large text area that displays the body text interpreted using the character set detected using the headers, the byte-order-marker, or an embedded META tag declaration. Pressing CTRL+G in the text area allows you to move the cursor to a specific line number. When right-clicking, the text area's context menu offers standard Cut, Copy and Paste options and a checkbox to enable or disable word wrapping. The menu also offers an option to send the currently selected text to the TextWizard tool.

Along the bottom of the Inspector is a bar that offers additional information and features. The first box shows the current cursor position in **Line:Column** format. The next box shows the current character offset within the content in **Offset/Total** format. The third box shows the character count of the current text selection, if any.

Next is a search box that allows you to select matching text within the content. The search text is case-insensitive and does not support regular expressions. Pressing the Up or Down arrow keys in the search box will scroll the text area above (to allow you to view search results in context). Matches are selected as you type, and the box will turn green if a match was found or red if no further matches were found. Pressing Enter or F3 will select the next match. Pressing CTRL+Enter will highlight all matches in the content.

The **View in Notepad** button saves the text content to a temporary file and opens a text editor to view the file. The text editor launched is controlled by the fiddler.config.path.texteditor preference; notepad.exe is the default.

The ... button at the right end of the bar saves the content to a temporary file and shows Windows' **Open With** prompt to allow you to select an application to load the file.

TRANSFORMER

Type	Response only
Allows Editing	Always

Background on Response Encodings

The HTTP specification defines a number of response encoding methods that can be used to improve performance.

- **Compression** algorithms like DEFLATE can be applied to HTTP bodies to shrink the number of bytes that must be transferred over the network. Text-based Content-Types like HTML, script, and CSS shrink by up to 80% when compressed.

- **Chunked Transfer-Encoding** allows transmission of a body without knowing its length ahead of time. Ordinarily, the body's size is sent as a Content-Length header, but pre-calculating a body's size could require a great deal of time and memory, particularly if the body is being generated by running a database query or other operation.

  Without Chunked Transfer-Encoding, a server returning a response of indeterminate size would be forced to send a Connection: close header and close the connection when the response is complete. Such closures break the HTTP Keep-Alive mechanism and introduce a performance bottleneck.

  Chunking works by sending one or more chunks of data, each preceded by a Length value specified as a hexadecimal number. A chunk length of 0 signals the end of the body. For instance, here's a response which has been chunked:

```
HTTP/1.1 200 OK
Content-Type: text/plain
Transfer-Encoding: chunked

2b
This is a response which has been delivered
21
using HTTP Chunked encoding. To r
38
educe overhead, the chunks should be larger than those in
0c
 this exampl
18
e; 2kb is a common size.
0
```

Adding and Removing Encodings using the Transformer

Encodings can make it more difficult for you to inspect entity bodies. The Transformer Inspector allows you to add or remove HTTP-based encodings from the response. At the top of the Transformer tab, the current body's size is listed; keep an eye on this number as you add or remove encodings.

```
Transformer    Headers    TextView

Entity Size: 11,487 bytes.
Transforms
  ☐ Chunked Transfer-Encoding

  HTTP Compression
  ◉ No Compression
  ○ GZIP Encoding
  ○ DEFLATE Encoding
  ○ BZIP2 Encoding
```

The **Chunked Transfer-Encoding** checkbox adds or removes Chunked Transfer-Encoding from the response. Toggling this checkbox applies or removes the encoding, then adds or removes the Transfer-Encoding and Content-Length response headers. After enabling chunking, the HTTP Compression box below the checkbox is disabled. To make changes to compression, you must first remove chunking, then adjust HTTP compression.

The radio buttons in the **HTTP Compression** box allow you to compress or decompress the body:

- **No compression**: the body is not compressed.

- **GZIP**: The body is compressed using GZIP. This encoding uses DEFLATE internally, but with slightly different binary formatting.

- **DEFLATE**: The body is compressed using the DEFLATE (RFC1951) algorithm.

- **BZIP2**: The body is compressed using the BZIP2 algorithm. BZIP2 typically provides better compression than GZIP or DEFLATE at the cost of additional CPU time. This format was briefly supported by the Google Chrome browser but is currently not supported by any mainstream browser or server. It exists in Fiddler mostly for comparison purposes and to enable testing to determine how clients handle unknown encodings.

Selecting a radio button applies or removes the compression from the body, then adds, updates, or removes the Content-Encoding header and adjusts the Content-Length header.

You can use this Inspector to determine how effective HTTP compression will be when applied to your content—for most textual types, compression reduces the body's size by 80% or so. Unlike most Inspectors, the Transformer Inspector allows you to modify ReadOnly (complete) responses without unlocking them first. This capability allows you to more simply remove encodings on Sessions for easy inspection.

Presently, the Transformer Inspector is available for responses only. Use of HTTP encodings for requests is extremely rare, and generally not supported by most clients or servers.

Other Ways to Remove Encodings

Because most of Fiddler's Inspectors do not function well with encoded content, when an encoded Session is selected, a yellow button will appear above the list of Inspectors. Clicking the button will immediately remove all encodings from the request or response.

You can remove encodings from both the request and response simultaneously by right-clicking the Session in the Web Sessions list and choosing **Decode Selected Sessions** from the context menu. Similarly, enabling the **Decode** option in the toolbar will automatically remove all encodings as Fiddler reads requests from the client and responses from the server.

WebForms

Type	Request only
Allows Editing	Yes

The WebForms Request Inspector parses the request's query string and body for any HTML form-data. If a form is found, it is parsed and the name/value pairs are displayed in the grid view. For instance, the following request:

```
POST /sandbox/FileForm.asp?Query=1 HTTP/1.1
Content-Type: application/x-www-form-urlencoded
Host: www.fiddler2.com
Content-Length: 54

2=Data%3e123&fileentry2=a%2etxt&_charset_=windows-1252
```

...is displayed as follows:

This Inspector works best with `application/x-www-form-urlencoded` data used by most simple web forms. Support for `multipart/form-data` forms, commonly used for file uploads, is limited to display only. To modify a file upload, use the HexView Inspector instead.

WEBVIEW

Type	Response only
Allows Editing	No

The WebView Response Inspector allows you to view responses in a web browser control, which provides a quick preview of how a given response may appear in a browser. The web browser control is configured to prevent additional downloads when rendering the response to prevent muddling your Web Sessions list-- this means that most images, styles, and objects will be missing from the displayed content. Additionally, scripting and navigation are blocked, providing a read-only preview of HTML pages.

Beyond plain XHTML and HTML, the WebView Inspector is able to render several additional media types if IE8 or later is present. If IE8 is present, the Inspector can render any binary image (png, jpg, gif, etc) smaller than 24kb. This limit exists because the Inspector uses a Data URI to render the image, and IE8's Data URI length limit is 32kb, which is equal to 24kb of binary.

When IE9 is present, the Inspector can display images up to 1.5gb in size. Additionally, it can display SVG documents and will generate preview pages for WOFF, TTF, and EOT font files, MP3 audio files, and h264 video files. For instance, inspecting a WOFF file will generate the following display:

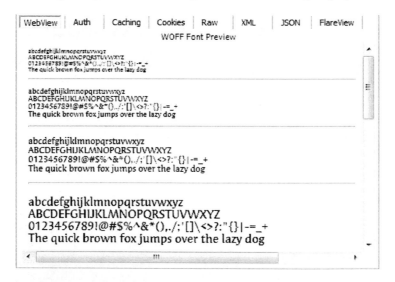

When previewing an audio or video file, an "AutoPlay" checkbox appears at the top-right of the tab. When this box is ticked, media files will automatically begin playback when loaded. When unticked, the media will be loaded but will not begin playing until the play button is clicked inside the preview.

XML

Type	Request & Response
Allows Editing	No

The XML Inspector interprets the selected request or response body as an Extensible Markup Language (XML) formatted string, showing a treeview of the XML document's nodes. If the body cannot be interpreted as XML, the treeview will remain empty.

Each XML element is represented as a node in the tree, and the attributes of the element are displayed in square brackets after the element's name.

Unlike most inspectors, the XML Inspector is able to render the data even if the request or response is compressed or has HTTP Chunked Encoding applied; you do not need to remove the encoding to display the content.

The treeview's context menu offers two options: **Copy**, to copy the selected node to the clipboard (or press CTRL+C), and **Send to TextWizard**, to send the selected node's content to the TextWizard window for encoding or decoding.

The **Expand All** button in the footer will expand all nodes of the tree, while the **Collapse** button will collapse all nodes of the tree. The XML tree will be automatically expanded if the body contains less than 2000 nodes; for performance reasons, you will have to manually expand the tree for larger documents.

Extensions

OVERVIEW

Fiddler's rich extensibility model enables developers to add powerful new features to Fiddler via easily installed add-ons.

Popular 3rd Party Extensions

Independent developers have built many Fiddler extensions, some of which are listed in the directory at `http://getfiddler.com/addons`. At the time of this writing, the most popular 3rd-party extensions enhance Fiddler's ability to test the performance and security characteristics of web applications.

Performance Add-ons

On its own, Fiddler can be used for many important performance-analysis and optimization tasks, but several extensions add even more power.

- **neXpert Performance Report Generator** – Written by a Microsoft Online Services testing team, neXpert will evaluate your websites' adherence to performance best-practices, generating a report which flags problems and recommends solutions. License: Freeware.

- **StresStimulus** – This load-testing extension permits you to record and run load-test scenarios against your website to evaluate its ability to scale to handle large numbers of simultaneous users. License: Free trial.

Security Add-ons

Many Security testing goals can be accomplished with Fiddler, and Web Security experts have built several powerful add-ons that enable even novices to discover and resolve security issues.

- **Watcher** – Developed by the Casaba Security team, Watcher is a "passive security auditor" which observes a browser's interactions with your site. The tool scans requests and responses, flagging potential security vulnerabilities. This powerful tool is used by professional security penetration testers to evaluate major sites. License: Open Source.

- **x5s** – Another add-on from Casaba Security, x5s evaluates your website's vulnerability to cross-site scripting bugs caused by character-set related issues. License: Open Source.

- **intruder21** – This add-on enables fuzz-testing of your web applications. After you identify target requests in Fiddler, this extension generates fuzzed payloads and launches those payloads against your site. License: Freeware.

- **Ammonite** – This add-on detects common website vulnerabilities including SQL injection, OS command injection, cross-site scripting, file inclusion, and buffer overflows. License: Free trial.

Extensions I've Built

The remainder of this chapter describes the most useful extensions that I have developed, all of which are available for free download from `http://getfiddler.com/addons`.

Some of the extensions will be useful for most users of Fiddler and aren't built into the tool simply for download size reasons. Other extensions are only useful for narrow scenarios, and providing their functionality via the add-on model allows me to prevent "bloat" in Fiddler—and ensure that Fiddler's add-on model is powerful enough to meet the needs of the development community.

Source code for many of these extensions is available so that they may serve as examples for developers who wish to extend Fiddler to better meet their own needs.

JavaScript Formatter

When the JavaScript Formatter is installed, you can right-click on any Session with a JavaScript response and choose **Make JavaScript Pretty**. This command reformats (or "beautifies") JavaScript to significantly improve its readability if it had been "crunched" or "minified". For instance, the following line of script:

```
1   /* Copyright (C) 2012 Microsoft Corporation */(function(){var b=window,e=
    b.jQuery,f=b.Debug,g=b.wLive={Core:{},Controls:{}},a=b.$Config;a.
    handlerBaseUrl=a.handlerBaseUrl||"";if(!a.sd){var d=document.domain,c=d.
    split(".");a.sd=c.length===1?"":"."+c[c.length-2]+".com"}a.mkt=a.mkt||"
    na";a.prop=a.prop||"X";if(typeof window.SymRealWinOpen!=="undefined")
    window.open=window.SymRealWinOpen}}();(function(){var a=window,e=a.
```

Is reformatted for readability:

```
 1   /* Copyright (C) 2012 Microsoft Corporation */
 2   (function() {
 3       var b = window, e = b.jQuery, f = b.Debug, g = b.wLive = {
 4           Core: {}, Controls: {}
 5       },
 6       a = b.$Config;
 7       a.handlerBaseUrl = a.handlerBaseUrl || "";
 8       if (!a.sd) {
 9           var d = document.domain, c = d.split(".");
10           a.sd = c.length === 1 ? "" : "." + c[c.length - 2] + ".com"
11       }
12       a.mkt = a.mkt || "na";
13       a.prop = a.prop || "X";
14       if (typeof window.SymRealWinOpen !== "undefined")
15           window.open = window.SymRealWinOpen
16   })();
```

To enable automatic reformatting of all script responses, enable the **Make JavaScript Pretty** option on Fiddler's Rules menu. When JavaScript is reformatted during download, the client will only see the reformatted form, which can be helpful when you are using the browser's script debugging tools.

You can manually control whether the JavaScript formatter runs on a response using the X-Format-JS session flag. When this flag is set to a value of 0, the extension will not format the response body, even if the **Make JavaScript Pretty** option is enabled on the Rules menu. Any other value will cause the JavaScript response body to be formatted, even if the **Make JavaScript Pretty** option is *not* enabled on the Rules menu.

This extension is not compatible with a very small number of responses, for which the reformatting process may introduce corruption. That problem arises in two scenarios: first, when a response is sent with a JavaScript MIME type but it's not actually JavaScript (seen on some Google properties). Second, the reformatting process may cause problems if the (very obscure) JavaScript line-continuation feature is used. Line continuation allows script developers to end a line with a backslash and the JavaScript engine will automatically concatenate that line with the following. The JavaScript Formatter's parser is not yet aware of this feature and will not format such lines properly.

GALLERY

The Gallery extension is designed to display any images that have been found in the selected Sessions. This extension is useful when you wish to interact with a large number of images, or wish to quickly select a Session based on the image it returned.

The extension has only a few options, displayed across the top of its tab:

By default, each image is shown as a 150x150 pixel thumbnail, and images smaller than 10kb in size are ignored. Clicking the **Filter sessions** link will select the Sessions for which images appear, unselecting any Sessions which do not represent images or whose thumbnails were removed from the view. Clicking the **Help** link shows text to explain the features of the extension.

Hovering over a thumbnail will show the Session ID, URL, dimensions, and image format in a balloon tip.

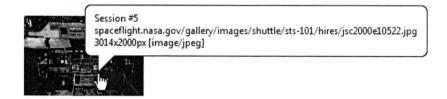

Middle-clicking on a thumbnail removes the image from the Gallery view. Right-clicking on a thumbnail will switch away from the Gallery to inspect the chosen image's Session using the Inspectors. If you hold Shift while right-clicking or double-clicking, the Inspectors will open in a popup window.

Full-Screen View

Double-clicking on a thumbnail enters the full-screen image viewer mode. If the image's Session has a Comment set, this comment is shown as a caption at the bottom of the screen.

While in full-screen mode, use the mouse or keyboard to control the view:

- Exit full screen mode by middle-clicking or pressing the Escape key.

- To advance to the next image, left-click, hit Spacebar, hit the Right arrow key, or hit Page Down. To go back to the previous image, right-click, hit Shift+Spacebar, hit the Left arrow key, or hit Page Up.

- Press the Z key, Enter, or use the mouse wheel to toggle the Zoom level (Actual Size, or Stretch-to-Fit). If the image is shown Actual Size and is larger than the screen, you can use the mouse to pan around the image.

- To start an automatically-advancing slideshow, press any number key 1 to 9, representing the number of seconds to linger on each image. Press the 0 key to cancel the slideshow's automatic advancement. By combining the slideshow with the Comment-displayed-as-Caption feature, you can use Fiddler as a basic photo presentation tool.

- Various options are available to temporarily change the appearance of an image. Press H to flip the displayed image horizontally, or V to flip the image vertically. Hit R to rotate the image by 90 degrees clockwise. Press I to invert the image's colors. Press S to apply a Sepia tone, and G to convert the image to grayscale. Pressing C will swap the green and blue colors in the image. Pressing E will convert the image to grayscale except for any Red pixels; this is a slow operation and may take several seconds for large images. Press U to undo all of the manipulations made to the display of the image.

- Press the Delete key to remove the image from the Gallery and advance to the next image.

CONTENT BLOCKER

The Content Blocker extension enables you to easily block selected content from download by returning a HTTP/404 response to the client. This functionality allows you to test your web applications' behavior if content is blocked by an ad-blocker or the Tracking Protection feature found in IE8 and later.

To install the extension, you must download it from the Fiddler website and copy the DLL into your \Program Files\Fiddler2\Scripts folder. After installing the extension, a new **ContentBlock** menu will appear on the Fiddler main menu.

The **ContentBlock** menu offers several simple options:

Enabled	When checked, blocking is enabled. When unchecked, no content will be blocked.
Block Paths	When checked, requests are blocked if the URL path contains the text /ad
Edit Blocked Hosts	When clicked, this menu item opens a new window that allows you to edit the list of hosts from which content will be blocked. The list consists of fully-qualified hostnames and is delimited by semicolons.
Always Block Flash	When checked, Adobe Flash content will be blocked, regardless of its origin.
Block X-Domain Flash	When checked, Adobe Flash content will be blocked if it originates from a different site than the requesting page. The Referer header is consulted in making this determination.
AutoTrim to 400 sessions	When checked, this extension will automatically trim the Web Sessions list such that it contains no more than 400 sessions. The **Keep Only** dropdown on the Fiddler toolbar offers the same functionality.
Hide Blocked Sessions	When checked, Sessions that are blocked will be hidden from the Web Sessions list.

You can easily add a host to the list of blocked hosts by right-clicking a Session in the Web Sessions list and choosing **Block this Host** from the context menu.

This extension was developed as an example of how to use the Fiddler extension model (its source is included in the download) and as such it offers some redundant functionality that can be found in other parts of Fiddler.

TRAFFIC DIFFER

The Traffic Differ extension aims to help you easily determine how two sets of captured traffic are different. This can be useful if, for instance, you have one SAZ file captured by a customer that encountered a problem from your site and another SAZ file captured which represents the "working" case.

The Traffic Differ enables you to load these two SAZ files and then compare the Sessions within them as a whole. Alternatively, you can drag and drop Sessions from the current Web Sessions list to either of the Session lists and use those Sessions for comparison.

Two side-by-side Session lists show each Session's status code, URL, response size, and a hash of the response body.

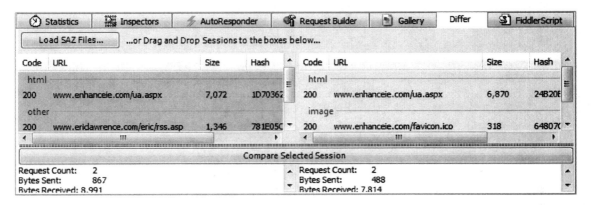

To compare any two individual Sessions between the two captures, select one Session in each list and then click the **Compare Selected Session** button. The file comparison tool will launch and compare the request and response headers and body text.

FIDDLERSCRIPT EDITORS

The Syntax Highlighting extensions package adds a new **FiddlerScript** tab to the main Fiddler UI and also provides a standalone **Fiddler2 ScriptEditor** application offering similar functionality. It also includes the SyntaxView Inspectors, described in the Inspectors chapter.

FiddlerScript Tab

The FiddlerScript tab allows you to easily view and update your FiddlerScript rules directly in the Fiddler UI. Across the top of the tab are a few UI controls:

Save Script button	Saves changes made to the script
Go to dropdown	This dropdown lists key methods in the FiddlerScript. Selecting an item from this list will scroll to the specified method. Choosing the ***FiddlerScript Reference** option will open the FiddlerScript reference web page. Hidden feature: If you double-click the Go to text label itself, the script source code will collapse to definitions.
Find... box	This box allows you to search your script for the specified text
ClassView button	This button toggles the visibility of the FiddlerScript ClassView sidebar.

Below these controls is a syntax-aware source code editor containing the current text of your FiddlerScript. The editor supports context-sensitive code completion and will show available properties, fields and methods in a popup window as you type:

Code lines that you've changed will show a yellow bar in the left margin:

```
import System;
import System.Windows.Forms;
import Fiddler;

// I've just typed this line
```

...until you save your changes, at which point the bar will turn green:

```
import System;
import System.Windows.Forms;
import Fiddler;

// I've just typed this line
```

If Fiddler encounters a script error when compiling your script, the FiddlerScript tab will activate and scroll to show the error.

ClassView Sidebar

The ClassView sidebar allows you to explore the key objects, properties, and methods available to your script. Note that the ClassView does not expose *all* available functionality, only the functionality that is most commonly used by scripts.

Clicking an item in the treeview will show the description of that item at the top of the sidebar. Pressing CTRL+C on an item will copy the item's name to the clipboard, allowing you to easily insert it in your script.

The sidebar's items are color-coded depending on their type:

Color	Type
Black	Method
Blue	Property
Green	Field
Purple	Event

Fiddler2 ScriptEditor

The Fiddler2 ScriptEditor program opens when you click **Rules** > **Customize Rules** or hit CTRL+R in Fiddler. You can also launch the Fiddler2 ScriptEditor from anywhere in Windows by tapping Windows+R and typing fse2 in the Windows Run prompt.

The standalone ScriptEditor offers the same general functionality as the FiddlerScript tab, with the convenience of running in its own window. Unlike the FiddlerScript tab, however, the standalone application is not notified of script compilation errors and will not notify you of any problems that Fiddler encounters when compiling your script.

The **Go** menu offers commands to navigate quickly to important methods in the FiddlerScript, and to scroll to a specific line.

The **View** menu offers options to adjust the display of the source code, including changing the font size, showing line numbers, and expanding and collapsing method blocks. It also includes the toggle which shows and hides the ClassView Explorer sidebar.

The **Insert** menu offers a number of pre-built snippets that you can add to your script. To use them, place the cursor where you'd like the snippet added, then click the menu item representing the desired snippet.

For instance, place the cursor just inside the Handlers class' opening brace:

Then click **Insert > Context Menu Item**:

The Editor will insert a template `ContextAction` block which will add a new menu item to the Web Sessions context menu:

```
class Handlers
{
        // Create a new item on the right-click menu of the Session List.
        public static ContextAction("&UNTITLED")
        function DoUNTITLED(oSessions: Fiddler.Session[]){
            for (var x = 0; x < oSessions.Length; x++){
                // Write your code here
            }
        }
}
```

SAZClipboard

The SAZClipboard is a simple extension that allows you to load a .SAZ file into a standalone Session list in its own window. The window enables you to drag Sessions between this clipboard and the main Fiddler UI. This functionality is convenient if you're using the Composer or AutoResponder features, both of which accept drops of Sessions for reuse.

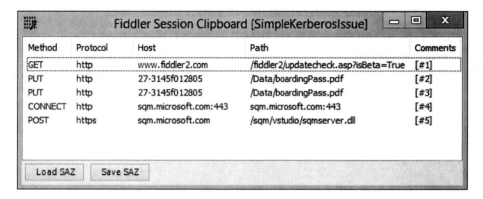

To use the extension, click **New SAZClipboard...** from Fiddler's **Tools** menu.

You can drag and drop from the Web Sessions list to the SAZClipboard, or load a SAZ directly into it using the button at the bottom.

AnyWHERE

Most modern browsers support geolocation, a feature that allows JavaScript to determine the user's real-world location. Most browsers implement this functionality by querying the operating system for a list of nearby Wi-Fi access points, then submitting that list to a webservice which maps the nearby access points to a longitude/latitude pair. The webservice provides that value to the browser, which then returns it to JavaScript.

Fiddler's AnyWHERE extension allows you to trivially spoof the responses to geolocation webservice queries, enabling you to "trick" the browser into thinking you're somewhere you are not. The window allows you to type in your current location, or select a location from a list of worldwide points-of-interest:

Because browser geolocation webservice queries travel over HTTPS, you must enable HTTPS decryption for this add-on to operate. This extension supports IE9+, FF4, Chrome, and Opera, but it will not work if the browser's geolocation feature is not based on webservice lookups. For instance, when IE10 is running on a Windows 8 device that includes GPS hardware, Windows will use that hardware rather than calling a webservice to determine the location.

Source code for this extension is provided in the download package.

Storing, Importing, and Exporting Traffic

SESSION ARCHIVE ZIP (SAZ) FILES

Fiddler's default save format is the Session Archive Zip (SAZ) file. SAZ files are simply Zip archives that are constructed in a particular way that Fiddler understands. By renaming a .SAZ file to .ZIP, you can use Windows Explorer or WinZip to explore the SAZ file to see how it works under the covers.

The SAZ format is Fiddler's most "lossless" format—it contains all of the headers and bodies for each Session that Fiddler captured, along with metadata including comments, color markers, and timing information. Because it contains all of the traffic, a SAZ file may grow quite large, especially if it contains images, sounds or video responses. In contrast, HTML, script, and CSS files tend to compress well, at about a 5:1 ratio. It is possible to store SAZ files with gigabytes of data and tens of thousands of Sessions, but because such files are unwieldy to load or transfer, you will generally want to use Fiddler's filtering features to minimize the amount of data stored in any given SAZ.

You can later reload a SAZ file into Fiddler to view the Sessions contained within; these sessions will be colored with a light grey background color for easy of identification. One thing Fiddler *won't* restore in Sessions loaded from a SAZ file is Session ID; when a SAZ is loaded, each session gets a new ID starting at the current index. Before sharing a SAZ file with someone else, use the **Comments** button or **Edit > Mark** menu to tag any Sessions of interest.

If Fiddler reloads a Session which does not already have a comment, it will automatically add a comment containing the original session's ID:

> Comments
>
> [#1]
> [#2]
> [#3]
> [#4]

Tip: The AutoResponder tab is able to import a SAZ file and replay the responses contained within to mimic the original traffic flow captured in the SAZ file.

Protecting SAZ Files

SAZ files contain all captured web traffic, which might include sensitive information like usernames, passwords, cookies, and account information, if such information was captured by Fiddler. Therefore, you should only share SAZ files with trusted people or organizations.

If a SAZ file must be stored in an unprotected location or transferred over an insecure connection, you can help keep it private by encrypting the contents before saving. To do so, select **Password-Protected SAZ** in the **Save as type** dropdown on the Save Session Archive prompt.

After choosing to save in encrypted format, a password will be requested:

Password-Protected SAZ files are encrypted using 128-bit AES encryption, a strong form of encryption that is also used for HTTPS traffic and by government and military organizations. Of course, to keep the file private, your password must be kept secret. If the file is being shared with someone else, you must securely communicate the password to the other person. Don't forget your password—there's no practical way (short of brute-force guessing) to reopen your SAZ file without it.

The preference `fiddler.saz.AES.Use256Bit` may be set to `true` to configure Fiddler to use 256-bit AES instead of 128bit. Alternatively, the legacy `CONFIG.bUseAESForSAZ` property may be set to `false` to configure Fiddler to use the legacy PKZIP obfuscation scheme, which is very fast but provides much weaker protection of the file's contents.

FIDDLERCAP

SAZ files have proven so useful in capturing and reproducing problems with web applications that I soon found that many web developers were requesting SAZ captures from novice PC users. In the hope of making that a more practical request, I built **FiddlerCap**. FiddlerCap is a lightweight tool designed to allow non-technical users to capture SAZ files for later analysis by experts using the full Fiddler debugger.

FiddlerCap offers a simplified user-interface and streamlined workflow for capturing web traffic; unlike Fiddler itself, it cannot modify traffic and has no extensibility mechanisms. Like Fiddler, you can use FiddlerCap to collect web traffic from any application developed using any technology. FiddlerCap is built atop the FiddlerCore library and uses a FiddlerCore proxy instance running on port 8889 to capture web traffic.

Install FiddlerCap by visiting `http://fiddlercap.com`, a simple page which provides simple step-by-step instructions on how to use the tool to capture web traffic. By default, FiddlerCap installs to a folder on your desktop and it does not require Administrative permissions. To simplify worldwide use, FiddlerCap has been localized to Spanish, French, Italian, Japanese, Portuguese, and Russian.

When the install completes, the tool automatically opens. The window is divided into three groups: **Capture**, **Capture Options**, and **Tools**.

The **Details** button at the bottom right of the FiddlerCap window will expand the window to show a simple Session list of the captured traffic. Sessions' content cannot be inspected, but individual sessions may be removed by selecting them and pressing the `Delete` key.

Capture Box

The Capture box offers the minimum set of controls needed to collect a capture. Press the **Start Capture** button to begin capturing web traffic. A new browser window will open for you to reproduce the problem, although FiddlerCap will capture traffic from any process that respects the system proxy setting—not just that single browser window. The FiddlerHook extension for Firefox is not available for FiddlerCap. To capture Firefox's network traffic, open the browser's **Tools** > **Options** > **Advanced** > **Network** > **Connection Settings** screen and select the **Use System Proxy Settings** option.

After the problem has been reproduced, click the **Stop Capture** button to end the capture of traffic. Lastly, click the **Save Capture** button to select where to save the .SAZ file. By default, the SAZ file will be saved on the desktop. To encrypt the SAZ file with a password, select the **Password-Protected SAZ** option in the **Save as type** dropdown:

Capture Options Box

The Capture Options box controls the options used in capturing.

The **Store binaries** checkbox (unticked by default) controls whether binary response bodies (e.g. images, audio, video, and application/octet-stream downloads) will be stored in the capture. Omitting these bodies (storing only their headers) can dramatically shrink the size of the final SAZ file, although obviously if the problem being reproduced depends on the content of such downloads, you should enable the Store binaries option.

The **Decrypt HTTPS traffic** checkbox (unticked by default) controls whether or not HTTPS traffic will be decrypted by FiddlerCap. When you check this box, an explanatory message is shown:

```
---------------------------
A note about HTTPS Decryption
---------------------------
HTTPS decryption will enable your debugging buddy to see the raw traffic sent
via the HTTPS protocol.

This feature works by decrypting SSL traffic and reencrypting it using a
locally generated certificate. FiddlerCap will generate this certificate
and remove it when you close this tool.

You may choose to temporarily install this certificate in the Trusted store
to avoid warnings from your browser or client application.
---------------------------
```

After this note is dismissed, a Windows Security prompt is presented to allow you to trust FiddlerCap's root certificate:

When FiddlerCap is closed, it will automatically delete all of the certificates it generated during the capture, prompting for permission to delete the root certificate from the Trusted Certificates store.

The **Store cookies and POSTs** option (checked by default) controls whether FiddlerCap will store POST request bodies and the HTTP headers Cookie, Set-Cookie, Set-Cookie2, Authorization, and Proxy-Authorization. Disabling this option can slightly shrink the capture and somewhat reduces the amount of privacy-impacting information stored in the capture. Even when this option is disabled, however, captures obviously may contain other sensitive information and thus they should only be shared with trusted parties.

The **Automatically discard traffic after # minutes** option allows you to control how many minutes of traffic are saved in the SAZ file. This option is most useful when trying to capture a problem that only happens intermittently. You can leave FiddlerCap running in the background and it will periodically expire older traffic to reduce the size of the capture and the amount of memory used. When you encounter the problem you are trying to capture, you can save just the last few minutes' worth of traffic to the archive.

Tools Box

The Tools box offers options that may be useful in reproducing a problem. The **Clear Cookies** button will purge all persistent cookies for Internet Explorer and other applications that are based on WinINET. The **Clear Cache** button will purge all cached files from the Internet Explorer / WinINET cache to help ensure that all responses are seen by FiddlerCap instead of possibly being pulled from the local cache.

The **Clear Capture** button is enabled only while FiddlerCap is capturing; it immediately clears all previously captured Sessions from the capture.

The **Snapshot** button will take a screenshot of whatever monitor FiddlerCap is running on and add it to the capture as a JPEG-formatted image. It will be stored in a new session whose URL contains the current timestamp in the format `http://localhost/Screenshot_h-mm-ss.jpg`.

The Flag button will prompt you to add a comment to the capture:

The comment text entered will be stored as the HTTP response body of a new Session with a URL of `http://USERCOMMENT/MARKER`.

FIDDLER'S VIEWER MODE

Ordinarily, only one instance of Fiddler may be started at a time; attempting to launch a new instance of Fiddler while it's already open will simply reactivate the existing Fiddler instance.

However, it is sometimes useful to open additional instances of Fiddler to view SAZ files or compose requests, independent of the existing Fiddler instance. To achieve those goals, Fiddler supports opening additional **Viewer** instances by passing the `-viewer` command line argument, or by right-clicking on a SAZ file in Windows Explorer and choosing **Open in Viewer** from the context menu.

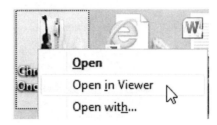

Viewer Mode instances can be identified by the Viewer Mode icon in the status bar: and by the text at the front of the toolbar. When no SAZ file is loaded, the text shows **FiddlerViewer:**

You can identify this Viewer instance by clicking on the text and entering a new title:

If you load a SAZ file into the instance, the text will change to the name of the SAZ file, with a tooltip showing the full path to the file:

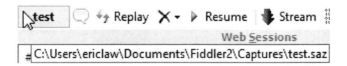

Fiddler Viewer instances cannot capture traffic, and most UI changes made in Viewer mode (e.g. hiding the toolbar or reordering columns in the Web Sessions list) will be discarded when the instance is closed.

Importing and Exporting Sessions

Beyond Fiddler's native SAZ format, the debugger offers a rich set of Importers and Exporters (known collectively as "Transcoders") that allow it to share captured network traffic with other tools. In addition to the Transcoders bundled with Fiddler, an extensibility mechanism permits support of additional formats to be added by other developers.

Fiddler's Import and Export functionality can be found on the File menu. The **Import Sessions...** command will allow you to load Sessions from other formats, while the **Export Sessions** submenu allows you to export either all Sessions or only the Sessions selected in the Web Sessions list.

Import Formats

The current version of Fiddler includes two Import formats: **HTTPArchive** and **F12 NetXML** format. HTTPArchive Format (HAR; `http://groups.google.com/group/http-archive-specification`) is a lossy JSON-based format which is supported by a number of tools including Firebug, Chrome's Developer tools, and HTTPWatch. Versions 1.1 and 1.2 of the format are supported.

The F12 NetXML Format is a very similar format exported by the IE 9 Developer Tools' Network tab; it's actually just an HTTPArchive file encoded using XML instead of JSON. This was not an intentional difference on Microsoft's part: the original HTTPArchive format spec defined the format using XML syntax. Only a small comment at the top of the specification noted that JSON should be used instead. Fiddler is the only popular tool to read the NetXML Format; you can use Fiddler to load NetXML and save it to a more common format like HAR. Note that both of these are lossy formats, so some data will be missing (in particular, large binary bodies like images will not be present).

After choosing a format to Import from, you will be prompted to select the file to import. The selected file will be parsed and the traffic will be added to the Web Sessions list.

Support for other Import formats can be added by any developer. I'm currently working on an Importer that allows import of Wireshark `.pcap` and NetMon `.cap` files.

Export Formats

Fiddler includes a broad set of Exporters that allow it to export traffic for use in other tools or applications. The remainder of this chapter describes the export formats supported by Fiddler itself.

HTML5 AppCache Manifest

HTML5 introduces the concept of an Application Cache, which allows a web developer to provide a manifest of pages that should be cached to permit offline use. The manifest specifies which resources the browser should download into the AppCache and which resources should always be retrieved from the network.

Manifests are simply text files and you can create them with your text editor of choice. However, this process can be tedious and begs for an automated solution. Fiddler's HTML5 AppCache Manifest Exporter makes the process of generating a manifest a straightforward exercise:

1. Clear your browser cache.

2. Start Fiddler.

3. Load your website in the browser.

4. In Fiddler, click **File** > **Export Sessions** > **All Sessions**....

5. In the Select Format window, pick **HTML5 AppCache Manifest**.

6. Click **Next**. In the **Adjust AppCache Manifest** window, check any resources that you wish to exclude from the CACHE section of the manifest; those will be added to the NETWORK section of the manifest:

7. If you'd like, use the text box at the bottom to specify a **Base URL** if the resource URLs should be relative to the manifest. For instance, in the example above, I will place the manifest in the folder `http://ie.microsoft.com/testdrive`, so I will use that as the Base URL.

8. Click the **Save** button to generate and display the manifest in your text editor:

```
IETestDrive.appcache - Notepad
File  Edit  Format  View  Help
CACHE MANIFEST
# Generated: 9/14/2011 6:36:33 PM

# Deploy so that URLs are relative to: http://ie.microsoft.com/testdrive

CACHE:
/
/Includes/Libraries/jquery-1.6.2.min.js
/Includes/Script/BrowserInfo.js
/Includes/Script/TestDriveCommon.js
/Includes/Styles/BaseStyles.css
/Views/Homepage/AllDemos.png
/Views/Homepage/Homepage.css
/Views/Homepage/Homepage.js
/Views/Homepage/Icons/Cookbook.png
/Views/Homepage/Icons/HandsOnWindows8.png
/Views/Homepage/Icons/SpellChecking.png
/Views/Homepage/Icons/WebSockets.png
/Views/Homepage/Wrapping.png

NETWORK:
*
```

9. If you're happy with the manifest, save it to your web server in the appropriate location. Ensure that your web server is configured to return the manifest file type with `Content-Type: text/cache-manifest`

10. In your web page, ensure that your page will run in Standards mode (e.g. using the HTML5 doctype) and add a `manifest` attribute on the `HTML` element pointing to your application's manifest.

```
<!DOCTYPE html>
<html manifest="app.manifest" >
<head>
```

Keep in mind that when the browser is using AppCached content, those resources will be reused from the cache and not pulled from the network (until the cache is expired). Because the content is cached locally, you will not see requests to re-download that content in Fiddler. If you wish to use Fiddler to modify such content, you will need to clear your browser's cache so that the browser is forced to re-download the content from the network on next use.

HTTPArchive v1.1 and v1.2
The HTTPArchive format is a JSON format that contains Web Sessions' headers, some bodies, and timing information. The primary difference between versions 1.1 and 1.2 of the format is that the newer version permits the inclusion of small binary bodies.

By default, Fiddler will store text bodies up to 1MB in length, and binary bodies up to 32768 bytes in length; these values can be changed by setting the appropriate preferences:

```
fiddler.importexport.HTTPArchiveJSON.MaxTextBodyLength
fiddler.importexport.HTTPArchiveJSON.MaxBinaryBodyLength
```

If a body is too long, it will not be stored in the file and instead a comment will be added to the Session noting the omission.

MeddlerScript

Meddler (`http://webdbg.com/Meddler/`) is a HTTP Traffic generation tool which I developed to allow building of tiny, self-contained reproductions of HTTP traffic. Meddler is essentially a "scripted socket" which allows very low-level manipulation of sockets, a capability useful for debugging browsers or other clients.

When you export Web Sessions to MeddlerScript, the result is an `.MS` file that can be loaded into Meddler to "play back" that traffic. Conceptually, this is very similar to using Fiddler's AutoResponder tab to play back previously captured traffic from a SAZ file, but Meddler scripts can be easier to automate and they permit low-level tweaks (e.g. "*Wait 300ms between sending the headers and the first byte of the body, then write the body in 2048 byte chunks each 10 seconds apart*") which cannot be easily replicated using Fiddler itself.

Unless you're building a browser or other HTTP client, exporting MeddlerScript probably will not be very useful for you.

Raw Files

The Raw Files Exporter allows you to store individual response bodies to files on disk. This can be tremendously useful when dumping media content to disk. For instance, say you've browsed around a photography website and collected a bunch of photos in the Web Sessions list. You can use filters and other features in Fiddler to select only the photos of interest (e.g. JPG files over 20k). You can then select **File** > **Export Sessions** > **Selected Sessions** and choose **Raw Files** in the **Select Export Format** box.

The **File Exporter** window allows you to configure the export process.

The **Path** box allows you to select the base path under which a new folder will be created. The folder will be automatically named `\Dump-MonthDay-Hour-Minute-Second\`.

The **Options** box contains two checkboxes. **Recreate Folder Structure** will create subfolders for each resource based on the hostname and path of the file. Use this to mimic a site's hierarchy on your local disk. The **Open folder when complete** option will open Windows Explorer to display the root folder into which files were exported when the export has completed.

Click the **Export >>** button to begin the export.

Beyond dumping media files, the **Raw Files** Exporter allows you to easily mirror a captured website to your disk. You can then drag/drop the contents of that folder to the AutoResponder tab, and Fiddler will then be able to play back that local content mirror based on inbound requests. This practice can be very convenient for debugging a website when you want to use other tools (e.g. Expression Web or Visual Studio) to edit HTML content locally.

Visual Studio WebTest

Generating a Visual Studio `.WebTest` file allows you to use the Visual Studio Web Test product to reissue previously captured requests for functional-testing and load-testing purposes. Visual Studio Web Test is included in some editions of Visual Studio 2008 and later.

WCAT Script

As explained on the tool's website:

> Web Capacity Analysis Tool (WCAT) is a lightweight HTTP load generation tool designed to measure the performance of a web server within a controlled environment. WCAT can simulate thousands of concurrent users making requests to a single web site or multiple web sites. The WCAT engine uses a simple script to define the set of HTTP requests to be played back to the web server.

Fiddler's WCAT Exporter allows you to easily generate request-generation scripts for WCAT to replay against your servers to verify their ability to handle load.

You can download the 32bit or 64bit WCAT installer from `http://fiddler2.com/r/?WCAT`.

FiddlerScript

Extending Fiddler with FiddlerScript

The earliest versions of Fiddler had no extensibility model at all; the features I coded were all that users had available. It didn't take long to recognize that I would never be able to keep up with the myriad feature requests coming in from Fiddler users who were using the tool to solve a huge variety of problems.

One of the biggest early limitations was that Fiddler only offered one filter (Hide Images) and thus it was easy to get overwhelmed by the sheer volume of traffic flowing through the tool. I had planned to build a filtering interface full of dropdown fields and textboxes which would allow users to filter traffic based on boolean criteria that I would make available. There were two obvious problems with this approach: first, it would require that I do a lot of tedious UI development, and second, I knew that most users wouldn't be happy with it. Advanced users find it very cumbersome to build complicated queries using UI controls, and novice users would be easily confused when trying to build complicated queries that involved nested AND, OR, and NOT operators.

Fortunately, laziness often leads to better engineering. I remember thinking one night: *"It's so easy for me to build complicated filter expressions inside Fiddler's code itself. If only users could just write code to do filtering."* Happily, this thought led to a *"eureka"* moment-- the recollection that the .NET Framework makes it very easy to build a script engine into an application, and exposing the application's object model to that script engine is easy. With a few dozen lines of code added in late 2003, Fiddler got infinitely more powerful.

Even as Fiddler was modernized over the last 9 years, including the introduction of Fiddler extensions and many built-in filtering capabilities, the FiddlerScript engine has remained an indispensable component of Fiddler. By mastering FiddlerScript, you will get much more out of Fiddler.

About FiddlerScript

As each Session flows through Fiddler, methods in the `CustomRules.js` script file are run, enabling you to hide, flag, or modify Sessions based on criteria of arbitrary complexity. Your rules script can be modified and recompiled dynamically at runtime without restarting Fiddler. This book does not provide a comprehensive reference to the JScript.NET language upon which FiddlerScript is based. If you plan to code especially powerful or complicated FiddlerScript, you should consider finding a copy of Microsoft JScript.NET Programming. That book presents a comprehensive view of the language, including useful information I haven't seen anywhere else. (I discovered it in 2012, ten years after its only printing. In one of those "small world" coincidences, it was authored by Justin Rogers, a colleague on the Internet Explorer team.)

JavaScript is a language familiar to most Fiddler users, and JScript.NET isn't syntactically much different than the C# language beloved by most .NET programmers. There are two deltas that JavaScript developers moving to JScript.NET should be aware of:

1. JScript.NET supports a C#-like mechanism for declaring classes that contain fields, properties and methods. Fiddler integrates your script by calling methods on a `static class` named `Handlers`, described below.

2. When declaring a variable, you may (and should) declare that variable's type. Type definition improves the performance of the generated code and allows the compiler to flag errors at compile time instead of runtime.

To set the type of a variable, just specify the type after the variable name and before any initial value, like so:

```
var sMyString: String = "StringValue";
var bMyBool: boolean = false;
var iMyInt: int = 42;
```

For ease of development, the FiddlerScript engine will automatically call specially-named functions in your script when events of interest occur. However, less-interesting events do not get this special treatment and you must directly attach handlers for such events. To supply an event handler in script, call the hidden *add_EventName* method generated by the compiler for each event. For instance, to handle the `OnClearCache` event, use the following code:

```
// Call the hidden method using the format Object.add_EventName(handlerFunction)
FiddlerApplication.add_OnClearCache(catchClearCache);

// Implement the event handler
static function catchClearCache(sender, args:CacheClearEventArgs) {
  MessageBox.Show("User cleared the cache.");
}
```

If you do attach any event handlers in this way, you'll need to use the *remove_EventName* method to remove the event handler in your script's `OnRetire` function.

Over the years, a variety of powerful features were added to FiddlerScript, including the ability to extend the Fiddler UI and accept automation commands from the `ExecAction.exe` command line tool. As Fiddler's scripting capabilities became more powerful, I began building some core features of Fiddler (for instance, UserAgent spoofing and performance simulations) in FiddlerScript because users often wanted to customize these features slightly. By implementing such features in the easily-updated script, Fiddler enables users to customize the tool to their exact needs.

Editing FiddlerScript

To see the current FiddlerScript loaded in Fiddler, choose **Customize Rules** on Fiddler's **Rules** menu. The configured script editor will launch and show the script. By default, Notepad will be used as the script editing program, but you can adjust this preference using the **Tools** > **Fiddler Options** > **Extensions** tab. If you plan to do any non-trivial modifications to the FiddlerScript, I highly recommend that you install the

Fiddler ScriptEditor, a syntax-highlighting editor that can either run standalone or on a tab within Fiddler itself. When installed, the Fiddler ScriptEditor will set itself as the default script editor.

Updating FiddlerScript at Runtime

When you save the `CustomRules.js` file, Fiddler will play a sound while reloading the source code and attempting to recompile it. If compilation succeeds, the new script will be used for all subsequent Sessions. If compilation fails, you'll be shown an error message and no script will run until the error is corrected and the script is recompiled.

The compiler's error message will show the offending line and attempt to explain the nature of the error:

Keep in mind that each time your script is recompiled, the previously-running script is first discarded. This means that the current values of variables or properties in the script will be reset to their default values every time the script is reloaded. If you need to preserve a variable's value from the old script to the new one, you should use a Preference to load and store the value. See the `OnRetire` method for more information.

Resetting to the Default FiddlerScript

Don't worry about "breaking" your script—if you make a mistake and corrupt the script to the point where you don't know how to fix it, simply delete the `CustomRules.js` file from the `%USERPROFILE%\My Documents\Fiddler2\Scripts` folder. The next time Fiddler is started, your `CustomRules.js` file will be recreated by copying the `SampleRules.js` file from the Fiddler application folder.

One important consequence of updating your `CustomRules.js` file is that when you install new versions of Fiddler, your old rules file will be preserved. Any new or updated rules stored in the `SampleRules.js` file will not be loaded unless you delete your `CustomRules.js` file or copy the updated content from the sample script.

FiddlerScript Functions

When FiddlerScript is compiled, Fiddler obtains references to several key static functions, all of which are found on a class named `Handlers`. Each of these functions and their use is described in this section.

Session Handling Functions

As each Session is processed, the Fiddler invokes specially-named functions in your FiddlerScript. If your script contains the named function, it will be invoked with one argument-- a reference to the current Session. Each function should be declared as a **public static function**.

These functions are called on the Session's background handler thread, not the UI thread, and thus you should avoid making any UI calls from within these functions.

OnPeekAtRequestHeaders

The `OnPeekAtRequestHeaders` function runs as soon as the request headers have been read from the client. This function generally runs before the request body has been read, so avoid manipulating the `oSession.requestBodyBytes` array to avoid causing a `null`-reference exception.

In practice, this function is rarely useful, because until the complete request has been read, there's not a lot your script can do.

OnBeforeRequest

The `OnBeforeRequest` function executes after the client's complete request has been read and before the request is sent to the server. This function gives you the opportunity to modify the request's headers or body before the server sees it.

OnPeekAtResponseHeaders

The `OnPeekAtResponseHeaders` function runs as soon as the response headers have been read from the server. This function generally runs before the response body has been read, so avoid manipulating the `oSession.responseBodyBytes` array to avoid causing a `null`-reference exception.

One of the best uses of this function is to examine the response headers to determine whether or not the response may be streamed as it is read from the server. If the response should be buffered so that its body may be modified by the `OnBeforeResponse` function, set `oSession.bBufferResponse=true` inside this function.

OnBeforeResponse

The `OnBeforeResponse` function *typically* executes after the server's full response has been read and before the response is sent to the client. This function gives you the opportunity to modify the response's headers or body before the client browser sees it.

When a Session has buffering disabled, the `OnBeforeResponse` function is called *after* the response has already been streamed to the client. Hence, if you modify the previously-streamed response in this function, only Fiddler will see the modified response—the client already got the unmodified original.

OnReturningError

The `OnReturningError` function executes in the event that a Fiddler-generated error message (for instance, "DNS Lookup Failed") is returned to the client. This provides the opportunity to customize the message that the client application sees. For instance, you could show a more friendly error page, log the error in a database, flag the error in the Web Sessions list, or undertake other actions.

General Functions

FiddlerScript includes a number of functions which run based on events in Fiddler itself, and not in response to any given session. Each function should be declared as a `public static function`.

Main

This function runs immediately after the script is successfully compiled. It provides an opportunity to reload variables in the script from the Preferences system, or perform other one-time initialization.

OnRetire

This function runs immediately before the script is unloaded, either because Fiddler is closing or because a new script is being loaded. It provides an opportunity to store variables from the script into the Preferences system, detach event handlers you've added, or perform other cleanup.

OnBoot

This function runs only when Fiddler first boots. If this function's script is changed at runtime, the new code will not execute until the next time you start Fiddler.

OnShutdown

This function runs when Fiddler is shutting down. In practice, there's rarely a need to put any code in this function.

OnAttach

This function runs after Fiddler registers as the system proxy. By default this will happen when Fiddler starts up, and if the user ever toggles capturing off and back on using the status bar button or by pressing the F12 key.

OnDetach

This function runs after Fiddler has unregistered as the system proxy and the default proxy is restored. By default this will happen when Fiddler shuts down, and if the user ever disables capturing using the status bar button or by pressing the F12 key.

OnExecAction(sParams: string[])

This function runs when the user enters a command in the QuickExec box beneath the Web Sessions list, or if a command is sent to Fiddler from the `ExecAction.exe` command line program. The single parameter passed into the function is an array of `strings` which are tokenized from input to the QuickExec box. The `OnExecAction` function is called after all extensions which implement the `IHandleExecAction` interface have the opportunity to handle (and optionally cancel) the command.

The default implementation of this function shows how you can use it to set script variables, run functions, or otherwise control Fiddler's behavior.

FiddlerScript and Automation Tools

Fiddler was designed primarily for interactive use, where you directly use the Fiddler user-interface to perform whatever debugging tasks you'd like to accomplish. However, Fiddler includes a limited set of features to support automated use.

Quiet Mode

First is the `-quiet` command line argument. When Fiddler is activated with this switch, the main Fiddler window is automatically minimized to the System Tray. Fiddler will automatically suppress most of its prompts and alerts when running in quiet mode; for instance, no Certificate Warnings or HTTP Errors will pop up message boxes in this mode. The `CONFIG.QuietMode` property can be respected by extensions or FiddlerScript to accommodate the quiet mode of operation.

Driving Fiddler from Batch Scripts

Of course, running Fiddler silently isn't usually enough to accomplish most automation goals—you also will need to enable your test harness or script to drive Fiddler. Depending on your framework, you might use UI Automation to drive Fiddler's existing interface directly, but there's a more robust and reliable option available. As we saw previously, the `OnExecAction` function in FiddlerScript is run whenever the user enters a command in the QuickExec box. However, that's not the only way to invoke script commands—you can also use the `ExecAction.exe` command line tool included with the default install of Fiddler.

For instance, if you wanted to invoke the `dump` command to save all of the Sessions in the Web Sessions list to a SAZ file, you can simply run:

```
"%PROGRAMFILES%\Fiddler2\ExecAction.exe" dump
```

The utility will pass the `dump` command into Fiddler's extensions and FiddlerScript, and the default handler in the FiddlerScript file will perform the specified action. If you need to pass multiple parameters into the tool, you can do so by quoting the arguments:

```
"%PROGRAMFILES%\Fiddler2\ExecAction.exe" "select text/html"
```

You may use the backslash character to escape quotation marks if you need them in your command:

```
ExecAction.exe "prefs set \"MyExt.UI.Title\" \"A Quoted Value\""
```

If you pass an incorrect number of arguments to the utility (zero or more than one), it will display help text and set the `ERRORLEVEL` to 1. If the utility cannot find the Fiddler window, it will display a message indicating that Fiddler could not be found and set the `ERRORLEVEL` to 2.

Driving Fiddler from Native or .NET Code

Under the covers, the ExecAction utility is extremely simple. If your test harness is written in C++ or any .NET language, you can easily pass messages directly to Fiddler without relying upon ExecAction.exe. Simply determine the main Fiddler window's handle, and then call SendMessage to pass a WM_COPYDATA structure containing the desired command's text.

Using C++, the barebones logic is as follows:

```
#include "stdafx.h"
int _tmain(int argc, _TCHAR* argv[])
{
  HWND hWndControl = FindWindow(NULL, L"Fiddler - HTTP Debugging Proxy");

  if (NULL == hWndControl)
  {
    printf("ERROR: Fiddler window was not found.\n");
    return 2;
  }

  tagCOPYDATASTRUCT oCDS;

  oCDS.dwData = 61181; // Use 61180 for ANSI; 61181 for Unicode
  oCDS.cbData = lstrlen(argv[1]) * sizeof(WCHAR);
  oCDS.lpData = argv[1];

  SendMessage(hWndControl, WM_COPYDATA, NULL, (WPARAM) wParam, (LPARAM) &oCDS);
  return 0;
}
```

If you're using .NET code, first you must define some functions and constants for PInvoke:

```
internal const int WM_COPYDATA = 0x4A;

[DllImport("user32.dll", EntryPoint = "SendMessage")]
internal static extern IntPtr SendWMCopyMessage(IntPtr hWnd, int Msg,
  IntPtr wParam, ref SendDataStruct lParam);

[DllImport("user32.dll")]
internal static extern IntPtr FindWindow(string lpClassName, string lpWindowName);

[StructLayout(LayoutKind.Sequential)]
internal struct SendDataStruct
{
  public IntPtr dwData;
  public int cbData;
  public string strData;
}
```

Then, simply use these methods to send the command string to the Fiddler window:

```
SendDataStruct oStruct = new Utilities.SendDataStruct();
oStruct.dwData = (IntPtr) 61181;
oStruct.strData = "TheString";
oStruct.cbData = Encoding.Unicode.GetBytes(oStruct.strData).Length;
IntPtr hWnd = FindWindow(null, "Fiddler - HTTP Debugging Proxy");
SendWMCopyMessage(hWnd, Utilities.WM_COPYDATA, IntPtr.Zero, ref oStruct);
```

You can use this technique to perform lightweight and ad-hoc automation of Fiddler. For more complicated jobs, you will likely instead choose to build a custom tool based on the FiddlerCore class library described in the final chapter of this book.

EXTENDING FIDDLER'S UI - MENUS

When Fiddler compiles your script, it looks for attributed methods that are used to create new entry-points in the Fiddler user-interface. You can add new items to the **Rules** menu, **Tools** menu, and **Web Sessions** context menu, as well as adding new top-level menus of your own.

Extending the Tools Menu

You can add new items to the Tools menu by adding a `ToolsAction` attribute to a method in your script. The attribute specifies the text of the item to show on the **Tools** menu, and it immediately precedes the method that will be run if the user clicks on the menu item. For instance, the following block, when placed inside your `Handlers` class, will add an item titled **Launch Opera** to the Tools menu:

```
// Launch Opera
ToolsAction("Launch Opera")
public static function DoLaunchOpera()
{
  System.Diagnostics.Process.Start("opera.exe", String.Empty);
}
```

Your method's signature may optionally specify a single parameter which will receive an array of the Sessions currently selected in the Web Sessions list when the menu item is invoked.

```
// Launch Opera to the URL of the first selected session
ToolsAction("Launch Opera to &URL")
public static function DoLaunchOperaToURL(oS: Session[])
{
  if (oS.Length > 0) {
      System.Diagnostics.Process.Start("opera.exe", oS[0].fullUrl);
  }
}
```

If the user clicks on your menu when no items are selected, the `oS` array will have a `Length` property value of 0.

To specify an accelerator key for your menu item, include an ampersand (&) in its name. The &U in the previous example creates the following menu item with the U key as an accelerator:

Extending the Web Sessions Context Menu

You may similarly extend the Web Sessions context menu by adding a **ContextAction** attribute to a method in your script. For instance, the following method will decompress and unchunk the HTTP request and response for each selected session:

```
ContextAction("Decode Selected Sessions")
public static function DoRemoveEncoding(oS: Session[])
{
  for (var x=0; x < oS.Length; x++) {
     oS[x].utilDecodeRequest();
     oS[x].utilDecodeResponse();
  }
}
```

The new context menu items created by your script are added to the top of the context menu.

Extending the Rules Menu

Your script may add new entries to the Rules menu, but they will work somewhat differently than the items added to the Tools menu and Web Sessions context menu. Instead of annotating a function using an attribute, you will instead annotate a variable (field) in your script using a RulesOption attribute. For instance, to add the **Hide 304s** menu item, the following script is used:

```
RulesOption("Hide 304s")
public static var m_Hide304s: boolean = false;
```

Two types of fields in your script may be bound to Rules menu items: booleans, and strings.

Note: The default value of the field is used to set the initial state of the menu item when the script is compiled. After that initial setting, the binding between the UI and the field is one-directional. That means that when the user clicks a field-bound menu item, the value of the bound boolean or string is changed, but if the script itself changes the boolean's or string's value, no change is made to the menu item's state.

Boolean-bound Rules

When Fiddler encounters a boolean variable in the script that is annotated with a RulesOption attribute, a menu item will be created using the text provided. The menu item's checked state will track the value of the boolean.

In the prior example, the boolean's value is false, so the menu item will be unchecked by default. When the user clicks the menu item, it will become checked, and Fiddler will change the value of the bound m_Hide304s variable to true. Every time your script is recompiled, the default values of your boolean variables are restored, and the checkmarks on the Rules menu will be updated accordingly.

Simply declaring the attributed m_Hide304s variable doesn't yet do anything useful—the variable simply tracks the state of the menu item. The *functionality* of the rule is provided by a block of code added to the OnBeforeResponse method found later in the script:

```
if (m_Hide304s && (304 == oSession.responseCode)) {

  oSession["ui-hide"] = "true";

  // Note: This block could be placed in the OnPeekAtResponseHeaders method,
  // since it does not depend upon the availability of the response body.
}
```

This block first checks to see if the rule is enabled and if so, checks that the server returned a HTTP/304. If so, the block sets the ui-hide flag on the Session, which causes it to be hidden from the Web Sessions list.

You can also use different forms of the RulesOption attribute to create submenus of options. To do so, provide the name of the submenu as the second parameter of the attribute. For instance, the following three fields create a Performance submenu that exposes the three options:

```
RulesOption("Simulate &Modem Speeds", "Per&formance")
public static var m_SimulateModem: boolean = false;

RulesOption("&Disable Caching", "Per&formance")
public static var m_DisableCaching: boolean = false;

RulesOption("&Show Time-to-Last-Byte", "Per&formance")
public static var m_ShowTTLB: boolean = false;
```

If you would like some of the items on your submenu to be mutually exclusive (showing as a radio group instead of a set of checkboxes), you can set a third boolean parameter to true, and you can add a splitter after a menu item by setting yet a fourth boolean parameter to true.

To create this menu:

Add the following script:

```
RulesOption("Option A", "MyMenu", true)
public static var m_OptionA: boolean = true;

RulesOption("Option B", "MyMenu", true)
```

```
public static var m_OptionB: boolean = false;

RulesOption("Option C", "MyMenu", true, true)  // Splitter after option
public static var m_OptionC: boolean = false;

RulesOption("Some other setting", "MyMenu", false)
public static var m_OtherSetting: boolean = true;
```

String-bound Rules

When Fiddler encounters a string in the script that is annotated with a `RulesString` attribute, a new submenu item will be created. The first parameter to the `RulesString` constructor is a string containing the submenu's name, while the second parameter is a boolean indicating whether an item labeled **Disabled** should be added to the submenu.

Possible values for the string's value are provided by adding one or more `RulesStringValue` attributes to the same variable. Each `RulesStringValue` will create a new mutually-exclusive menu item on the new submenu. When the user checks one of the menu items, the variable will be updated to the string value selected and all other menu items on the menu will be unchecked.

For instance, this script:

```
RulesString("MyStringRule", true)
RulesStringValue("MyMenuText1", "MyValue1")
RulesStringValue("MyMenuText2", "MyValue2")
RulesStringValue("MyMenuText3", "MyValue3")
public static var m_StringRule: String = String.Empty;
```

…creates the following menu:

By default, the menu's items will be sorted alphabetically by the menu text. In some cases, you may wish to specify a different order. To do so, use the `RulesStringValue` overload that accepts an integer ordering parameter. For instance, you can create a menu that looks like this:

...using this script:

```
RulesString("MyStringRule", true)
RulesStringValue(1, "First Item", "one")
RulesStringValue(2, "Second Item", "two", true)
RulesStringValue(3, "Third Item", "three")
RulesStringValue(4, "Fourth Item", "four")
RulesStringValue(5, "Ask me...", "%CUSTOM%")
public static var m_StringRule: String = "two";
```

This script also shows how to set one of the entries as the default (see the last parameter on the "Second Item" RulesStringValue). Also, note the magic value %CUSTOM% used for the "Ask me…" menu item. When clicked, the user will be prompted to enter a value for the variable:

When the prompt is shown, the current value of the string variable will be presented for the user to modify.

Fiddler's **Rules** > **User-Agents** feature is implemented using a string variable named sUA bound to a RulesString submenu. Inside the OnBeforeRequest method, script checks whether the bound variable is set, and if so, uses its value to overwrite the request's User-Agent header:

```
if (null != sUA) {
    oSession.oRequest["User-Agent"] = sUA;
}
```

Creating New Top-Level Menus

Using FiddlerScript, you can also easily add new top-level menus that expose actions of your choice. To do so, add a QuickLinkMenu attribute to your method that specifies the name of the top-level menu. Then, add one or more QuickLinkItem attributes that specify the text of a menu item and a string to pass into the method if the user selects the specified item.

For instance, the following text will add a new **Links** menu containing two items:

```
QuickLinkMenu("&Links")
QuickLinkItem("IE GeoLoc TestDrive",
  "http://ie.microsoft.com/testdrive/HTML5/Geolocation/Default.html")
QuickLinkItem("FiddlerCore", "http://fiddler.wikidot.com/fiddlercore")
public static function DoLinksMenu(sText: String, sAction: String)
{
  Utilities.LaunchHyperlink(sAction);
}
```

When the user clicks on the FiddlerCore item, the DoLinksMenu function will run, passing in the URL associated with that menu item in the second parameter to the function. Items in the menu are sorted alphabetically by their menu text.

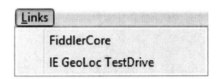

Of course, you're not limited to creating menus of links. You can create a Browser Launch menu that will allow you to launch the browser of your choice to the URL of the first selected session:

```
QuickLinkMenu("&Browse")
QuickLinkItem("&IE", "iexplore.exe")
QuickLinkItem("&Firefox", "firefox.exe")
QuickLinkItem("&Opera", "Opera.exe")
QuickLinkItem("&Chrome", "Chrome.exe")
public static function DoBrowsersMenu(sText: String, sAction: String)
{
  var oS = FiddlerApplication.UI.GetSelectedSessions();
  var sURL = String.Empty;

  if (oS.Length > 0) { sURL = oS[0].fullUrl; }

  System.Diagnostics.Process.Start(sAction, sURL);
}
```

Similarly, you could use a switch() statement to dispatch command invocations for handling by other functions.

Extending Fiddler's UI - Adding Columns to the Web Sessions List

FiddlerScript can also be used to add new columns to the Web Sessions list, either by using attributes or by making a method call.

Binding Columns using Attributes

The `BindUIColumn` attribute is used to create a new column in the Web Sessions list and bind to it a method in the script that will calculate the text for that column. The method must accept a `Session` object as a parameter, and return a `string` as its result.

The following script adds a new column to the Web Sessions list that shows the HTTP Method for each Session:

```
BindUIColumn("Method", 60)
public static function FillMethodColumn(oS: Session) {
  if ((oS.oRequest != null) && (oS.oRequest.headers != null))
  {
    return oS.oRequest.headers.HTTPMethod;
  }
  return String.Empty;
}
```

After this function is added to the script, a new **Method** column is added to the UI and values are added to the column for each subsequent Session:

#	Method	Protocol	Host
26	GET	HTTP	www.fiddler2.com
27	CONNECT	HTTP	Tunnel to
28	CONNECT	HTTP	Tunnel to
29	POST	HTTPS	beta.urs.microsoft.com
30	POST	HTTPS	beta.urs.microsoft.com
31	GET	HTTP	www.fiddler2.com

Your method must be robust against being called before the data it relies upon is ready. For instance, if you were to add a column that counts the number of times the word `fuzzle` appears in the HTTP response, your method should immediately return an empty string every time it is called until the `responseBodyBytes` array is created after the response is read from the server. Otherwise, the method will throw a Null Reference Exception every time it is called before the server response is completed.

Because your function will run multiple times for each Session as the Session proceeds from one state to the next, you should ensure that it runs as quickly as possible. One strategy to minimize the work of this function is to cache values using a new flag on the `Session` object. Obviously, the benefit of caching a computed value will increase as the complexity of the computation of that value increases. For instance, if the calculation involves converting the `responseBodyBytes` array to plaintext and searching that text for a string, this can be a very expensive operation which will greatly benefit from caching its result.

The following is an example which converts a non-binary response body to a string and then searches it for the word "`fuzzle`", caching the result of the search in a flag on the `Session` object:

```
BindUIColumn("HasFuzzle", 60)
public static function FillFuzzleColumn(oS: Session) {

  // Check the cache and return the value if we already computed it
  if (oS.oFlags.ContainsKey("HasFuzzle"))
  {
    return oS.oFlags["HasFuzzle"];
  }

  // Exit if we don't yet have a response
  if (!oS.bHasResponse)
  {
    return String.Empty;
  }

  // Avoid looking inside binary content
  if (Utilities.IsBinaryMIME(oS.oResponse.MIMEType))
  {
    oS.oFlags["HasFuzzle"] = "n/a";
    return "n/a";
  }

  var s = oS.GetResponseBodyAsString();
  var i = -1;

  if (s.Length > 0)
  {
    i = s.IndexOf("fuzzle", StringComparison.OrdinalIgnoreCase);
    if (i >= 0)
    {
      oS.oFlags["HasFuzzle"] = "Yes!";
      return "Yes!";
    }
  }

  oS.oFlags["HasFuzzle"] = "Nope";
  return "Nope";
}
```

This example first checks the cache for a previously computed value, and if one is found, it is immediately returned. Next, the example validates that the data it needs for the calculation is available. If not, it returns an empty string. Next, it checks to see whether the response body is advertising a binary Content-Type; if so, it caches an "n/a" result and returns it. Finally, it converts the response body to a string and hunts for the target word. It caches and returns the result of the search.

The complete set of `BindUIColumn` constructors includes versions that allow you to indicate that the column's contents should be sorted as integers, and to specify the column's width and its relative display ordering amongst the other columns.

```
public BindUIColumn(string sTitle)
public BindUIColumn(string sTitle, bool bSortNumerically)
public BindUIColumn(string sTitle, int iWidth)
public BindUIColumn(string sTitle, int iWidth, int iDisplayOrder)
public BindUIColumn(string sTitle, int iWidth,
                    int iDisplayOrder, bool bSortColumnNumerically)
```

Binding Columns using AddBoundColumn

In addition to adding columns by annotating a function with the `BindUIColumn` attribute, you can also add a column directly by calling the `AddBoundColumn` method on the Web Sessions listview. Various overloads of the function define the title of the column, its width, its relative display ordering amongst the other columns, its sort behavior, and a flag or function to which the column will be bound.

The call:

```
FiddlerObject.UI.lvSessions.AddBoundColumn("ClientPort", 50, "X-CLIENTPORT");
```

...adds a new column with the title **ClientPort** and a default width of 50 pixels. The contents of the column are bound to the value of each session's `X-ClientPort` flag, which will be empty if the flag does not exist. The third parameter allows you to specify either a Session Flag name, or the name of a request or response header using the `@request` or `@response` prefixes. For instance:

```
FiddlerObject.UI.lvSessions.AddBoundColumn("Server", 50, "@response.Server");
```

...will create a column with the title **Server**, displaying the contents of the response's `Server` header, if present.

Similarly,

```
FiddlerObject.UI.lvSessions.AddBoundColumn("Reason", 50,
  "@request.X-Download-Initiator");
```

...will create a column with the title **Reason**, displaying the request's `X-Download-Initiator` header's value, if present. You can configure IE9+ to emit this header on each request; it provides a terse explanation of why a given request was made. For instance, it will indicate if the request was caused by navigation, an IMG tag's download, etc. See `http://fiddler2.com/r/?InitiatorHeader` to download configuration scripts that enable and disable sending of this header.

You may also call AddBoundColumn and provide a callback function's name, along with a boolean indicating that the column's values should be interpreted and sorted as numbers. For instance:

```
// Callback function that returns the "Time to first byte" value
static function getTTLB(oS: Session): String
{
  var iMS = Math.round((oS.Timers.ServerDoneResponse
                    - oS.Timers.FiddlerBeginRequest).TotalMilliseconds);
  if (iMS > 0) return iMS.ToString();
  return 0;
}

FiddlerObject.UI.lvSessions.AddBoundColumn("TTLB", 0, 50, true, getTTLB);
```

The true parameter indicates that the column's values are numeric, while the 0 parameter indicates that this should be inserted as the first column displayed in the Web Sessions list. Note that the display order parameter is *relative*, not absolute, so calling:

```
FiddlerObject.UI.lvSessions.AddBoundColumn("4", 0, 50, func4);
FiddlerObject.UI.lvSessions.AddBoundColumn("3", 0, 40, func3);
FiddlerObject.UI.lvSessions.AddBoundColumn("2", 0, 30, func2);
FiddlerObject.UI.lvSessions.AddBoundColumn("1", 0, 20, func1);
```

…will result in four new columns of increasing width, titled 1, 2, 3, and 4, in that order from left to right.

If you'd like to change a column's width or ordering within the Web Sessions list, you can use the SetColumnOrderAndWidth method. The method takes three parameters: the title of the column to adjust, the new position, and the new width. The latter two parameters may be set to -1 to leave the order or width unchanged.

For instance, to move the Protocol column to the far left of the Web Sessions list without changing its width, call:

```
FiddlerApplication.UI.lvSessions.SetColumnOrderAndWidth("Protocol", 0, -1);
```

Again, keep in mind that column ordering behaves as an insertion operation. So, if you call:

```
FiddlerApplication.UI.lvSessions.SetColumnOrderAndWidth("#",        0, -1);
FiddlerApplication.UI.lvSessions.SetColumnOrderAndWidth("Result",   1, -1);
FiddlerApplication.UI.lvSessions.SetColumnOrderAndWidth("Protocol", 0, -1);
FiddlerApplication.UI.lvSessions.SetColumnOrderAndWidth("Host",     0, -1);
```

The final ordering is [Host, Protocol, #, Result], because the Host column was inserted at index 0, pushing the Result and Protocol columns rightward.

FIDDLEROBJECT FUNCTIONS

The FiddlerScript engine itself provides a number of simple utility functions and properties that you may use to accomplish common tasks. These methods and properties are exposed by the `FiddlerObject` object and include:

FiddlerObject.ReloadScript()
This method instructs Fiddler to reload the script file from disk and recompile it, resetting all variables to their default values.

FiddlerObject.StatusText
This property allows you to set the text on Fiddler's status bar. It may safely be set from any thread, as it will internally call `BeginInvoke` on the UI thread if set from a background thread. The default Fiddler-Script file sets the status bar text when the script is first compiled:

```
static function Main() {
  var today: Date = new Date();
  FiddlerObject.StatusText = " CustomRules.js was loaded at: " + today;
}
```

The `OnExecAction` handler in the default script uses the `StatusText` property to communicate the results of commands to the user.

FiddlerObject.log(sTextToLog)
This method allows you to log text to Fiddler's event log. The first character of the provided text may be an exclamation mark, underscore, or forward slash to cause the Log tab to format the text in bold, underlined, or italic text respectively.

The following example:

```
static function OnPeekAtResponseHeaders(oSession: Session) {
  FiddlerObject.log("_Underlined\t#" + oSession.id.ToString());
  FiddlerObject.log("!Bolded\t" + oSession.fullUrl);
  FiddlerObject.log("/Italicized\t" + oSession.oResponse.MIMEType);
}
```

Yields the following output:

FiddlerObject.playSound(sSoundFilename)
This method loads and plays the specified .wav audio file. This can be useful if your script needs to draw the user's attention to an exceptional event.

FiddlerObject.flashWindow()
This method flashes the Fiddler window's entry in the Windows task bar to help draw the user's attention.

FiddlerObject.alert(sMessage)
This method displays the provided message in a message box with the title "FiddlerScript."

FiddlerObject.prompt(sMessage)
This method and its overloads:

```
FiddlerObject.prompt(sMessage, sDefaultValue)
FiddlerObject.prompt(sMessage, sDefaultValue, sTitle)
```

…allow you to prompt the user for a string using the prompt message provided in the first parameter. The second and third overloads allow you to optionally specify a default value and the title of the prompt dialog box.

For instance, this line will prompt the user for a HTML tag name:

```
var sTagName: String =
  FiddlerObject.prompt("Enter a HTML tag name", "<br />", "Specify Tag");
```

When the prompt is displayed, Fiddler will flash its window's entry in the Windows task bar to help draw the user's attention. If the user presses Cancel on the prompt, the supplied default value (or String.Empty) will be returned.

FiddlerObject.createDictionary()
This method allows you to create a simple Dictionary<string, object> object suitable to pass to the DoImport and DoExport methods on the FiddlerApplication object. This method is necessary because the JScript.NET language does not expose any other way to create a generic Dictionary<> object.

The following example generates a HAR file on the desktop containing all of the captured sessions:

```
var oSessions = FiddlerApplication.UI.GetAllSessions();
var oExportOptions = FiddlerObject.createDictionary();
oExportOptions.Add("Filename", "C:\\users\\ericlaw\\desktop\\out1.har");
```

```
oExportOptions.Add("MaxTextBodyLength", 0);
oExportOptions.Add("MaxBinaryBodyLength", 0);
FiddlerApplication.DoExport("HTTPArchive v1.2", oSessions, oExportOptions, null);
```

FiddlerObject.WatchPreference(sPrefBranch, oFunc)

This method allows you to provide a callback method which will be notified when any change occurs within the specified branch of Preferences.

```
static function Main() {
   FiddlerObject.WatchPreference("fiddler.script", ObservePrefChange);
}

static function ObservePrefChange(oSender: Object, oPCEA: PrefChangeEventArgs) {
   var sMsg: String = oPCEA.PrefName + " changed to " + oPCEA.ValueString;
   MessageBox.Show(sMsg, "A pref was changed");
}
```

This method exists because, if your FiddlerScript were to call `FiddlerApplication.Prefs.AddWatcher` directly, the entire script engine would be leaked each time the script is recompiled. That leak would occur because the callback event could not be garbage-collected due to the outstanding reference held by the Preferences object.

REFERENCING ASSEMBLIES

The .NET Framework offers a huge library of functionality that you can take advantage of in your Fiddler-Script. For instance, you can use the classes in System.Data to log traffic to a database, or use classes in the System.IO namespace to write files to disk.

To reference an assembly that is installed in the system's Global Assembly Cache, simply add the appropriate namespace to the list of #import statements at the top of your script:

```
import System;
import System.Windows.Forms;
import Fiddler;
import System.IO;
```

Then use the classes as needed:

```
static function OnBeforeResponse(oSession: Session)
{
    File.WriteAllBytes("C:\\temp\\Session"+oSession.id.ToString()+".dat",
        oSession.responseBodyBytes);
```

You can also use methods in your own assembly DLLs even if those assemblies are not loaded into the global assembly cache. There are two ways to enable FiddlerScript to find the assembly.

The first is to add the Assembly's full path inside **Tools > Fiddler Options > Extensions**:

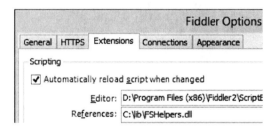

Alternatively, you may use a Preference to specify the default library path used to find assemblies. The Preference fiddler.script.LibPath should be set to the fully-qualified path that contains your DLLs. For instance, type the following in the QuickExec box below the Web Sessions list:

```
prefs set fiddler.script.LibPath "C:\src\Library DLLs\"
```

...and when your FiddlerScript is next compiled, Fiddler will look for referenced assemblies in the Library DLLs folder.

EXAMPLE SCRIPTS

While you can use FiddlerScript to build nearly any type of functionality you want, in most cases you will use script to modify either the request or response. This section contains a few examples to get you started.

Request Scripts

Place these snippets inside the OnBeforeRequest function so that they run before the request is sent to the server.

Add (or Overwrite) a Request Header

You can modify request headers very easily using the indexer property on the oRequest object:

```
oSession.oRequest["HeaderName"] = "New value";
```

This will add the specified header, or overwrite the first existing header named HeaderName.

To add the Session's ID to the outbound request headers so that they will be captured in the server's logs, use the line:

```
oSession.oRequest["X-Fiddler-SessionID"] = oSession.id.ToString();
```

Remove Request Headers

You can remove all headers of a specified name:

```
oSession.oResponse.headers.Remove("Cookie");
```

Flag Requests that Send Cookies

Session flags can be set based on request headers:

```
if (oSession.oRequest.headers.Exists("Cookie"))
{
  oSession["ui-color"]="red";
  oSession["ui-customcolumn"] = oSession.oRequest["Cookie"];
}
```

Rewrite a Request from HTTP to HTTPS

You can modify the UriScheme property for requests to change the protocol used:

```
if (!oSession.isHTTPS && !oSession.HTTPMethodIs("CONNECT") &&
    oSession.HostnameIs("myServer"))
{
  oSession.oRequest.headers.UriScheme = "https";
}
```

Swap the Host Header

When Fiddler gets a request whose URL doesn't match its Host header, the original Host value is stored in the session flag X-Original-Host and then the Host value is replaced with the host parsed from the URL. The following script reverses behavior by routing the request to the host specified by the original Host header.

```
if (oSession.BitFlags & SessionFlags.ProtocolViolationInRequest) {
  var sOverride = oSession["X-Original-Host"];
  if (!String.IsNullOrEmpty(sOverride)) {
    oSession["X-overrideHost"] = sOverride;
    oSession["ui-backcolor"] = "yellow";

    // Be sure to bypass the gateway, otherwise overrideHost doesn't work
    oSession.bypassGateway = true;
  }
}
```

Drop a Connection

FiddlerScript can drop the client's connection, like the AutoResponder Actions *drop and *reset.

```
if (oSession.uriContains("DropIt") && (null != oS.oRequest.pipeClient)) {

  // Use this to close the connection using TCP/IP RST
  oS.oRequest.pipeClient.EndWithRST();

  // or use this to close the connection using TCP/IP FIN
  // oS.oRequest.pipeClient.End();

  // So that the UI shows what we did, create a placeholder
  // response for display purposes:
  if (this.state < SessionStates.SendingRequest) {
    oS.utilCreateResponseAndBypassServer();
  }

  oS.oResponse.headers.HTTPResponseCode = 0;
  oS.oResponse.headers.HTTPResponseStatus = "0 Connection dropped by script";
  oS.responseBodyBytes = new byte[0];
  oS.state = SessionStates.Aborted;
  return;
}
```

Prevent Response Streaming

To ensure that the server's response is buffered to permit tampering, you must set the Session object's bBufferResponse field *before* the response is read from the server:

```
if (oSession.HostnameIs("myServer") && oSession.uriContains(".aspx"))
{
  oSession.bBufferResponse = true;
}
```

Response Scripts

You can modify responses just as easily. If your code only needs to access the response's headers, use the `OnPeekAtResponse` headers function. If you need access to the response body, place your code inside the `OnBeforeResponse` function. There, the script will run after the response body is read from the server but before the response is returned to the client. That is, unless buffering is disabled, in which case the function will run after the response has been streamed to the client, hiding any modifications you make to the body from the client.

Hide Sessions that Returned Images

You can set the `ui-hide` flag to hide traffic from the Web Sessions list:

```
if (oSession.oResponse.MIMEType.Contains("image"))
{
  oSession["ui-hide"] = "Script hiding images";
}
```

Flag Redirections

Examine the `responseCode` property to identify redirects:

```
if ((oSession.responseCode > 299) && (oSession.responseCode < 400)) {

  oSession["ui-customcolumn"] = oSession.oResponse["Location"];
  oSession["ui-bold"] = "redirect";
}
```

Replace Text in Script, CSS, and HTML

Change any CSS vendor-prefixes from `-Moz-` and `-WebKit-` to `-MS-`:

```
if ( !Utilities.IsBinaryMIME(oSession.oResponse.MIMEType)  )
{
  oSession.utilDecodeResponse();
  oSession.utilReplaceInResponse("-moz-", "-ms-");
  oSession.utilReplaceInResponse("-webkit-", "-ms-");
}
```

Remove All DIV Elements

Use regular expressions to modify the response body:

```
if (oSession.oResponse.MIMEType.Contains("html")) {
  var oBody = oSession.GetResponseBodyAsString();

  // Replace all content of DIV tags with an empty string.
  // WARNING: Doesn't work well with nested DIVs.
  var oRegEx =  /<div[^>]*>(.*?)<\/div>/gi;
  oBody = oBody.replace(oRegEx, "");

  // Set the response body to the div-less string
  oSession.utilSetResponseBody(oBody);
}
```

More Examples

You can find more FiddlerScript sample code:

- In the `SampleRules.js` file installed with Fiddler

- At `http://fiddler2.com/r/?FiddlerScriptCookbook`

Extending Fiddler with .NET Code

EXTENDING FIDDLER WITH .NET

While FiddlerScript provides a simple and lightweight means of extending Fiddler, extending Fiddler with .NET assemblies offers significantly more power and an improved debugging experience. That's especially true if you plan to distribute your logic to other users.

Extending Fiddler with .NET enables you to build your extension in any .NET language (C# and VB.NET are the most common choices) and take advantage of the powerful IntelliSense and debugging features of Visual Studio. If your extension limits itself to the classes in the v2.0 Framework, it should work properly on every Fiddler user's system. While both FiddlerScript and .NET extensions may use any of the classes in the .NET Framework, it can be cumbersome to use many Framework classes from FiddlerScript. Compiled .NET extensions typically exhibit significantly faster load-time and run-time performance as compared to building equivalent functionality in FiddlerScript, because the latter must be recompiled each time Fiddler starts.

Extensions can be installed to users' machines without the hassle of manual modifications of the user's FiddlerScript source file, and can be uninstalled using the system's Control Panel. Each extension's assembly declares the minimum version of Fiddler with which it is compatible, and users will be prompted to update if an extension requiring a later Fiddler version is encountered. This versioning feature helps prevent problems where code that works great on your computer fails spectacularly on another user's machine because they're clinging to an outdated version of Fiddler.

Project Requirements and Settings

Writing extensions for Fiddler requires Visual Studio .NET 2005 or later, or the free .NET Framework v2 command-line compilers.

Fiddler2 loads only .NET Common Language Runtime (CLR) v2.0 assemblies; assemblies that target the v1.1 or v4.0 CLR will not be loaded. Fiddler itself requires only that the user have .NET Framework **2.0 SP1** installed. Your extension *may* target the .NET Framework 3.5 (which includes LINQ and other useful features) since that framework also runs on the v2.0 CLR. However, if it takes such a dependency, *your* installer must ensure that the user has the required Framework version installed, or the user will encounter "Class not found" exceptions as your extension loads.

You should also ensure your project targets **AnyCPU** to ensure that Fiddler loads it when running on a 64bit system.

Debugging Extensions

To avoid annoying end-users with warnings that they cannot do anything about, Fiddler silently handles a variety of problems when it loads and calls into extensions. However, these warnings can be extremely useful to extension developers, pointing out problems that prevent extensions from functioning properly.

Extension developers should set the `fiddler.debug.extensions.showerrors` preference to `true` ensure that exceptions and other extension-related errors are not silently caught. Additionally, they should set the `fiddler.debug.extensions.verbose` preference to `true` to spew logging information and warnings to Fiddler's Log tab.

Best Practices for Extensions

On the Internet Explorer team, we've found that over 75% of browser crashes and nearly all major performance problems are caused by buggy browser extensions. Fortunately, extension quality in the Fiddler ecosystem is much better, but it's still the case that an extension can cause Fiddler to crash or perform more slowly. I'm relying on you to help ensure that users have a great experience when your extension is running inside Fiddler.

The simplest way to minimize your extension's performance impact is to ensure that it does not run when it's not being used. There are two key strategies for doing that: offer an enable switch, and use a delay-load pattern.

Best Practice: Use an Enable Switch

With very few exceptions, users should not be forced to uninstall your extension to disable it-- most users will only want your extension to run at certain times. Extensions should offer an **Enable** switch; when that switch is off, the extension should do as little work as possible. For instance, inside the ContentBlock extension, each method that handles a Session first checks to see whether blocking is enabled:

```
public void AutoTamperRequestBefore(Session oSession)
{
  // Return immediately if no rule is enabled
  if (!bBlockerEnabled) return;
  // ...
```

This best practice is followed by Fiddler itself—the AutoResponder and Filters tabs have enabling checkboxes at their top and only process Sessions when enabled.

Best Practice: Use Delay Load

Extensions and Inspectors are loaded as Fiddler starts up, so your code can directly impact the time that Fiddler takes to load. Because some users will restart Fiddler dozens of times per day, load time is a very important factor in their experience with the tool.

In many cases, a user may not use your Inspector or Extension at all within a given session. For instance, perhaps the user installed your Silverlight-troubleshooter Inspector for one project, but then gets pulled away to go help with a HR system that uses only WCF Web Services and no Silverlight at all. If your Inspector uses a lot of memory and takes a long time to load, the user will be paying a penalty for having it installed even when it's not used. To avoid that problem, use the Delay Load pattern, in which expensive operations are only undertaken if needed. This pattern can be effectively applied to both Inspectors and other types of extensions.

For instance, the **FiddlerScript** tab uses a syntax-highlighting component to display the source of your script file; this component requires hundreds of millions of cycles and several megabytes of memory to load. If this component was loaded every time Fiddler starts, these cycles and memory are wasted if the user doesn't interact with the tab. To mitigate this problem, the FiddlerScript tab only creates the syntax-highlighting component when the user first activates the extension's tab.

The OnLoad handler for the extension creates its tab, adds a "Loading..." label to it, and adds a handler to the SelectedIndexChanged event to detect when its tab is being activated.

```
public void OnLoad()
{
  myPage = new TabPage("FiddlerScript");
  myPage.ImageIndex = (int)Fiddler.SessionIcons.Script;
  this.lblLoading = new System.Windows.Forms.Label();
  this.lblLoading.Text = "Loading...";
  myPage.Controls.Add(lblLoading);
  FiddlerApplication.UI.tabsViews.TabPages.Add(myPage);

  TabControlEventHandler evtTCEH = null;
  evtTCEH = delegate(object s, TabControlEventArgs e) {
    if (e.TabPage == myTabPage)
    {
      // Create heavyweight components used to display UI
      EnsureReady();

      // Remove the unneeded event handler.
      FiddlerApplication.UI.tabsViews.Selected -= evtTCEH;
    }
  };

  // Subscribe to tab-change events
  FiddlerApplication.UI.tabsViews.Selected += evtTCEH;
}
```

Only when the extension's tab is activated does the EnsureReady method run to create the heavyweight component, hiding the "Loading..." label:

```
private void EnsureReady()
{
  if (null != oEditor) return;     // Exit if we've already been made ready

  lblLoading.Refresh();            // Force repaint of "Loading..." label

  // Create the extension's UI (slow)
  oEditor = new RulesEditor(myPage);
  lblLoading.Visible = false;      // Remove the "Loading..." label
}
```

This pattern is also used by the SyntaxView, HexView, and WebView Inspectors, all of which depend upon components that are expensive to construct. Other extensions do not bother with the Delay Load pattern if they use only a few lightweight controls and the complexity of the Delay Load pattern isn't necessary.

Best Practice: Beware "Big Data"
The user's web traffic may include giant responses (e.g. videos or other files that are hundreds of megabytes in size) that you might not have anticipated when building your extension. Requests *can* be quite large as well, but in practice, enormous downloads are much more common than large uploads.

If your extension doesn't defend itself from "big data," your code could hang Fiddler when the user selects such a Session. There are several best practices to help prevent hangs:

- Ensure that your extension "fails fast" if it encounters a response of a type or size that it wasn't designed to handle.

- Avoid making unnecessary copies of data. In most places, Fiddler uses a "copy on write" architecture to prevent unneeded duplication of data, and your extensions should do the same.

- If your extension attempts to render data by replacing embedded nulls using the Unicode replacement character (0xFFFD, rendered as �), ensure that you limit how much data you attempt to show. Otherwise, rendering a binary file will result in massive memory use, because the embedded nulls will not terminate the text passed to a textbox or other UI control.

Fiddler's default extensions all follow these best practices to help ensure that the debugger remains responsive even when dealing with huge responses.

Best Practice: Use the Reporter Pattern for Extensions
A common goal when building an extension is to display summary data about the currently selected Sessions in the Web Sessions list. For instance, the Statistics tab shows the timing data and size of the selected sessions, while the Timeline tab shows the start time and duration of each selected Session. Extensions of this sort are called **Reporters** because they generate a report on the currently-selected Sessions.

A naïve implementation of a Reporter would recalculate its data each time a session is selected or unselected. The problem with that approach is that if the user hits CTRL+A to select all of the sessions in the Web Sessions list (or CTRL+X to clear it) the Reporter will end up doing billions of redundant calculations whose results are never displayed to the user.

To avoid that problem, instead handle the FiddlerApplication.CalculateReport event. This event is dispatched as the user selects and unselects Sessions, but it is suppressed during certain bulk operations (like loading a SAZ file or clearing the Web Sessions list), ensuring that it is dispatched only after the bulk update is completed. The event is also suppressed when Fiddler shuts down, helping to ensure that you don't perform expensive work as Fiddler is unloading and disposing of its objects.

Your event handler implementation must have the following signature:

```
public delegate void CalculateReportHandler(Session[] _arrSessions);
```

Your event handler will be called at the appropriate intervals, and an array of the currently selected Sessions will be passed as the only parameter. You should still avoid doing any redundant work—for instance, if your tab isn't presently active, you should suppress calculations until it is activated.

The Statistics tab's `CalculateReport` handler looks a bit like this:

```
void UpdateStatsTab(Session[] _arrSessions)
{
  // If we're not showing the Stats tab right now, bail out.
  if (FiddlerApplication.UI.tabsViews.SelectedTab !=
      FiddlerApplication.UI.pageStatistics)
  {
    return;
  }

  try
  {
    if (_arrSessions.Length < 1)
    {
      ClearStatsTab();
      return;
    }

    Dictionary<string, long> dictResponseSizeByContentType;
    long cBytesRecv;
    string sStats = BasicAnalysis.ComputeBasicStatistics(
    _arrSessions, true, out dictResponseSizeByContentType, out cBytesRecv);

    txtReport.Text = String.Format("{0}\r\n, sStats);
  }
  catch (Exception eX)
  {
    Debug.Assert(false, eX.Message);
  }
}
```

By using the `CalculateReport` event, your extension can avoid performing unnecessary work, helping to keep Fiddler running fast.

Interacting with Fiddler's Objects

Most FiddlerScript and extensions use Fiddler's object model to interact with the user-interface, Session objects, the FiddlerScript engine, and features like the TextWizard. This section outlines the properties, flags, fields, and events that your code may rely upon.

The Web Sessions List

Because the Web Sessions list is the most important component of the Fiddler user-interface, your code will often need to interact with the list's entries. Fiddler exposes methods on the `FiddlerApplication.UI` object to interact with the Web Sessions list.

Session[] GetAllSessions()

This method will return an array containing all of the Sessions in the Web Sessions list. If the Web Sessions list is empty, the array's `Length` will be 0.

Session GetFirstSelectedSession()

This method will return the first selected Session in the Web Sessions list, or `null` if no entries are selected.

Session[] GetSelectedSessions()

This method will return an array containing all of the Sessions that are currently selected in the Web Sessions list. If no entries are selected, the array's `Length` will be 0.

Session[] GetSelectedSessions(int iMax)

This method will return an array containing all of the Sessions that are currently selected in the Web Sessions list, up to the maximum number specified. If no entries are selected, the array's `Length` will be 0.

void actSelectAll()

Selects all Sessions in the Web Sessions list.

void actSelectSessionsMatchingCriteria(doesSessionMatchCriteriaDelegate oDel)

This powerful method allows you to supply a delegate function (similar to a predicate delegate) that is evaluated for each Session in the Web Sessions list. For each entry, if your delegate returns `true`, the Session's entry will be selected. If it returns `false`, the Session's entry will be unselected.

For instance, say that you want to select all Sessions that use the POST request method. You can use the following code:

```
FiddlerApplication.UI.actSelectSessionsMatchingCriteria(
  delegate(Session oS)
  {
    return oS.HTTPMethodIs("POST");
  });
```

Or, if you want to select all Sessions that have a HTTP/200 response status, use this:

```
FiddlerApplication.UI.actSelectSessionsMatchingCriteria(
  delegate(Session oS)
  {
    return (200 == oS.responseCode);
  });
```

void actRemoveSelectedSessions()

Removes all selected Sessions from the Web Sessions list.

void actRemoveUnselectedSessions()

Removes all unselected Sessions from the Web Sessions list.

bool actLoadSessionArchive(string sFilename)

Loads the sessions from the specified SAZ file and adds them to the Web Sessions list.

void actSaveSessionsToZip()

Saves the currently selected Sessions to a SAZ file whose filename is provided by the user in a Save File prompt. The "Zip" part of this method's name reflects the fact that a SAZ file is merely a structured Zip archive.

void actSaveSessionsToZip(string sFilename, string sPwd)

Saves the currently selected Sessions to a SAZ file named by the provided filename. If the password parameter is non-null, the SAZ file will be encrypted using the specified password.

void actSessionCopyURL()

Copies the URLs of the currently selected Sessions to the clipboard, one per line.

void actSessionCopySummary()

Copies all of the text from the Web Sessions listview to the clipboard for each of the selected Sessions. The data is copied in both tab-delimited text and HTML formats, suitable for pasting into either documents or spreadsheets.

void actSessionCopyHeadlines()

Copies a terse listing of the selected Sessions to the clipboard. For instance, when loading the Fiddler homepage, the data copied is:

```
GET http://www.fiddler2.com/
302 Object moved to /fiddler2/

GET http://www.fiddler2.com/fiddler2/
200 OK (text/html)

CONNECT http://sqm.telemetry.microsoft.com:443
```

```
200 Connection Established ()

GET http://www.fiddler2.com/Fiddler2/Fiddler.css
200 OK (text/css)

GET http://www.fiddler2.com/Eric/images/rss.gif
200 OK (image/gif)
```

int FiddlerApplication.UI.lvSessions.SelectedCount

This property appears directly on the Web Sessions listview and returns the count of selected Sessions without returning those items. This provides a quick way to get a count of selected Sessions without copying those sessions into an array as the `GetSelectedSessions` method does.

SimpleEventHandler FiddlerApplication.UI.lvSessions.OnSessionsAdded

By default, Fiddler queues updates to the list for a short period of time to help ensure UI responsiveness. This event fires whenever one or more Sessions is visibly added to Web Sessions list. If you choose to provide a handler for this event, ensure that the handler does not perform any expensive computations, as doing so will block the UI thread and severely impair performance.

Session Objects

Each Web Session is represented by a `Session` object which exposes fields, properties, and methods which control how the Session is processed and record information about it.

oRequest

The `oRequest` object represents the client's request. It exposes key properties including the `headers` object which contains the Request's headers. The headers themselves may be accessed by the indexers on the `oRequest` or `Session` objects:

```
oSession.oRequest["HeaderName"] == oSession.oRequest.headers["HeaderName"]
    == oSession["REQUEST", "HeaderName"];
```

The `oRequest` object's `pipeClient` field, if set, represents Fiddler's connection to the client.

requestBodyBytes

This byte array contains the raw bytes of the client's request. Because the body may be encoded, typically the `GetRequestBodyAsString` and `utilSetRequestBody` methods are used instead of manipulating the byte array directly.

oResponse

The `oResponse` object represents the server's response. It exposes key properties including the `headers` object which contains the Response's headers. The headers themselves may be accessed by the indexers on the `oResponse` or `Session` objects:

```
oSession.oResponse["HeaderName"] == oSession.oResponse.headers["HeaderName"]
    == oSession["RESPONSE", "HeaderName"];
```

The oResponse object's MIMEType property returns the MIME-type portion of the response's Content-Type header. The object's pipeServer field, if set, represents Fiddler's connection to the server.

responseBodyBytes
This byte array contains the raw bytes of the server's response. Because the body may be encoded, typically the GetResponseBodyAsString and utilSetResponseBody methods are used instead of manipulating the byte array directly.

oFlags
This StringDictionary contains flags that describe the Session. A full list of Session flags can be found in Appendix C. You may access this collection directly, or via one of the two indexer properties exposed by the Session object.

```
oSession.oFlags["FlagName"] == oSession["FlagName"]
    == oSession["SESSION", "FlagName"];
```

Note: If the requested Flag does not exist, the indexers have slightly different behavior:

```
if (!oSession.oFlags.ContainsKey("SomeKey")
{
  Debug.Assert(oSession["SomeKey"] == null);
  Debug.Assert(oSession.oFlags["SomeKey"] == null);
  Debug.Assert(oSession["Session", "SomeKey"] == String.Empty);
}
```

void Abort()
Aborts processing of the current Session. This closes both client and server connections (if any) and moves the Session's state to Aborted.

bBufferResponse
This boolean field controls whether the response will be streamed to the client as it is read from the server.

bHasReponse
This readonly property returns true if the Session's state > ReadingResponse and oResponse is not null.

bypassGateway
This boolean field controls whether the request will be sent to the upstream gateway proxy server, if any such server is configured.

clientIP
This string records the IP address from which the request originated.

clientPort
This integer records the port from which the request originated.

bool COMETPeek()

Call this method while in the `ReadingResponse` state to update the `responseBodyBytes` array with the partially-read response.

fullUrl

This property stores the complete request URI, including protocol/scheme, in the form `http://www.host.com/filepath?query`. To retarget this request to a different URL, adjust this property before the request is sent.

PathAndQuery

This property contains the path and query string from the request URL.

port

This property contains the port to which the request is targeted.

host

This property stores the host specified in the request headers; this value may include a port number.

hostname

This property stores the hostname specified in the request headers; this value will never include a port number.

bool HostnameIs(string)

This method compares the supplied hostname to the hostname of the request, returning `true` if a case-insensitive match is found.

bool HTTPMethodIs(string)

This method compares the supplied HTTP Method name to the HTTP Method of the request, returning `true` if a case-insensitive match is found.

bool uriContains(string)

This method searches the request URI for the supplied string, and returns `true` if a case-sensitive match is found.

id

This readonly integer property returns the Session's automatically-generated identification number.

isFTP

This readonly property returns `true` if the Session targets the FTP protocol.

isHTTPS

This readonly property returns `true` if the Session targets the HTTPS protocol.

isTunnel
This readonly property returns `true` if the Session is a `CONNECT` tunnel used for HTTPS or WebSocket traffic.

LocalProcessID
This readonly integer property returns the process ID of the local process from which the request originated. If the request was generated from a remote client, this property will return 0.

bool utilDecodeRequest()
Call this method to remove any HTTP compression or Chunked Encoding from the request body.

bool utilDecodeResponse()
Call this method to remove any HTTP compression or Chunked Encoding from the response body.

responseCode
This integer property contains the HTTP status code from the server's response.

state
Each Session's `state` property tracks its progress through the following `SessionStates`:

SessionState	Description
Created	The `Session` has been created but nothing's happening yet.
ReadingRequest	Fiddler is reading the request from the client.
AutoTamperRequestBefore	Fiddler extensions that provide an `AutoTamperRequestBefore` method are processing the request.
HandTamperRequest	The user may manually edit the request using the Fiddler Inspectors.
AutoTamperRequestAfter	Fiddler extensions that provide an `AutoTamperRequestAfter` method are processing the request.
SendingRequest	Fiddler is sending the request to the server.
ReadingResponse	Fiddler is reading the response from the server.
AutoTamperResponseBefore	Fiddler extensions that provide an `AutoTamperResponseBefore` method are processing the request.
HandTamperResponse	The user may manually edit the response using the Fiddler Inspectors.
AutoTamperResponseAfter	Fiddler extensions that provide an `AutoTamperResponseAfter` method are processing the request.
SendingResponse	Fiddler is sending the response to the client.
Done	The Session is complete.
Aborted	The Session was aborted (the client disconnected before reading the response, there was a fatal error in processing, etc.)

The Session moves from one state to the next until it reaches the `Done` state; in the event of an error, the Session jumps immediately to the `Aborted` state. The Session object's `OnStateChanged` event fires any time the Session's `state` property changes.

BitFlags

Each Session's `BitFlags` property holds zero or more `SessionFlags` that supply commonly-queried state information. The `SessionFlags` enumeration includes:

SessionFlags	Description
None	No flags are set.
IsHTTPS	The request's URI has a HTTPS target.
IsFTP	The request's URI has a FTP target.
ClientPipeReused	The request was read from a previously used connection from the client.
ServerPipeReused	The request reused an existing connection to the server.
ResponseStreamed	The response was not buffered and was instead streamed to the client as it was read from the server.
RequestGeneratedByFiddler	The request was generated by Fiddler itself (e.g. from the Composer tab).
ResponseGeneratedByFiddler	The response was generated by Fiddler itself (e.g. AutoResponder or the `utilCreateResponseAndBypassServer` method).
LoadedFromSAZ	This previously-captured Session was reloaded from a SAZ file.
ImportedFromOtherTool	The Session was imported by a Transcoder.
SentToGateway	The request was sent to an upstream (CERN) gateway proxy.
IsBlindTunnel	This CONNECT tunnel "blindly" shuttles bytes across without decryption.
IsDecryptingTunnel	This CONNECT tunnel decrypts HTTPS traffic as it flows through.
ServedFromCache	The response was served from a client cache, bypassing Fiddler. Fiddler only "sees" this Session if other software reports it to Fiddler, because Fiddler only observes network traffic.
ProtocolViolationInRequest	There was a HTTP Protocol violation in the client's request.
ProtocolViolationInResponse	There was a HTTP Protocol violation in the server's response.
ResponseBodyDropped	The response body was dropped, e.g. because the Preference `fiddler.network.streaming.ForgetStreamedData` is set.
IsWebSocketTunnel	This CONNECT tunnel is used for WebSocket traffic.
SentToSOCKSGateway	The request was proxied using the SOCKS protocol.

The Session object exposes two methods to evaluate the Session's `BitFlags`. The `isAnyFlagSet` method accepts a set of flags and returns `true` if *any* of the specified flags are set, and `false` otherwise. The `isFlagSet` method accepts one or more flags and returns `true` if *all* of the specified flags are set, and `false` otherwise.

For example:

```
bool bHadAnyHTTPErrors =
    oSession.isAnyFlagSet(SessionFlags.ProtocolViolationInRequest
                     | SessionFlags.ProtocolViolationInResponse);

bool bReusedBothConnections =
    oSession.isFlagSet(SessionFlags.ClientPipeReused
                     | SessionFlags.ServerPipeReused);
```

Timers

Fiddler records timestamps as the Session is processed using the Session's `Timers` object. These timestamps can help shed light on performance issues in your website or application, and can be seen in the Session's Properties window or the Statistics tab.

SessionTimers	Description
ClientConnected	Timestamp at which the client's connection to Fiddler was first established.
ClientBeginRequest	Timestamp at which the request's first socket Send() operation was serviced by Fiddler. If this request was issued on a reused connection, this timestamp could be much later than the ClientConnected value.
FiddlerGotRequestHeaders	Timestamp at which Fiddler completed reading the headers from the client.
ClientDoneRequest	Timestamp at which Fiddler completed reading the entire request from the client.
GatewayDeterminationTime	The number of milliseconds spent determining which gateway proxy should be used to handle this request. In many cases this value will be 0, but it may be hundreds or thousands of milliseconds if a WPAD Proxy Configuration script is being used to determine the upstream proxy.
DNSTime	The number of milliseconds spent determining the IP address of the remote host. Due to caching of DNS records, this value is often 0 for all but the first connections to a host.
TCPConnectTime	The number of milliseconds spent waiting for TCP/IP connection establishment to the server.
HTTPSHandshakeTime	The number of milliseconds elapsed while performing the HTTPS handshake with the server. This value will be 0 if Fiddler is not configured to decrypt HTTPS traffic. If decryption is enabled, when a CONNECT tunnel is being used for HTTPS traffic, Fiddler will populate this value.
ServerConnected	Timestamp at which the TCP/IP connection to the server or upstream gateway proxy was established.
FiddlerBeginRequest	Timestamp at which Fiddler began sending the request to the server. If this request is being sent on a reused server connection, this timestamp could be much later than the ServerConnected value.
ServerGotRequest	Timestamp at which Fiddler completed sending the request to the server.
ServerBeginResponse	Timestamp at which Fiddler read the first packet of the server's response.
FiddlerGotResponseHeaders	Timestamp at which Fiddler completed reading the headers from the server.
ServerDoneResponse	Timestamp at which Fiddler completed reading the entire response from

	the server.
`ClientBeginResponse`	Timestamp at which Fiddler began sending the response to the client. If buffering is disabled for the current Session, this timestamp will be earlier than the `ServerDoneResponse` timestamp.
`ClientDoneResponse`	Timestamp at which Fiddler completed sending the response to the client.

The `ToString()` method of the `Timers` returns all of the timer values in a comma-delimited string; pass `true` as an optional parameter to return the values as a multi-line string instead.

Note: Fiddler captures timestamps using the default system clock, which typically has a precision of 15.6 milliseconds. If a given operation takes less than 15.6ms to complete, it may appear that the operation took no time at all. Fiddler has not been updated to take advantage of high-precision timers because any task for which that level of precision is required should be accomplished via other means. The Observer Effect of introducing the Fiddler proxy between the client and server exceeds the limited resolution of the default timers.

Sending Strings to the TextWizard

In many cases, your Extension will display text that has been encoded using one of several high-level encodings. If the encoding is expected and understood, your extension may want to encode and decode the text itself—for instance, the WebForms Inspector will encode and decode form fields automatically. In other cases, however, the encoding may not be known in advance. In such cases, it can be helpful to provide a **Send to TextWizard** command which will send text to Fiddler's TextWizard window, without requiring that the user copy/paste the text manually. Most of the Inspectors included with Fiddler offer such a command.

To launch the TextWizard from your Extension, simply call the following API:

```
FiddlerApplication.UI.actShowTextWizard(string sDefaultInput)
```

…passing the selected text in the `sDefaultInput` parameter. An instance of the TextWizard will open, enabling the user to easily encode or decode the text.

Logging

Fiddler's Log tab collects logged message strings that are generated by extensions, FiddlerScript, or Fiddler itself. Fiddler logs messages including application events (e.g. when a SAZ file is saved or loaded) as well as system events (e.g. when the system's network connectivity is lost or restored). An extension can log text to the Log tab using either of the following two methods:

```
FiddlerApplication.Log.LogString(string sMsg)
FiddlerApplication.Log.LogFormat(string sFormat, params object[] args)
```

These methods may be safely called from any thread and can be called before Fiddler itself has loaded; the Log object will queue any messages and publish them when a Log listener is first attached.

If you are writing an extension or a FiddlerCore-based application and wish to receive notice of logged messages, add a handler to the `FiddlerApplication.Log.OnLogString` event. Your handler will be passed the logged string as the `LogString` property of a `LogEventArgs` object.

```
public event EventHandler<LogEventArgs> OnLogString;

public class LogEventArgs:EventArgs
{
  internal LogEventArgs(string sMsg);
  public string LogString { get; }
}
```

Keep in mind that this event will often fire from background threads, so your handler must `Invoke` or `BeginInvoke` onto the UI thread if any visual updates are required.

Fiddler's Log tab uses a very simple formatting mechanism when interpreting the strings it receives in its `OnLogString` handler:

- Strings prefixed with an underscore (_) will render in an <u>underlined</u> font.

- Strings prefixed with an exclamation mark (!) will render in a **bold** font.

- Strings prefixed with a forward slash (/) render in an *italic* font.

Your extension can use this simple feature to draw attention to messages based on their importance. The Log tab also supports simple macro commands:

- Logging the string `@Log.Clear` will clear the Log tab's contents.

- Logging the string `@Log.Save` will generate a new Session in the Web Sessions list. Its response body will contain the Log tab's text.

- Logging the string `@Log.Export filename` will save the Log tab's text to the specified filename. Use a filename ending in `.rtf` to save in Rich Text Format, preserving font size and weight.

Interacting with the FiddlerScript Engine

Extensions may subscribe to events related to the compilation of FiddlerScript. For instance, this allows the Fiddler ScriptEditor extension to capture and display script compilation errors.

The `FiddlerApplication.scriptRules` object exposes three events, two of which will fire as a script file is loaded and either compiles successfully or encounters an error:

```
public event RulesBeforeCompileHandler BeforeRulesCompile;
```

```
public event RulesAfterCompileHandler AfterRulesCompile;
public event RulesCompileFailedHandler RulesCompileFailed;
```

Because the script engine was developed before I knew how to use EventArgs properly, each event has its own custom delegate:

```
public delegate void RulesBeforeCompileHandler(string sFilename);
public delegate void RulesAfterCompileHandler();
public delegate void RulesCompileFailedHandler(string sDescription, int iLine,
                                               int iStartColumn, int iEndColumn);
```

The BeforeRulesCompile event fires when Fiddler is instructed to load a new script file. The event handler delegate contains one parameter, the name of the script file that is to be loaded and compiled.

The AfterRulesCompile event fires after Fiddler successfully compiles a script file, runs its Main function, and updates the Fiddler UI based on the contents of the script. The event handler delegate has no parameters.

The RulesCompileFailed event fires if Fiddler encounters an error when compiling the script file. The event handler delegate has four parameters: the human-readable description of the problem, the line number of the error within the script file, and the starting and ending column on that line. If you plan to handle this event, please be aware that RulesCompileFailed usually fires very shortly after the BeforeRulesCompile event. If your extension loads the new script's text in its handler for the first event, ensure that you have successfully updated your copy of the script text before attempting to display the error information to the user.

Fiddler includes a Preferences system which is accessible to FiddlerScript and extensions. The system is designed to be somewhat similar to the system used in Firefox (e.g. type about:config in Firefox to view its preferences).

Fiddler's Preferences are automatically serialized to and deserialized from the registry.

Preference Naming

Keep the following in mind as you name your preferences:

- Preference names are case-insensitive.
- Preference names must contain ASCII A-to-Z, numbers, dots, and dashes only.
- Preference names must be between 1 and 255 characters in length.
- Preference names containing ephemeral will not be saved to or loaded from the registry.
- Preference names containing internal cannot be created or updated by extensions or script.

You should name your preferences using a logical hierarchy, of the format:

```
myCompany.myExtension.Feature.SettingName
```

Careful naming makes it simpler to find your Preferences and improves performance if your extension or script wants to monitor Preferences for changes (more on that in a moment).

The IFiddlerPreferences Interface

Fiddler's preferences are accessed using FiddlerApplication.Prefs, an object which implements the IFiddlerPreferences interface.

```
public interface IFiddlerPreferences
{
  // Indexer
  string this[string sName] {get; set; }

  // Setters
  void SetBoolPref(string sPrefName, bool bValue);
  void SetInt32Pref(string sPrefName, Int32 iValue);
  void SetStringPref(string sPrefName, string sValue);
  void RemovePref(string sPrefName);

  // Getters
  bool GetBoolPref(string sPrefName, bool bDefault);
  string GetStringPref(string sPrefName, string sDefault);
  Int32 GetInt32Pref(string sPrefName, Int32 iDefault);
```

```
    // Methods to enable change notifications
    PreferenceBag.PrefWatcher AddWatcher(string sPrefixFilter,
                            EventHandler<PrefChangeEventArgs> pcehHandler);
    void RemoveWatcher(PreferenceBag.PrefWatcher wliToRemove);
}
```

Storing and Removing Preferences

You can store preferences using the SetStringPref, SetBoolPref, and SetInt32Pref methods. Each accepts the name of the preference and the value to store:

```
FiddlerApplication.Prefs.SetStringPref("example.str", "Remember me!");
FiddlerApplication.Prefs.SetBoolPref("example.bool", true);
FiddlerApplication.Prefs.SetInt32Pref("example.int", 5);
```

Alternatively, you can use the default indexer to store a string directly:

```
FiddlerApplication.Prefs["example.str"] = "value";
```

Internally, all preference values are stored as strings; the bool and int methods simply cast and parse the string's value.

Call RemovePref or store a value of null to remove a preference:

```
// These three lines are equivalent
FiddlerApplication.Prefs.RemovePref("NameToRemove");
FiddlerApplication.Prefs.SetStringPref("NameToRemove", null);
FiddlerApplication.Prefs["NameToRemove"] = null;
```

Retrieving Preferences

You can retrieve preferences using the GetStringPref, GetBoolPref, and GetIntPref methods. Each accepts the name of the preference and a default value to return if the requested preference does not exist.

```
string sStr = FiddlerApplication.Prefs.GetStringPref("example.str", "demo");
bool bBool = FiddlerApplication.Prefs.GetBoolPref("example.bool", false);
int iNum = FiddlerApplication.Prefs.GetInt32Pref("example.int", 0);
```

Alternatively, you can use the default indexer to retrieve a string preference directly:

```
string sStr = FiddlerApplication.Prefs["example.str"];
```

If the requested preference does not exist, the indexer will return null.

Watching for Preference Changes

In many cases, it's desirable for extensions or FiddlerScript to be notified when a preference of a specified name is created, updated, or removed. To avoid the overhead of constantly polling preference values, you can instead "watch a branch" of preferences whose name contains a specified prefix. For instance, watching the fiddler.ui.toolbar prefix will raise an event whenever any preference whose name starts with that prefix is created, removed, or has its value modified. By thoughtfully naming your preferences, you can help ensure that your code is only notified of relevant changes.

Notifications in Extensions

Extensions may subscribe to receive notifications when preferences under a given prefix change by attaching a PrefWatcher.

```
oWatcher = FiddlerApplication.Prefs.AddWatcher(
  string sPrefixToMatch, EventHandler<PrefChangeEventArgs> fnToNotify);
```

The event handler you supply in fnToNotify will be invoked for every preference change under the specified prefix. The EventArgs' PrefName property contains the name of the preference which has changed. The ValueString property contains the preference's new value, or null if the preference was removed. The ValueBool convenience property interprets the new value as a boolean.

To permit garbage-collection of objects, be sure to remove your PrefWatcher when it is no longer needed:

```
FiddlerApplication.Prefs.RemoveWatcher(oWatcher);
```

Notifications in FiddlerScript

To ensure that PrefWatcher references do not prevent garbage-collection of obsolete script engines, FiddlerScript code should call the WatchPreference function rather than calling the AddWatcher method.

```
// This callback function is called on Pref changes
// under the branch we specified.
static function FnChange(o: Object, pceA: PrefChangeEventArgs) {
  if (null != pceA) {
      MessageBox.Show(pceA.PrefName + " changed to: " + pceA.ValueString);
  }
  else {
      MessageBox.Show("Unexpected.");
  }
}

static function Main() {
  // Attach a callback to the preference change
  FiddlerObject.WatchPreference("fiddler.", FnChange);
}
```

Fiddler automatically disposes of the callback function when the FiddlerScript engine unloads on shutdown or because the script has been modified and must be recompiled.

BUILDING EXTENSION INSTALLERS

You may install your extensions using any technology you like. Fiddler simply requires that its Assembly .dll appear in the correct folder to load it next time that Fiddler launches.

Fiddler and all of the extensions I've written are installed using setup programs built using the Nullsoft Scriptable Install System (NSIS). You can get this great freeware from http://nsis.sourceforge.net /Download. NSIS allows you to write a script that is compiled into a compressed executable file containing all of the binaries that make up your project. The resulting setup program is small and works properly across all versions of Windows.

The only significant shortcoming I've encountered with NSIS is that it does not support Unicode, so you may need to use a different technology like WIX (http://wix.sourceforge.net/) if you want your installer to use non-Latin characters (e.g. Japanese).

A full explanation of how to use NSIS is beyond the scope of this book—the tool's website offers plenty of documentation at http://nsis.sourceforge.net/Docs/. However, I'll share an example setup script you can use to get started.

```
; In a NSIS Script, the semi-colon is a comment operator
Name "MyExtension"

; TODO: Set a specific name for your installer's executable
OutFile "InstallMyExtension.exe"
; Point to an icon to use for the installer, or omit to use the default
Icon "C:\src\MyExt\MyExt.ico"
XPStyle on                      ; Enable visual-styling for a prettier UI

; Explicitly demand admin permissions because we're going to write to
; Program Files. This prevents the "Program Compatibility Assistant" dialog.
; Note, you can use "user" here if you'd like, but then you must only write
; to HKCU and per-user writable locations on disk.
RequestExecutionLevel "admin"

; Maximize compression
SetCompressor /solid lzma

BrandingText "v1.0.1.0"         ; Text shown at the bottom of the Setup window

;
; TODO: Set the install directory to the proper folder.
;
; To install to the Extensions folder, use:
InstallDir "$PROGRAMFILES\Fiddler2\Scripts\"
InstallDirRegKey HKLM "SOFTWARE\Microsoft\Fiddler2" "LMScriptPath"

; To install to the Inspectors folder, use:
```

```
;InstallDir "$PROGRAMFILES\Fiddler2\Inspectors\"
;InstallDirRegKey HKLM "SOFTWARE\Microsoft\Fiddler2" "PluginPath"
;

Section "Main"
SetOutPath "$INSTDIR"

SetOverwrite on
;
; The next line embeds MyExt.dll from the output folder into the installer.
; When the installer runs, the file will be extracted to $INSTDIR\MyExt.dll
;
File "C:\src\MyExt\bin\release\MyExt.dll"
;
;
; TODO: List any other files your extension depends upon here.
; Be sure to also add those files to the list removed by the
; uninstaller at the bottom of this script
;


;
; Write information about the extension to the Add/Remove Programs dialog
;
WriteRegStr HKLM "Software\Microsoft\Windows\CurrentVersion\Uninstall\MyExt"
"DisplayName" "My Fiddler Extension"
WriteRegStr HKLM "Software\Microsoft\Windows\CurrentVersion\Uninstall\MyExt"
"Comments" "My Extension to Fiddler"
WriteRegStr HKLM "Software\Microsoft\Windows\CurrentVersion\Uninstall\MyExt"
"Publisher" 'MyCo'
WriteRegStr HKLM "Software\Microsoft\Windows\CurrentVersion\Uninstall\MyExt"
"InstallLocation" '$INSTDIR'
WriteRegDWORD HKLM "Software\Microsoft\Windows\CurrentVersion\Uninstall\MyExt"
"NoModify" 1
WriteRegDWORD HKLM "Software\Microsoft\Windows\CurrentVersion\Uninstall\MyExt"
"NoRepair" 1


;
; TODO: Update this line with the name of your uninstaller, set below
;
WriteRegStr HKLM "Software\Microsoft\Windows\CurrentVersion\Uninstall\MyExt"
"UninstallString" '"$INSTDIR\UninstallMyExt.exe"'


;
; TODO: Update this line to set a *unique* name for your uninstaller.
; Be sure to update the UninstallString value above to match.
; Also, update "Remove the uninstaller executable" line below to match.
;
WriteUninstaller "UninstallMyExt.exe"

SectionEnd ; end of default section

; ----------------------------------------------
; Perhaps surprisingly, this string cannot appear
```

```
; within the Uninstall section itself
UninstallText "This will uninstall My Fiddler Extension from your system"

Section Uninstall
Delete "$INSTDIR\MyExt.dll"
;
; TODO: Delete the other files you installed here.
;

; Remove the uninstaller regkey
DeleteRegKey HKLM "SOFTWARE\Microsoft\Windows\CurrentVersion\Uninstall\MyExt"
Delete "$INSTDIR\UninstallMyExt.exe"          ; Remove the uninstaller .exe

SectionEnd                ; eof
```

The resulting setup program will copy your assembly into the specified folder, and also add an item to the system's Add/Remove Programs applet to allow the user to uninstall the extension later.

Save the script to a file named `InstallMyExtension.nsi`. Next, create a batch file named `Build Installer.bat` to run the NSIS compiler and sign the resulting setup program. If you do not have a code-signing certificate, you can omit everything after the call to `MakeNSIS.exe`:

```
@title MyExtension Builder
@cd c:\src\MyExt\
@c:\src\NSIS\MakeNSIS.EXE /V2 InstallMyExtension.nsi
@if %ERRORLEVEL%==1 goto done
@CHOICE /M "Would you like to sign?"
@:sign
@signcode -spc C:\src\mycert.spc -v C:\src\mykey.pvk -n "Fiddler Extension" -i
    "http://mysite.com/myext/" -a sha1 -t http://timestamp.comodoca.com/authenticode
    InstallMyExtension.exe

@if %ERRORLEVEL%==-1 goto sign
@:done
@title Command Prompt
```

Run `BuildInstaller.bat` and the NSIS compiler will compile your script into the `InstallMyExtension.exe` setup program. It will then sign that new program to prevent tampering and avoid security warnings in browsers.

> **Warning**: Windows keeps track of the origins of the DLL file using a data stream known as the "Mark of the Web." If you don't build an installer and instead ask the user to copy your extension's .DLL from a ZIP file or network share, you may find that it fails to load in Fiddler v4. Before your assembly is loaded, .NET v4 sees the "This file is from an untrusted location" marker and will refuse to load the file by default.

BUILDING INSPECTORS

Developing custom Inspectors for Fiddler is simple-- you need only implement one class and one interface. Over the years, the Inspector model has evolved to allow for more powerful Inspectors while maintaining backward compatibility, so be aware that some of the APIs you encounter will seem a bit redundant.

There are two types of Inspectors: Request Inspectors and Response Inspectors; the former are used to view and/or modify a Session's request, while the latter are used to view and/or modify a Session's response. Both types of Inspector are derived from the abstract `Inspector2` base class. Request Inspectors must also implement the `IRequestInspector2` interface, while Response Inspectors implement the `IResponse Inspector2` interface. The `Inspector2` base class contains just two methods you must implement:

```
public abstract void AddToTab(TabPage o);
public abstract int GetOrder();
```

The `AddToTab` method is called when Fiddler has created a tabpage for your Inspector. In your implementation of this method, create your UI and add it to the `TabPage` provided. Most of Fiddler's default Inspectors consist of one class that implements the Inspector interfaces, and one `UserControl` that contains all of the UI for the Inspector. When `AddToTab` is called, it creates an instance of the `UserControl` and adds it to the `TabPage`:

```
public override void AddToTab(TabPage oPage)
{
  // Title my tab
  o.Text = "Raw";

  // Create my UserControl and add it to my tab
  myControl = new RawView(this);
  oPage.Controls.Add(myControl);
  oPage.Controls[0].Dock = DockStyle.Fill;
}
```

The `GetOrder` method is called when Fiddler sorts the tabs for display within the UI. Inspectors with lower numbers will display to the left of the tab set while Inspectors with larger numbers will display toward the right. Fiddler itself returns integers between -1000 and 110 for its own Inspectors. You may return any value you like, although you should strive to use a unique number. In the event that two Inspectors return the same value, ordering is non-deterministic and can change between instances.

In addition to the abstract methods your Inspector *must* implement, the base class exposes a number of virtual methods which you *may* implement if you'd like. These include:

```
public virtual void ShowAboutBox()
```

```
public virtual void SetFontSize(float flSizeInPoints)

public virtual int ScoreForSession(Session oS)
public virtual int ScoreForContentType(string sMIMEType)

public virtual void AssignSession(Session oS)
public virtual bool CommitAnyChanges(Session oS)
public virtual bool UnsetDirtyFlag()
public virtual InspectorFlags GetFlags()
```

The ShowAboutBox method runs when the user right-clicks on the Inspector's tab and clicks **Inspector Properties** on the context menu. If you don't override this method, when the user clicks the menu item, a message box will show the Inspector's full type name and information about the Assembly that contains it.

The SetFontSize method runs if the user changes Fiddler's font-size at runtime; override this method to adjust your Inspector's UI font size. This method was created before the Fiddler Preference System was created, and Inspectors may instead watch the preference fiddler.ui.font.size if you prefer.

The ScoreForSession method runs when the user double-clicks or hits Enter on a Session in the Web Sessions list. When this action occurs, each Inspector is polled to determine how eager it is to display a given request or response; the higher the value, the stronger the Inspector's desire to handle the Session. This method enables an Inspector to evaluate any aspect of a Session in making its decision. It should return 0 if it has no interest in a given Session (meaning *"I can't handle that at all"*) and should return 100 if it is confident that it is the *best* handler for a given Session.

The ability to consider any aspect of a session is a powerful one, as it enables your Inspector to consider factors beyond HTTP headers when deciding whether to render a Session. For instance, the WebView Inspector is able to render previews of WOFF Font files, but most servers are not configured to return the correct Content-Type for such files. Therefore, the WebView Inspector checks the first 4 bytes of any response body to detect the WOFF signature bytes.

```
static byte[] arr_WOFF_MAGIC =
    new byte[4] {(byte)'w', (byte)'O', (byte)'F', (byte)'F'};

public override int ScoreForSession(Session oS)
{
  // Check for WOFF Magic Bytes
  if (Utilities.HasMagicBytes(oS.responseBodyBytes, arr_WOFF_MAGIC)) {
    return 60;
  }

  // If not found, consult at the response's Content-Type
  return ScoreForContentType(oS.oResponse.MIMEType);
}
```

Avoid performing any expensive computations in your ScoreForSession method, as it runs often and users expect that inspecting a session will occur instantly. For example, your implementation of this method should not attempt to search a response body of arbitrary size for specific text, and should not perform network or disk operations.

If you do not override the ScoreForSession method, the base implementation calls the ScoreFor ContentType method, passing the Content-Type header.

The ScoreForContentType method predates the introduction of the ScoreForSession method, but it performs the same general function—it allows the Inspector to indicate how applicable it is for a given Session. Again, scores between 0 and 100 should be returned. Avoid returning an overly-confident value for a general type; for instance, the JSON Inspector returns only 55 when the type is application/json while the ImageView Inspector returns 80 for image types. Only return 100 if the MIME Content-Type is something that your extension will *uniquely* understand—for instance, if you have invented a custom MIME type and no other Inspector could be expected to be useful for your type.

The WebView Inspector's implementation of ScoreForContentType is as follows:

```
public override int ScoreForContentType(string sMIMEType)
{
  if (sMIMEType.StartsWith("audio/", StringComparison.OrdinalIgnoreCase)) {
    return 60;
  }

  if (sMIMEType.StartsWith("video/", StringComparison.OrdinalIgnoreCase)) {
    return 60;
  }

  // Just in case a site sent a malformed MP3 type, check the whole string
  if (sMIMEType.IndexOf("mp3", StringComparison.OrdinalIgnoreCase) > -1)
    return 60;
  }

  return 0;
}
```

If you do not implement the ScoreForContentType method, a default score of 0 is assumed and a different Inspector will be activated by default. The user may still manually choose your Inspector whenever needed.

The IRequestInspector2 and IResponseInspector2 interfaces both inherit from the IBaseInspector2 interface, which contains the following properties and method that your Inspectors must implement:

```
bool bReadOnly { get; set; }
bool bDirty { get; }
byte[] body { get; set; }
void Clear();
```

The inherited IRequestInspector2 interface adds one property:

```
HTTPRequestHeaders headers { get; set; }
```

Similarly, the inherited `IResponseInspector2` interface adds one property:

```
HTTPResponseHeaders headers { get; set; }
```

Inspectors may be readonly or read/write. Read/write Inspectors enable the user to modify the request or response under inspection when the Session is paused at a breakpoint. An Inspector's `bReadOnly` property is set to control whether the Inspector should permit the user to modify the request or response; readonly inspectors can simply ignore changes to the property. When `bReadOnly` is set to `false`, your Inspector should not permit the user to modify the headers or body. You can communicate the readonly status to the user by setting controls to readonly mode, and setting their background color to the color value stored in the `Fiddler.CONFIG.colorDisabledEdit` field. When `bReadOnly` is set to `true`, your Inspector may enable read/write mode for controls and allow the user to change the headers or body. If an Inspector is "display only" without modification capabilities, the `bReadOnly` property setter can be a no-op.

An Inspector's `bDirty` property is queried by Fiddler before it attempts to commit any modifications the Inspector has made to the `headers` or body. If your Inspector doesn't permit edits, or if the user has not made any modifications, return `false` when this property is queried.

The `headers` property allows Fiddler to provide the `HTTPRequestHeaders` or `HTTPResponseHeaders` for the Session being inspected. When a Session is assigned to your Inspector, the `headers` property will be set first. When Fiddler attempts to commit any changes to the Session because the Inspector's `bDirty` property returned `true`, Fiddler will query the `headers` property for the headers. If the Inspector does not wish to make any changes to the headers, simply return `null` in the getter for this property.

Warning: Fiddler does not currently clone the Session's headers when assigning to the `headers` property. Your Inspector must be coded to either clone the headers when assigned, or must avoid making any changes to the headers object reference it receives.

The **body** property accepts a byte array that contains the request or response body for the Session being inspected. When a Session is assigned to your Inspector, the `body` property will be set after the `headers`. When Fiddler attempts to commit any changes to the Session because the Inspector's `bDirty` property returned `true`, Fiddler will query the `body` property for the new byte array to use. If the Inspector does not wish to make any changes to the body, simply return `null` in the getter for this property. To store an empty body, return `new byte[0]`.

Warning: Fiddler does not currently clone the Session's body when assigning to the `body` property. Your Inspector must be coded to either clone the body array when assigned, or must avoid making any changes to the bytes in the body array reference it receives.

The Clear method is called by Fiddler when the user has unselected the current Session and your Inspector should be reset. In response to this method call, clear all data from the Inspector's UI, and indicate to the user that no Session is selected.

Inspecting the Session Object

In the original Inspectors API, the Inspectors were never provided a reference to the Session object under Inspection-- only the headers and body would be provided. This provided for a simple, easily understood API contract, but this simplicity presented a number of shortcomings. For instance, it was impossible for an Inspector to get or set flags on the Session object, and even examining properties of the Session was impossible. For instance, the Caching Response Inspector was unable to determine whether the inspected traffic used HTTPS because the URL (and thus the protocol scheme) only appears in the *request* headers, which were never available to a Response Inspector.

To resolve these shortcomings, the Inspector2 base class was augmented with four additional virtual methods:

```
public virtual void AssignSession(Session oS)
public virtual bool CommitAnyChanges(Session oS)
public virtual bool UnsetDirtyFlag()
public virtual InspectorFlags GetFlags()
```

These methods allow an Inspector to be passed a Session object rather than having individual header and body properties set using the IRequestInspector2 and IResponseInspector2 interfaces. If your Inspector *does not* override these virtual methods, Fiddler will simply access the headers and body properties on the interface, and you need not implement any of the four virtual methods. If your Inspector *does* override the AssignSession method, it must still implement all of the legacy properties because not all codepaths in Fiddler call the newer virtual methods. Specifically, when editing a response using the AutoResponder tab, no Session object is available, so the legacy properties will be used.

The AssignSession method is called when the user selects a session in the Web Sessions list when your Inspector's tab is visible. In your overridden method, your Inspector should update its UI based on the headers and/or body of the session. Note that your Inspector must *itself* examine the Session's state to determine whether the Inspector should be readonly, as shown in the following snippet:

```
public override void AssignSession(Session oSession)
{
  if ((null == oSession) || !oSession.bHasResponse)
  {
    Clear();
    return;
  }

  UpdateUIFromHeaders(oSession.oResponse.headers);
  UpdateUIFromBody(oSession.responseBodyBytes);
```

```
    bool bIsReadOnly = ((oSession.state != SessionStates.HandTamperResponse)
                    && !oSession.oFlags.ContainsKey("x-Unlocked"));

    UpdateReadOnlyState(bIsReadOnly);
}
```

If you do not override the `AssignSession` method, the base `Inspector2` class' implementation will automatically assign to the `headers`, `body`, and `bReadOnly` properties instead:

```
public virtual void AssignSession(Session oS)
{
  if (this is IRequestInspector2)
  {
    IRequestInspector2 oRI = (this as IRequestInspector2);
    oRI.headers = oS.oRequest.headers;
    oRI.body = oS.requestBodyBytes;
    oRI.bReadOnly = ((oS.state != SessionStates.HandTamperRequest)
                    && !oS.oFlags.ContainsKey("x-Unlocked"));
    return;
  }

  if (this is IResponseInspector2)
  //...
```

The `CommitAnyChanges` method is called when the Inspector should commit any changes to the request or response. If the Inspector has any uncommitted edits, they should be stored to the Session when this method is called and it should return `true`. If no changes were committed, return `false`. If you do not override this method, after Fiddler consults the `bDirty` property of the Inspector, and if it is `true`, and if the Session is in a `state` that permits editing, the default implementation will update the Session's headers and body using those properties of the Inspector.

The `UnsetDirtyFlag` method is called when Fiddler wishes to mark your Inspector as non-dirty (e.g. because it updated the Session's `headers` and `body` from those properties of the Inspector). If your Inspector overrides this method and can successfully clear its dirty state, do so and return `true`. This method exists because some Inspectors may not be able to easily reset their dirty state, and thus the `bDirty` property is readonly-- only the Inspector may change it. The benefit of implementing this method is that it prevents unneeded *"Do you want to save changes?"* prompts when the user edits an AutoResponder response using a popup Inspectors window.

The `GetFlags` method retrieves flags that describe the Inspector's behavior. Currently, this method is only overridden by the Transformer Inspector. You should not override this method for your own Inspectors.

Most Inspectors cannot properly parse a chunked or compressed response body into a higher-level format like XML or JSON text. For most Inspectors, the user is simply encouraged to decode the response manually before inspecting:

```
if (oHeaders.Exists("Transfer-Encoding") || oHeaders.Exists("Content-Encoding"))
{
  lblDisplayMyEncodingWarning.Visible = true;
  return;
}
```

Fiddler allows the user to easily remove the compression and chunking by clicking the yellow notification bar or using the **Transformer** Inspector.

However, it is possible to make a copy of the body and decode it for your Inspector's private use. Be wary of the cost of decoding large bodies; you'd be better off having the user do it manually just once instead of every time the response is loaded in your Inspector.

There are three ways to get the uncompressed and unchunked body.

Decoding a Copy of the Body

All Inspectors are provided a copy of the headers and body. Using this information, the body may be cloned and decoded using the Utilities.utilDecodeHTTPBody static method. If the body needs to be interpreted as a string, the getEntityBodyEncoding and GetStringFromArrayRemovingBOM methods can be used to convert the body bytes to a string.

Here's what the JSONView Inspector does in its body property setter. In this example, the oHeaders object is a reference to the headers stored by the headers property setter, and the incoming value object refers to the new body byte array that is being assigned to the Inspector:

```
if (null != oHeaders)
{
  // Check for no body
  if ((null == value) || (value.Length < 1)) return;

  if (!oHeaders.ExistsAndContains("Content-Type", "application/json")
      && !oHeaders.ExistsAndContains("Content-Type", "javascript"))
  {
    // Not JSON
    return;
  }

  if (oHeaders.Exists("Transfer-Encoding") || oHeaders.Exists("Content-Encoding"))
  {
```

```
      // Create a copy of the body to avoid corrupting the original
      byte[] arrCopy = (byte[])value.Clone();
      try
      {
        // Decode. Warning: Will throw if value cannot be decoded
        Utilities.utilDecodeHTTPBody(oHeaders, ref arrCopy);
        value = arrCopy;
      }
      catch
      {
        // Leave value alone.
      }
    }
  }

  // Okay, now the body stored in "value" is unchunked
  // and uncompressed. We need to convert it to a string,
  // keeping in mind that the HTTP response might have
  // been in a non-Unicode codepage.

  oEncoding = Utilities.getEntityBodyEncoding(oHeaders, value);
  sJSON = Utilities.GetStringFromArrayRemovingBOM(value, oEncoding);
  myControl.SetJSON(sJSON);

  //...
```

The Session's headers are not modified by this code, which means that they may refer to encodings that have been removed from the Inspector's copy of the body.

Using the GetRe*BodyAsString Methods

If your Inspector overrides the AssignSession method, then you can get the body as a string using one of the following two methods:

```
string sRequestBody = oSession.GetRequestBodyAsString();
string sResponseBody = oSession.GetResponseBodyAsString();
```

These methods consult the headers to determine what encodings are in use, then copy the body bytes to a temporary array and decode them. Next, the Content-Type header and the body are inspected for clues as to what codepage the content uses, and the body bytes are converted to a .NET string (Unicode) and returned as the result of the function.

.NET strings are immutable. You don't need to worry about corrupting the original HTTP body by manipulating the returned string, since any modifications will yield a new string.

Using the utilDecode* Methods

If your Inspector overrides the AssignSession method, then your code may call the Session object's utilDecodeRequest and utilDecodeResponse methods to decode the request or response bodies respectively. These methods will decompress and unchunk the body and update the Session's headers to remove the reference to the now-removed encodings.

Your Inspector should not automatically call these methods when a Session is assigned to your Inspector. If it did, your Inspector would permanently change the Session even when the Inspector is meant to be in a readonly state. Instead, call these methods only if the user takes an explicit action, like clicking on a button or link that indicates that a permanent change will be made.

Inspector Assemblies

When looking for Inspectors, Fiddler loads all assembly .DLLs from the %PROGRAMFILES%\Fiddler2\ Inspectors and %USERPROFILE%\My Documents\Fiddler2\Inspectors folders and enumerates all public classes within them to find Request and Response Inspectors.

Install to the %PROGRAMFILES% location to make your Inspectors available to all users on the machine, or the %USERPROFILE% folder to make them available only to the current user.

In addition to placing your Inspector assemblies in the appropriate folder, you must also mark your assembly to indicate the minimum version of Fiddler required by your Inspectors. Set the Required Version attribute as follows:

```
// Inspector requires methods introduced in v2.3.9.0...
[assembly: Fiddler.RequiredVersion("2.3.9.0")]
```

If Fiddler loads an assembly for which the RequiredVersion attribute indicates a later version of Fiddler is needed, the user will be notified that an update is required and no Inspectors will be loaded from the assembly. Assemblies in the \Inspectors\ folder which lack a RequiredVersion attribute are silently ignored.

Fiddler skips enumeration of DLLs named with a leading underscore character (_) when loading Inspectors. Many Inspectors may rely upon 3rd party assemblies that do not themselves contain any Fiddler-related code. To avoid the performance cost of Fiddler enumerating such assemblies to look for Inspectors, name those assemblies using a leading underscore.

BUILDING EXTENSIONS

When you need to add functionality to Fiddler and an Inspector isn't the appropriate way to expose that functionality, build an extension instead. Extensions can enhance Fiddler with anything from simple features (like a new menu item) to extremely complicated business logic and reporting infrastructures.

Getting started is easy. The simplest Fiddler extension must implement only one interface whose methods are called to load and unload the extension:

```
public interface IFiddlerExtension
{
  void OnLoad();
  void OnBeforeUnload();
}
```

The OnLoad function is called when Fiddler has finished loading and its UI is fully available. At this point, you can safely add menu items, tabbed pages, or other elements to the Fiddler UI. The OnBeforeUnload function will be called when Fiddler is shutting down and unloading all extensions.

The IAutoTamper interface inherits from the IFiddlerExtension interface, and permits your extension to receive callbacks as each Session is processed, enabling modifications, logging, or other operations.

```
public interface IAutoTamper : IFiddlerExtension
{
  void AutoTamperRequestBefore(Session oSession);
  void AutoTamperRequestAfter(Session oSession);
  void AutoTamperResponseBefore(Session oSession);
  void AutoTamperResponseAfter(Session oSession);
  void OnBeforeReturningError(Session oSession);
}
```

The difference between the *Before and *After methods is that the former execute before the user has a chance to manually tamper with a breakpointed Session using the Inspectors, while the latter methods execute after any such modifications are completed. If you to permit the user to manually undo any modifications your method makes, use the *Before methods, otherwise, use the *After methods.

The IAutoTamper2 interface inherits from IAutoTamper and adds one additional method that is called when Fiddler has read the server's response headers, (usually) before the response body is available:

```
public interface IAutoTamper2 : IAutoTamper
{
  void OnPeekAtResponseHeaders(Session oSession);
}
```

A common use of the OnPeekAtResponseHeaders method is to examine the response's headers to decide whether the response should be buffered or streamed. For instance, to stream all image files, you could write the following code:

```
void OnPeekAtResponseHeaders(Session oSession)
{
  if (oSession.oResponse.MIMEType.StartsWith("image/"))
  {
    bBufferResponse = false;
  }
}
```

Be careful not to attempt to read the responseBodyBytes array in this method, because a Null Reference Exception is likely to ensue. Additionally, you should avoid manipulating headers related to the response's length (e.g. Content-Length, Transfer-Encoding, Connection) because the subsequent attempt to read to the response body from the server will likely fail.

The IAutoTamper3 interface inherits from IAutoTamper2 and adds one additional method that is called when Fiddler has read the client's request headers, (usually) before the request body is available:

```
public interface IAutoTamper3 : IAutoTamper2
{
  void OnPeekAtRequestHeaders(Session oSession);
}
```

This method is only useful in certain niche scenarios; in most cases, the availability of the request's headers alone is not sufficient to do anything useful.

Understanding Threading

The IAutoTamper interfaces' methods are called on background, non-UI threads. If you wish to update UI, you *must* use Invoke or BeginInvoke to update the UI. Also, note that the IAutoTamper interfaces' methods can be called *before* the OnLoad event fires-- Fiddler allows traffic to flow before the UI is fully available. Therefore, most extensions will initialize objects and UI inside their constructor and wait until OnLoad only to insert their UI into the main Fiddler UI.

Integrating with QuickExec

Extensions that implement the IHandleExecAction interface are called when the user has entered a command into the QuickExec box or invoked a command using the ExecAction.exe command-line tool.

```
public interface IHandleExecAction
{
    bool OnExecAction(string sCommand);
}
```

If your extension would like to handle the command (and prevent further processing by other extensions and Fiddler itself) return `true` from your implementation of this method. The `Utilities` class includes a helper function for interpreting the `sCommand` parameter:

```
public static string[] Parameterize(string sCommand)
```

The `Parameterize` method tokenizes a string into tokens. The string is split by whitespace characters, unless the spaces are contained within quotation marks, in which case the entire quoted string is stored as a token. Use a backslash character (\) to escape quotation marks so that they may appear literally within a string.

Example Extension

The following is a simple extension which examines all responses as they are received. It determines whether the responses attempt to set cookies, and if so, whether a valid P3P Compact Policy statement has been provided. This example adds an item to the top-level menu, adds a column to the Web Sessions list, and modifies Sessions as they are processed.

```
using Fiddler;
using System;
using System.Text;
using System.IO;
using System.Collections;
using System.Globalization;
using System.Collections.Generic;
using System.Windows.Forms;
using System.Diagnostics;
using System.Text.RegularExpressions;

[assembly: Fiddler.RequiredVersion("2.3.9.0")]
[assembly: AssemblyVersion("1.0.1.0")]
[assembly: AssemblyDescription("Scans for Cookies and P3P")]

public class TagCookies : IAutoTamper2
{
  private bool bEnabled = false;
  private bool bEnforceP3PValidity = false;
  private bool bCreatedColumn = false;
  private MenuItem miEnabled;
  private MenuItem miEnforceP3PValidity;
  private MenuItem mnuCookieTag;

  private enum P3PState
  {
    NoCookies,
    NoP3PAndSetsCookies,
    P3POk,
    P3PUnsatisfactory,
    P3PMalformed
  }
```

```csharp
public void OnLoad()
{
  /*
     NB: OnLoad might not get called until ~after~ one of
     the AutoTamper methods was called, because sessions are
     processed while Fiddler is loading.
     This is okay for us, because we created our mnuCookieTag
     in the constructor and its simply not
     visible anywhere until this method is called and we
     merge it onto the Fiddler Main menu.
  */

  FiddlerApplication.UI.mnuMain.MenuItems.Add(mnuCookieTag);
}

// We don't need to do anything on unload, since Fiddler only presently
// unloads extensions at shutdown, and the GC will dispose of our UI.
public void OnBeforeUnload() { /*noop*/ }

private void InitializeMenu()
{
  this.miEnabled = new MenuItem("&Enabled");
  this.miEnforceP3PValidity = new MenuItem("&Rename P3P header if invalid");

  this.miEnabled.Index = 0;
  this.miEnforceP3PValidity.Index = 1;

  this.mnuCookieTag = new MenuItem("Privacy");
  this.mnuCookieTag.MenuItems.AddRange(new MenuItem[] {
    this.miEnabled, this.miEnforceP3PValidity });

  this.miEnabled.Click += new System.EventHandler(this.miEnabled_Click);
  this.miEnabled.Checked = bEnabled;

  this.miEnforceP3PValidity.Click +=
    new System.EventHandler(this.miEnforceP3PValidity_Click);

  this.miEnforceP3PValidity.Checked = bEnforceP3PValidity;
}

public void miEnabled_Click(object sender, EventArgs e)
{
  miEnabled.Checked = !miEnabled.Checked;
  bEnabled = miEnabled.Checked;
  this.miEnforceP3PValidity.Enabled = bEnabled;
  if (bEnabled) { EnsureColumn(); }
  FiddlerApplication.Prefs.SetBoolPref("extensions.tagcookies.enabled",
                                        bEnabled);
}

public void miEnforceP3PValidity_Click(object sender, EventArgs e)
{
```

```csharp
    miEnforceP3PValidity.Checked = !miEnforceP3PValidity.Checked;
    bEnforceP3PValidity = miEnforceP3PValidity.Checked;
    FiddlerApplication.Prefs.SetBoolPref(
      "extensions.tagcookies.EnforceP3PValidity", bEnforceP3PValidity);
}

private void EnsureColumn()
{
  // If we already created the column, bail out.
  if (bCreatedColumn) return;

  // Add a new Column to the Web Sessions list, titled "Privacy Info",
  // that will automatically fill with each Session's X-Privacy flag string
  FiddlerApplication.UI.lvSessions.AddBoundColumn(
                                    "Privacy Info", 1, 120, "X-Privacy");
  bCreatedColumn = true;
}

public TagCookies()
{
  this.bEnabled = FiddlerApplication.Prefs.GetBoolPref(
    "extensions.tagcookies.enabled", false);

  this.bEnforceP3PValidity = FiddlerApplication.Prefs.GetBoolPref(
    "extensions.tagcookies.EnforceP3PValidity", true);

  InitializeMenu();

  if (bEnabled)
      { EnsureColumn(); } else
      { this.miEnforceP3PValidity.Enabled = false; }
}

private void SetP3PStateFromHeader(string sValue, ref P3PState oP3PState)
{
  // If there was no P3P header, bail out
  if (string.IsNullOrEmpty(sValue)) { return; }

  string sUnsatCat = String.Empty;
  string sUnsatPurpose = String.Empty;
  sValue = sValue.Replace('\'', '"');

  string sCP = null;

  // Use a Regular Expression to search the header for a CP attribute
  Regex r = new Regex("CP\\s?=\\s?[\"]?(?<TokenValue>[^\";]*)");
  Match m = r.Match(sValue);
  if (m.Success && (null != m.Groups["TokenValue"]))
  {
    sCP = m.Groups["TokenValue"].Value;
  }

  // If we didn't find a Compact Policy statement, bail out.
```

```
      if (String.IsNullOrEmpty(sCP)) { return; }

      // Okay, we've got a compact policy string. Evaluate each token.
      oP3PState = P3PState.P3POk;
      string[] sTokens = sCP.Split(new char[] { ' ' },
          StringSplitOptions.RemoveEmptyEntries);

      foreach (string sToken in sTokens)
      {
        // Reject clearly invalid tokens...
        if ((sToken.Length < 3) || (sToken.Length > 4))
        {
          oP3PState = P3PState.P3PMalformed;
          return;
        }

        // Track any tokens with "Unacceptable" privacy category
        if (",PHY,ONL,GOV,FIN,".IndexOf("," + sToken + ",",
            StringComparison.OrdinalIgnoreCase) > -1)
        {
          sUnsatCat += (sToken + " ");
          continue;
        }

        // Track any tokens with "Unacceptable" privacy purposes
        if (",SAM,OTR,UNR,PUB,IVA,IVD,CON,TEL,OTP,".IndexOf("," + sToken + ",",
            StringComparison.OrdinalIgnoreCase) > -1)
        {
          sUnsatPurpose += (sToken + " ");
          continue;
        }

        // TODO: Check each token against the list of 70-some valid tokens and
        // reject if it's not found.
      }

      // If a cookie contains an unsatisfactory purpose and an unsatisfactory
      // category, tag it. Learn more about "Unsatisfactory cookies" at
      // http://msdn.microsoft.com/en-us/library/ie/ms537343(v=vs.85).aspx
      if ((sUnsatCat.Length > 0) && (sUnsatPurpose.Length > 0))
      {
        if (oP3PState == P3PState.P3POk)
        {
          oP3PState = P3PState.P3PUnsatisfactory;
        }
      }
    }

// On each HTTP response, examine the response headers for attempts to set
// cookies, and check for a P3P header too. We do this
// in OnPeekAtResponseHeaders rather than OnBeforeResponse because we only
// need the headers and do not need to wait for the responseBodyBytes to
// be available.
```

```
public void OnPeekAtResponseHeaders(Session oSession)
{
  // If our extension isn't enabled, bail fast
  if (!bEnabled) return;

  P3PState oP3PState = P3PState.NoCookies;
  if (!oSession.oResponse.headers.Exists("Set-Cookie")) { return; }

  oP3PState = P3PState.NoP3PAndSetsCookies;

  if (oSession.oResponse.headers.Exists("P3P"))
  {
    SetP3PStateFromHeader(oSession.oResponse.headers["P3P"], ref oP3PState);
  }

  // Based on the cookie/P3P state, set the background color of item in the
  // Web Sessions list. Also set the X-Privacy flag which is shown in the
  // column that we created.
  switch (oP3PState)
  {
    case P3PState.P3POk:
      oSession["ui-backcolor"] = "#ACDC85";
      oSession["X-Privacy"] = "Sets cookies & P3P";
    break;

    case P3PState.NoP3PAndSetsCookies:
      oSession["ui-backcolor"] = "#FAFDA4";
      oSession["X-Privacy"] = "Sets cookies without P3P";
    break;

    case P3PState.P3PUnsatisfactory:
      oSession["ui-backcolor"] = "#EC921A";
      oSession["X-Privacy"] = "Sets cookies; P3P unsat. for 3rd-party use";
    break;

    case P3PState.P3PMalformed:
      oSession["ui-backcolor"] = "#E90A05";
      if (bEnforceP3PValidity)
      {
        oSession.oResponse.headers["MALFORMED-P3P"] =
            oSession.oResponse.headers["P3P"];
        oSession["X-Privacy"] = "MALFORMED P3P: " +
            oSession.oResponse.headers["P3P"];

        // Delete the invalid header to prevent the client from seeing it.
        oSession.oResponse.headers.Remove("P3P");
      }
    break;
  }
}

// Our extension doesn't need any of the other AutoTamper* methods.
public void AutoTamperRequestBefore(Session oSession) {/*noop*/}
```

```
      public void AutoTamperRequestAfter(Session oSession) {/*noop*/}
      public void AutoTamperResponseAfter(Session oSession) {/*noop*/}
      public void AutoTamperResponseBefore(Session oSession) {/*noop*/}
      public void OnBeforeReturningError(Session oSession) {/*noop*/}
   }
```

If your extension needs to extend to the Web Sessions list's context menu, add your new menu items to `FiddlerApplication.UI.mnuSessionContext`. If your extension needs to create a new top-level tab, it can add one to the `tabsViews` control. Here's how the Timeline tab adds its tab with a title and icon:

```
   public void OnLoad()
   {
     oPage = new TabPage("Timeline");
     oPage.ImageIndex = (int)Fiddler.SessionIcons.Timeline;
     FiddlerApplication.UI.tabsViews.TabPages.Add(oPage);
   }
```

If your tab contains any non-trivial UI, you should use the Delay Load pattern described in the Best Practices for Extensions section to ensure that the heavyweight initialization only occurs if and when the user switches to your new tab.

Extension Assemblies

When looking for extensions, Fiddler loads all assembly `.DLLs` from the `%PROGRAMFILES%\Fiddler2\Scripts` and `%USERPROFILE%\My Documents\Fiddler2\Scripts` folders and enumerates all `public` classes within them to find extensions.

Install to the `%PROGRAMFILES%` location to make your extension available to all users on the machine, or the `%USERPROFILE%` folder to install it for the current user only.

In addition to placing your extension assemblies in the appropriate folder, you must also mark your assembly to indicate the minimum version of Fiddler required by your extension. Set the `Required Version` attribute as follows:

```
   // Extension requires methods introduced in v2.3.9.0...
   [assembly: Fiddler.RequiredVersion("2.3.9.0")]
```

If Fiddler loads an assembly for which the `RequiredVersion` attribute indicates a later version of Fiddler is needed, the user will be notified that an update is required and no extensions will be loaded from the assembly. Assemblies in the `\Scripts\` folder which lack a `RequiredVersion` attribute are silently ignored.

Fiddler skips enumeration of DLLs named with a leading underscore character (_) when loading extensions. Many extensions may rely upon 3rd party assemblies that do not themselves contain any Fiddler-related code. To avoid the performance cost of Fiddler enumerating such assemblies to look for extensions, name those assemblies using a leading underscore.

BUILDING IMPORT AND EXPORT TRANSCODERS

One of the most common goals when building an extension is to export captured data out of Fiddler, or import data captured by other tools. While there's no reason you *can't* build such an extension using the general IFiddlerExtension interface, there are shortcomings in doing so:

- Such extensions have a performance cost, even when unused
- Such extensions require a lot of boilerplate code
- Inconsistent import/export UI leads to user confusion

To combat these shortcomings, Fiddler offers a specific extension type called a **Transcoder**. Fiddler ships with a number of these Transcoders by default, and developers can build new Transcoders easily. A Transcoder is simply an object that implements either or both of the ISessionImporter and ISession Exporter interfaces. Transcoder Assemblies are only loaded when invoked by the user via the **Import Sessions** and **Export Sessions** entry points on the File menu. Delay-loading means that Transcoders do not have a performance impact on Fiddler boot time or memory usage.

Direct Fiddler to load your Transcoder assemblies

Fiddler loads Transcoder assembly DLLs from the %PROGRAMFILES%\Fiddler2\ImportExport\ and %USERPROFILE%\My Documents\Fiddler2\ImportExport\ folders. Install to the %PROGRAMFILES% location to make your Transcoder available to all users on the machine, or the %USERPROFILE% folder to install it for the current user only.

Be sure to set the RequiredVersion attribute as follows:

```
// Transcoders require methods introduced in v2.3.9.0...
[assembly: Fiddler.RequiredVersion("2.3.9.0")]
```

...and ensure that your Transcoder classes are marked public.

The ProfferFormat Attribute

Each Transcoder class must be decorated with one or more ProfferFormat attributes that specify Format Name and FormatDescription strings that describe the Transcoder. These strings are shown to the user in the Select Format window. For instance, the HTTPArchive format exporter is decorated with two ProfferFormat attributes:

```
[ProfferFormat("HTTPArchive v1.1", "A lossy JSON-based HTTP traffic
archive format. Standard is documented @ http://groups.google.com/group/http-
archive-specification/web/har-1-1-spec")]

[ProfferFormat("HTTPArchive v1.2", "A lossy JSON-based HTTP traffic
archive format. Standard is documented @ http://groups.google.com/group/http-
archive-specification/web/har-1-2-spec")]
```

```
public class HTTPArchiveFormatExport: ISessionExporter
{
    ///...
```

Each of these two attributes identifies a format supported by the Transcoder, and each is displayed in the Select Format window's dropdown:

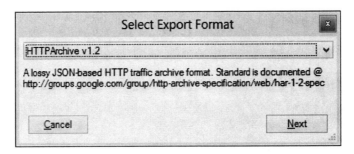

When the user invokes the Transcoder, the FormatName is provided to the ImportSessions or Export Sessions method so that a Transcoder that supports multiple formats may know which format the user has requested.

The ISessionImporter Interface

Transcoders that implement the ISessionImporter interface are invoked when the user invokes the **File > Import Sessions...** menu command. The interface defines one method:

```
public interface ISessionImporter : IDisposable
{
    Session[] ImportSessions(string sFormatName,
        Dictionary<string, object> dictOptions,
        EventHandler<ProgressCallbackEventArgs> evtProgressNotifications);
}
```

... and it also inherits the Dispose method from IDisposable.

The ImportSessions method should return an array of Session objects created from the import of the data, or null if there was an error in loading the data.

When the user chooses **File > Import Sessions...**, Fiddler will call the Transcoder and then add the Sessions returned by the Transcoder to the Web Sessions list.

The ISessionExporter Interface

Transcoders that implement the ISessionExporter interface are called when the user invokes the **File > Export Sessions** menu command. The interface defines one method:

```
public interface ISessionExporter : IDisposable
{
```

```
    bool ExportSessions(string sFormatName,
        Session[] oSessions,
        Dictionary<string, object> dictOptions,
        EventHandler<ProgressCallbackEventArgs> evtProgressNotifications);
}
```

… and it also inherits the `Dispose` method from `IDisposable`.

The `ExportSessions` method should return `true` if the export of the Sessions passed in the `oSessions` parameter is successful. If the data could not be exported for some reason, the Transcoder should log an explanation to Fiddler's Log and return `false`.

Handling Options

The `ImportSessions` and `ExportSessions` methods' second parameter is a `string-to-object` `Dictionary` that permits callers (FiddlerScript, other Extensions, or a FiddlerCore-based application) to pass options into the Transcoder.

The provided `dictOptions` dictionary may be `null`, or may contain a set of string-keyed objects. Most Importers support specification of a filename like this:

```
dictOptions["Filename"] = "C:\\test.file";
```

When a filename is provided through this mechanism, the Transcoder can suppress its normal UI and respect the provided option. Similarly, many Transcoders support a `Silent` key, which, if present, ensures that no warning or error UI is shown to the user.

Other Transcoders have other options, depending on their individual needs. For instance, FiddlerScript can invoke the HTTPArchive Transcoder, passing in the filename string and maximum response size integers thusly:

```
var oSessions = FiddlerApplication.UI.GetAllSessions();
var oExportOptions = FiddlerObject.createDictionary();
oExportOptions.Add("Filename", "C:\\users\\ericlaw\\desktop\\out1.har");
oExportOptions.Add("MaxTextBodyLength", 1024);
oExportOptions.Add("MaxBinaryBodyLength", 16384);

FiddlerApplication.DoExport("HTTPArchive v1.2", oSessions, oExportOptions, null);
```

As you can see in this example, the `DoExport` method on the `FiddlerApplication` object enables script or an extension to invoke a Transcoder by passing the `FormatName`. Similarly, the `DoImport` method permits invocation of a Transcoder to import Sessions.

The HTTPArchive Transcoder's code checks whether its caller has set any options like so:

```
public bool ExportSessions(string sFormat, Session[] oSessions,
```

```
      Dictionary<string, object> dictOptions,
      EventHandler<ProgressCallbackEventArgs> evtProgressNotifications)
   {

     //...
     string sFilename = null;
     int iMaxTextBodyLength = DEFAULT_MAX_TEXT_BYTECOUNT;
     int iMaxBinaryBodyLength = DEFAULT_MAX_BINARY_BYTECOUNT;

     if (null != dictOptions)
     {
       if (dictOptions.ContainsKey("Filename"))
       {
         sFilename = dictOptions["Filename"] as string;
       }

       if (dictOptions.ContainsKey("MaxTextBodyLength"))
       {
         iMaxTextBodyLength = (int)dictOptions["MaxTextBodyLength"];
       }

       if (dictOptions.ContainsKey("MaxBinaryBodyLength"))
       {
         iMaxBinaryBodyLength = (int)dictOptions["MaxBinaryBodyLength"];
       }
     }

   //...
```

Providing Progress Notifications

A caller may subscribe to progress notifications from your Transcoder by passing in an EventHandler delegate via evtProgressNotifications. As the import or export proceeds, your Transcoder should construct ProgressCallbackEventArgs objects to report on the progress the operation.

```
     public class ProgressCallbackEventArgs: EventArgs
     {
       public ProgressCallbackEventArgs(float flCompletionRatio, string sProgressText)
       public string ProgressText { get; }
       public string PercentComplete { get; }
       public bool Cancel { get; set; }
     }
```

When creating the EventArgs object, set flCompletionRatio to the fraction of the operation that is complete (ranging from 0 to 1.0). If the completion ratio cannot be determined, simply set flCompletionRatio to 0 or a "guess" between 0 and 1.0. Set sProgressText to provide status text (for instance "Adding session #1234" or "Compressing output."

After constructing the EventArgs, invoke the provided event handler if it is non-null.

If the handler sets the `Cancel` property to `true`, your Transcoder should gracefully abort the current operation as soon as possible, returning `null` or `false` to the caller.

Notes on Threading and Transcoders in FiddlerCore

Currently, methods of the `ISessionImporter` and `ISessionExporter` interfaces are called on the application's UI thread. This is almost certain to change in the future, so you should ensure that your classes are thread-safe and that they do not attempt to directly manipulate any UI.

Transcoders may be cross-compiled to work with FiddlerCore which has no UI and thus any attempt to manipulate the Fiddler UI will throw an exception. To cross-compile with FiddlerCore, create two variants of your project, one referencing `Fiddler.exe` and one referencing `FiddlerCore.dll`. To support FiddlerCore, it's also advised that you support the `Filename` key (with string value of a fully-qualified path) in the `dictOptions` parameter, and consider supporting a key named `Silent` (with a boolean value).

Beyond Files

While most Transcoder objects are designed to import or export *files* of various formats, there's no requirement that files are the source or destination of Transcoding. For instance, you can build a Transcoder whose `ISessionExporter` implementation stores the captured traffic to a remote database by calling a web service. Similarly, you could develop an `ISessionImporter` that reloads previously-stored traffic out of that database and adds it back to the Web Sessions list.

Example Transcoder

To build a simple Transcoder, follow these steps:

1. Start Visual Studio (version 2005 or later).

2. Create a new **Project** of type **Visual C# Class Library**.

3. Right-click the project's **References** folder in the **Solution Explorer**.

4. Choose the **Browse** tab and find `Fiddler.exe` in the `%PROGRAMFILES%\Fiddler2\` folder. If you want to build a version of your Transcoder that works with FiddlerCore instead, reference `FiddlerCore.dll`.

5. Click **Ok** to add the reference.

6. In the Solution Explorer, right click the project. Choose **Properties**.

7. On the **Application** tab, ensure that the project's **Target Framework** is **.NET Framework 2.0**. Note that if you need to change this value, Visual Studio may prompt you to reload the project.

8. On the **Build** tab, ensure that the **Platform Target** is **Any CPU**.

9. On the **Build Events** tab, add the following as the **Post-build event** command line:

```
         copy "$(TargetPath)"
           "%USERPROFILE%\My Documents\Fiddler2\ImportExport\$(TargetFilename)"
```

This will ensure that every time you successfully build your project, your new assembly is copied to the proper location for Fiddler to load. You will, of course, need to close Fiddler between each build or the command to copy the assembly to the target folder will fail with a "File in use" error.

10. On the **Debug** tab, click **Start external program** and enter %PROGRAMFILES%\Fiddler2 \Fiddler.exe as the target program. When you hit F5 to test your Transcoder, Fiddler will launch.

11. Save the project.

Modify the default class1.cs (or create a new class) in your project as follows:

```
using System;
using System.IO;
using System.Text;
using System.Reflection;
using System.Collections.Generic;
using System.Windows.Forms;
using Fiddler;

[assembly: AssemblyVersion("1.0.0.0")]
[assembly: Fiddler.RequiredVersion("2.3.9.5")]

// Note that this Transcoder only works when loaded by Fiddler itself; it will
// not work from a FiddlerCore-based application. The reason is that the output
// uses the columns shown in Fiddler's Web Sessions list, and FiddlerCore has
// no such list.

// Ensure your class is public, or Fiddler won't see it!
[ProfferFormat("TAB-Separated Values", "Session List in Tab-Delimited Format")]
[ProfferFormat("Comma-Separated Values",
    "Session List in Comma-Delimited Format; import into Excel or other tools")]
public class CSVTranscoder: ISessionExporter
{
  public bool ExportSessions(string sFormat, Session[] oSessions,
      Dictionary<string, object> dictOptions,
      EventHandler<ProgressCallbackEventArgs> evtProgressNotifications)
  {
    bool bResult = false;
    string chSplit;

    // Determine if we already have a filename
    // from the dictOptions collection
    string sFilename = null;
    if (null != dictOptions && dictOptions.ContainsKey("Filename"))
    {
      sFilename = dictOptions["Filename"] as string;
```

```
    }

    // If we don't yet have a filename, prompt the user
    // with a File Save dialog, using the correct file extension
    // for the export format they selected
    if (sFormat == "Comma-Separated Values")
    {
      chSplit = ",";
      if (string.IsNullOrEmpty(sFilename))
        sFilename = Fiddler.Utilities.ObtainSaveFilename(
          "Export As " + sFormat, "CSV Files (*.csv)|*.csv");
    }
    else
    {
      // Ensure caller asked for Tab-delimiting.
      if (sFormat != "TAB-Separated Values") return false;
      chSplit = "\t";
      if (string.IsNullOrEmpty(sFilename))
        sFilename = Fiddler.Utilities.ObtainSaveFilename(
          "Export As " + sFormat, "TSV Files (*.tsv)|*.tsv");
    }

    // If we didn't get a filename, user cancelled. If so, bail out.
    if (String.IsNullOrEmpty(sFilename)) return false;

    try
    {
      StreamWriter swOutput = new StreamWriter(sFilename, false, Encoding.UTF8);
      int iCount = 0;
      int iMax = oSessions.Length;

      #region WriteColHeaders
      bool bFirstCol = true;
      foreach (ColumnHeader oLVCol in FiddlerApplication.UI.lvSessions.Columns)
      {
        if (!bFirstCol)
        {
          swOutput.Write(chSplit);
        }
        else
        {
          bFirstCol = false;
        }

        // Remove any delimiter characters from the value
        swOutput.Write(oLVCol.Text.Replace(chSplit, ""));
      }

      swOutput.WriteLine();
      #endregion WriteColHeaders

      #region WriteEachSession
      foreach (Session oS in oSessions)
```

```
    {
      iCount++;

      // The ViewItem object is the ListViewItem in the Web Sessions list
      // Obviously, this doesn't exist in FiddlerCore-based applications
      if (null != oS.ViewItem)
      {
        bFirstCol = true;
        ListViewItem oLVI = (oS.ViewItem as ListViewItem);
        if (null == oLVI) continue;
        foreach (ListViewItem.ListViewSubItem oLVC in oLVI.SubItems)
        {
          if (!bFirstCol)
          {
            swOutput.Write(chSplit);
          }
          else
          {
            bFirstCol = false;
          }

          // Remove any delimiter characters from the value
          swOutput.Write(oLVC.Text.Replace(chSplit, ""));
        }

        swOutput.WriteLine();
      }

      // Notify the caller of our progress
      if (null != evtProgressNotifications)
      {
        ProgressCallbackEventArgs PCEA =
          new ProgressCallbackEventArgs((iCount/(float)iMax),
            "wrote " + iCount.ToString() + " records.");
        evtProgressNotifications(null, PCEA);

        // If the caller tells us to cancel, abort quickly
        if (PCEA.Cancel) { swOutput.Close(); return false; }
      }
    }
    #endregion WriteEachSession

      swOutput.Close();
      bResult = true;
    }
    catch (Exception eX)
    {
      // TODO: Replace alert with FiddlerApplication.Log.LogFormat(...
      MessageBox.Show(eX.Message, "Failed to export");
      bResult = false;
    }
```

```
        return bResult;
    }

    public void Dispose() { /*no-op*/ }
}
```

This simple example defines an ISessionExporter that offers two text formats: "comma-separated values" and "tab-separated values." When ExportSessions is called, the method examines the dictOptions provided and prompts the user for any missing information (like the target filename) required to complete the export. It then processes each Session in the oSessions array, reporting progress of the export back to Fiddler using the callback event handler provided.

FiddlerCore

Overview

As you've seen in prior chapters, you can extend Fiddler's functionality with both script and .NET code, and this is the best approach for building new functionality for most users. However, in some scenarios, like test automation, it would be more natural to add proxy functionality into an existing tool or test harness instead of using the entirety of Fiddler for the job.

Enter **FiddlerCore**. FiddlerCore is a class library that you can reference in your .NET applications to add Fiddler-like proxy functionality to .NET programs with none of the Fiddler user-interface. This diagram shows the difference between extending Fiddler with your code and extending your code with FiddlerCore:

Fiddler application with extensions | Your application hosting FiddlerCore

If you've previously built a Fiddler extension, you'll find that programming against FiddlerCore is an easy adjustment. Many FiddlerCore-based applications are first prototyped as a Fiddler extension before being moved into a standalone program. Building your code on Fiddler first allows you to easily see what is happening to web traffic using Fiddler's Inspectors. Once you're using FiddlerCore, you can only see the web traffic by adding logging functionality to your application (unless you chain your FiddlerCore application to an upstream or downstream Fiddler instance!).

Legalities

Before adopting any library, you should always understand its license terms to ensure that your use of the library is permitted. Fortunately, FiddlerCore has a simple license. You may freely redistribute the

FiddlerCore assembly with your application, without payment of any royalties, subject to the terms in the License.txt file included in the package. The license terms are quite liberal, and amount to a statement that the library is provided with no warranty and you may not use it for any illegal purpose.

FiddlerCore's certificate generation code used to intercept HTTPS traffic depends upon Microsoft's makecert.exe. If you do not need to decrypt HTTPS traffic, your program does not need to take a dependency on makecert. The utility is a licensed Visual Studio 2008 redistributable[1], so if you have a license to that tool you may redistribute makecert with your FiddlerCore-based applications. If you do not have the appropriate license, you should either speak to your lawyer or supply a different certificate generation tool.

Getting Started with FiddlerCore

You can download FiddlerCore from http://getfiddler.com/core/. The download package contains two copies of the library, one compiled for the v4 .NET Common Language Runtime, and one compiled for the v2 .NET CLR. The package also contains source code for a demonstration program which exercises FiddlerCore's functionality, and the makecert.exe utility.

You should also take the opportunity to download the separate documentation package, which will install the FiddlerCore.chm file. This file is an HTML Help file[2] that shows all of the classes, properties, methods, and fields available in FiddlerCore for your application to call.

After installing these packages, you'll have a new folder named FiddlerCoreAPI on your desktop.

Compiling the Sample Application

Explore the SampleApp subfolder of the FiddlerCoreAPI folder, and open the Demo.csproj file to launch Visual Studio. The Demo project contains a Console Application which demonstrates FiddlerCore's basic functionality. Scroll to the static void Main function in Program.cs to see how FiddlerCore is configured and used.

The very first thing you'll need to do is attach the event listeners that handle events raised by FiddlerCore. A key thing you must keep in mind is that FiddlerCore typically calls event handlers on the background threads in which Sessions are processed, so if you make any calls that modify shared objects (e.g. a list of Sessions) or update the application's UI, you must do so using thread-safe mechanisms. To update shared data-structures, use a Mutex or lock; to update WinForms-based UI, use the BeginInvoke method on the control being updated.

Supplying event handlers for FiddlerCore's OnNotification and LogString events allows you to see error messages and other information which is very useful for troubleshooting problems in your application:

---

[1] See redist.txt in the Microsoft Visual Studio program files folder.
[2] Built using the very cool Sandcastle Help File Builder tool. http://shfb.codeplex.com/

```
FiddlerApplication.OnNotification += delegate(object s,
  NotificationEventArgs oNEA)
{
  Console.WriteLine("** NotifyUser: " + oNEA.NotifyString);
};

FiddlerApplication.Log.OnLogString += delegate(object s, LogEventArgs oLEA)
{
  Console.WriteLine("** LogString: " + oLEA.LogString);
};
```

The next step is to attach event handlers that fire as each Session is processed. It's common to attach event handlers for the BeforeRequest and BeforeResponse events.

One of the most common behaviors of the BeforeRequest event handler is to set the bBufferResponse property to false if you want responses to stream to the client, or to true if you want the Before Response event handler to be able to modify the response before the client gets it. If your application will keep a list of Sessions, you should add the new Session to your list in the BeforeRequest handler.

```
FiddlerApplication.BeforeRequest += delegate(Session oS)
{
  // Buffer response to allow response tampering
  oS.bBufferResponse = true;

  // Use a thread-safe mechanism to update my List<Session>
  Monitor.Enter(oAllSessions);
  oAllSessions.Add(oS);
  Monitor.Exit(oAllSessions);
}
```

A BeforeResponse handler enables you to modify a Session's response:

```
FiddlerApplication.BeforeResponse += delegate(Fiddler.Session oS)
{
  oS.utilDecodeResponse();
  // Note: This change only takes effect properly if
  // oS.bBufferResponse was set to true earlier!
  oS.utilReplaceInResponse("<title>", "<title>INJECTED!!");
};
```

After your event handlers are ready, your next step is to start the FiddlerCore proxy instance. First calculate the desired behavior flags:

```
// The default flags are your best bet
FiddlerCoreStartupFlags oFCSF = FiddlerCoreStartupFlags.Default;

// ...but if, say, we don't want FiddlerCore to Decrypt
// HTTPS traffic, we can unset that flag at this point
oFCSF = (oFCSF & ~FiddlerCoreStartupFlags.DecryptSSL);
```

Then call the Startup method, passing in the desired port and your flags:

```
// Start listening on port 8877
FiddlerApplication.Startup(8877, oFCSF);
```

If you don't care which port FiddlerCore listens on, freeing you from handling errors when that port is already in use, pass 0 for the port and FiddlerCore will automatically select an available port. The port chosen can be retrieved using the property FiddlerApplication.oProxy.ListenPort.

When using the default flags, the Startup method will immediately register the new proxy as the system's default proxy. Any BeforeRequest and BeforeResponse event handlers will begin to fire as traffic is captured.

After you're done with FiddlerCore, you should call the Shutdown method to unregister as the system proxy and close the listening proxy port:

```
FiddlerApplication.Shutdown();
```

Note that the Shutdown method cannot gracefully terminate any in-progress Web Sessions. Those sessions' background threads will continue to run (potentially calling into your event handlers) but will likely eventually be aborted by either an ObjectDisposedException or NullReferenceException when they attempt to access the now-null FiddlerApplication.oProxy object. If you'd prefer, you might instead call:

```
FiddlerApplication.oProxy.Detach();
```

...to unregister as the system proxy. Wait a few seconds to permit in-progress Sessions to complete before calling the Shutdown method.

FiddlerCoreStartupFlags

The FiddlerCoreStartupFlags enumeration allows you to specify the behavior of the FiddlerCore proxy endpoint. The enumeration exposes the following flags:

None	No options are set.
RegisterAsSystemProxy	When Startup is called, FiddlerCore will register as the system proxy.
DecryptSSL	FiddlerCore will attempt to decrypt any HTTPS traffic that flows through the proxy.
AllowRemoteClients	Permit connections from remote PCs or devices. You may need to enable a firewall exception for your application to receive remote traffic.
ChainToUpstreamGateway	Automatically adopt the system's existing proxy settings as an upstream gateway proxy.
MonitorAllConnections	Register as the default proxy for all WinINET connections, including dialup and VPN connections. When not set, only the LAN connection is set to point

	at the FiddlerCore proxy instance.
HookUsingPACFile	This option is not presently implemented.
CaptureLocalhostTraffic	Add `<-loopback>` to the system's proxy exceptions list, enabling IE9+ to send loopback traffic to FiddlerCore.
Default	This flag encompasses the following flags: `RegisterAsSystemProxy` | `DecryptSSL` | `AllowRemoteClients` | `ChainToUpstreamGateway` | `MonitorAllConnections` | `CaptureLocalhostTraffic`

Using `FiddlerCoreStartupFlags.Default` is the recommended approach as it sets the options desired by most applications. Even if you don't want all of the flags in the default set, your best bet is to start with `Default` and use bit-manipulation to mask off unwanted options:

```
FiddlerCoreStartupFlags oFlags =
    (FiddlerCoreStartupFlags.Default & ~FiddlerCoreStartupFlags.DecryptSSL);
```

This approach has the benefit that as new options are introduced in future versions of FiddlerCore, your application will automatically be opted-in (upon recompile) to new default options.

The static `FiddlerApplication` class provides many useful event handlers, static methods, and properties that control FiddlerCore's behavior. Most of these APIs are also available for use by extensions running inside Fiddler itself.

FiddlerApplication Events

`FiddlerApplication` fires events raised by the FiddlerCore engine and each Session as it is processed. Most of these events fire on background threads so you must take care to ensure that your event handlers are thread-safe. Use `BeginInvoke` or `Invoke` to update any user-interface elements on the UI thread.

RequestHeadersAvailable Event

This event fires after FiddlerCore has read the complete set of request headers from the client. It is rarely useful because it fires so early in request processing.

BeforeRequest Event

This event fires after the request has been completely read from the client, before the server is contacted. This provides the opportunity to modify the client's request or generate a local response without contacting the server.

OnValidateServerCertificate Event

This event fires as FiddlerCore evaluates a HTTPS server's certificate. Your event handler may accept or reject the server's certificate based on the criteria of your choosing.

```
FiddlerApplication.OnValidateServerCertificate += new
  System.EventHandler<ValidateServerCertificateEventArgs>(CheckCert);

void CheckCert(object sender, ValidateServerCertificateEventArgs e)
{
  // If there's an obvious issue with the presented certificate,
  // it will be rejected unless overridden here.
  if (SslPolicyErrors.None != e.CertificatePolicyErrors)
  {
    return;        // Certificate will be rejected
  }

  // Check if the Convergence Certificate Notary services have
  // an opinion about this certificate chain.
  bool bNotariesAffirm = GetNotaryConsensus(e.Session,
    e.ServerCertificate, e.ServerCertificateChain);

  FiddlerApplication.Log.LogFormat("Notaries have indicated that the "
    + "certificate presented for {0} is {1}", e.ExpectedCN,
    bNotariesAffirm ? "VALID" : "INVALID");

  if (!bNotariesAffirm)
  {
```

```
      e.ValidityState = CertificateValidity.ForceInvalid;
      return;
  }

  e.ValidityState = CertificateValidity.ForceValid;
}
```

OnReadResponseBuffer Event

This event fires on every read of the server's response stream. It is generally not handled because the event provides only a raw buffer of bytes which hasn't yet been parsed into headers and body.

The event can be useful when low-level logging (of say, timing information) is desired.

```
FiddlerApplication.OnReadResponseBuffer += new
  EventHandler<RawReadEventArgs>(OnRead);

static void OnRead(object sender, RawReadEventArgs e)
{
  Console.WriteLine(String.Format("Read {0} response bytes for session {1}",
    e.iCountOfBytes, e.sessionOwner.id));

  // NOTE: arrDataBuffer is a fixed-size array. Only bytes 0 to
  // iCountOfBytes should be read/manipulated.

  // Just for kicks, lowercase every ASCII char. Note that this will
  // obviously mangle any binary MIME files and break many types of markup
  for (int i = 0; i < e.iCountOfBytes; i++)
  {
    if ((e.arrDataBuffer[i] > 0x40) && (e.arrDataBuffer[i] < 0x5b))
    {
      e.arrDataBuffer[i] = (byte)(e.arrDataBuffer[i] + (byte)0x20);
    }
  }
}
```

ResponseHeadersAvailable Event

This event fires when FiddlerCore has read the complete set of response headers from the server. It provides the opportunity to set the Session's bBufferResponse property based on the contents of the headers:

```
FiddlerApplication.ResponseHeadersAvailable += delegate(Session oS)
{
  // Disable streaming for HTML responses on a target server so that
  // we can modify those responses in the BeforeResponse handler
  if (oS.HostnameIs("example.com") && oS.oResponse.MIMEType.Contains("text/html"))
  {
    oS.bBufferResponse = true;
  }
};
```

When this event fires, the response body is not yet available from the server. Attempting to modify the responseBodyBytes or modify headers that influence the download of the body (Content-Length, Transfer-Encoding, and Content-Encoding) inside this event will almost certainly result in an exception or other error.

BeforeResponse Event

This event fires after the response has been completely read from the server. If you plan to modify the server's response in your handler for this event, you must first disable streaming of the response by setting oSession.bBufferResponse to true in the ResponseHeadersAvailable or BeforeRequest events.

If the Session's bBufferResponse property is false, as it is by default in FiddlerCore, the response will stream to the client as it is read from the server, *before* your BeforeResponse event handler has the chance to modify it. On streaming responses, the BeforeResponse event handler (non-intuitively but necessarily) fires *after* the response is sent to the client.

BeforeReturningError Event

This event fires when FiddlerCore generates an error (e.g. a DNS lookup failure notice) to return to the client. The event provides the opportunity to customize the error message that will be returned to the client.

```
FiddlerApplication.BeforeReturningError += delegate(Session oS)
{
  string sErrMsg = oS.GetResponseBodyAsString();

  oS.utilSetResponseBody("<!doctype html><title>AcmeCorp Error Page</title>"
    + "<body>Sorry, this page or service is presently unavailable. Please try"
    + " again later. <br /><pre>" + sErrMsg + "</pre></html>");
};
```

Your event handler might also take other actions, like logging the error to a database.

AfterSessionComplete Event

This event fires when the processing of a Session is complete. It provides the opportunity to perform any necessary logging of the final state of the Session.

FiddlerAttach Event

This event fires when FiddlerCore has registered as the system's default proxy.

FiddlerDetach Event

This event fires when FiddlerCore has unregistered as the system's default proxy.

OnClearCache Event

This event fires when the Fiddler.WinINETCache.ClearCacheItems method is called; properties of the EventArgs object indicate what elements of the cache should be cleared. The event allows your application to provide its own handling (e.g. clearing an auxiliary cache) instead of or in addition to the default handling, in which FiddlerCore deletes the requested items from the WinINET cache.

OnNotification Event

This event fires when FiddlerCore logs a notification event. Since FiddlerCore runs in silent mode by default, most notifications of errors or configuration problems are raised using this event.

Developers often contact me to complain that *"FiddlerCore isn't working properly."* After attaching a handler for this event, the source of the problem is often obvious.

FiddlerApplication Methods

Startup()

This method is used to configure the default FiddlerCore proxy listener and instruct it to begin capturing requests. Various overloaded versions of this method are available—I recommend that you use the overload that accepts `FiddlerCoreStartupFlags`.

Shutdown()

This method detaches the default FiddlerCore listener (if attached) and disposes of it.

IsStarted()

This method returns `true` if the default FiddlerCore listening endpoint has been created, otherwise it returns `false`.

IsSystemProxy()

This method returns `true` if FiddlerCore is running and attached as the system proxy, otherwise it returns `false`.

CreateProxyEndpoint()

This method allows you to create additional FiddlerCore proxy endpoints that can accept requests from clients. When calling this method, supply a port number and a boolean indicating whether remote connections should be permitted.

You may also supply either a string containing a hostname or an `X509Certificate2`. If either is supplied, the endpoint will automatically perform a HTTPS handshake with the client on each connection, presenting either the provided certificate or an automatically generated certificate containing the specified hostname. Use this overload when running FiddlerCore as a reverse proxy for a HTTPS site.

```
Proxy oSecureEP = FiddlerApplication.CreateProxyEndpoint(8777, true, "localhost");
if (null != oSecureEP)
{
  FiddlerApplication.Log.LogString("Created secure endpoint listening "
    + "on port 8777, which will send a HTTPS certificate for 'localhost'");
}
```

If you do not supply a hostname or certificate, the endpoint will act as a normal proxy endpoint and will not masquerade as a HTTPS server.

Sessions accepted by the endpoints created using this method will be processed using the normal Session-processing pipeline. Your Session-processing event handlers can determine which endpoint a given request was received upon by examining its `LocalPort` property:

```
FiddlerApplication.Log.LogFormat("Session {0} received by EndPoint on Port #{1}",
    oSession.id,
    (null != oSession.oRequest.pipeClient) ?
        "n/a" : oSession.oRequest.pipeClient.LocalPort
);
```

DoImport()
This method enables import of Sessions using the Importer architecture. When calling this method, supply an Import Format name, a `StringDictionary` containing options, and a progress event callback to receive updates on the progress of the import.

DoExport()
This method enables export of Sessions using the Exporter architecture. When calling this method, supply an Export Format name, the array of Sessions, a `StringDictionary` containing options, and a progress event callback to receive updates on the progress of the export.

GetVersionString()
This method returns a string describing the FiddlerCore version. For instance:

```
FiddlerCore/2.3.9.9 (+SAZ)
```

GetDetailedInfo()
This method returns a string describing the FiddlerCore version and the configuration of the default listening endpoint. This method is used by logging or for display in an application's About box.

ResetSessionCounter()
This method resets the Session ID counter to 0. Use this method sparingly, because duplicate session IDs can be very confusing.

FiddlerApplication Properties and Fields

isClosing
This boolean is set to `true` when the application is shutting down. When set to `true`, FiddlerCore will attempt to avoid unnecessary processing of Sessions and will suppress errors as gracefully as possible.

Log
This object provides access to Fiddler's logging system. The `LogString` and `LogFormat` methods allow your code to record new messages. The `OnLogString` event permits your application to detect when messages are logged. See the **Logging** section on page 220 for more information.

oDefaultClientCertificate

When set, FiddlerCore will use the supplied `X509Certificate` when performing client authentication to a HTTPS server.

oProxy

This object represents Fiddler's default listening proxy endpoint. Its `SendRequest` methods allow your application to generate and inject new requests into the processing pipeline.

oTranscoders

This object represents Fiddler's Import/Export subsystem. Your application may register Transcoder assemblies using the `ImportTranscoders` method on this object. Invoke Import or Export operations using the `DoImport` and `DoExport` methods of the `FiddlerApplication` object.

Prefs

This object provides access to Fiddler's Preferences system. See **Programming with Preferences** on page 223 for more information.

The Rest of the Fiddler API

With the exception of a few FiddlerCore-specific APIs, Fiddler and FiddlerCore share a common object model. Code developed as a Fiddler extension can often be ported to run in a FiddlerCore-based application simply by eliminating any dependencies upon Fiddler user-interface objects.

COMMON TASKS WITH FIDDLERCORE

Keeping track of Sessions

Unlike Fiddler, FiddlerCore does not keep a Session list automatically. If you want a Session list, simply create a List<Fiddler.Session> and add new Sessions to it as they are captured. The multi-threaded nature of FiddlerCore means that you must Invoke to a single thread, use thread-safe data structures, or use a Monitor or other synchronization mechanism (as shown below) to update or enumerate a list of Sessions safely.

```
// Inside your main object, create a list to hold the Sessions
// The generic list type requires you are #using System.Collections.Generic
List<Fiddler.Session> oAllSessions = new List<Fiddler.Session>();

// Add Sessions to the list as they are captured
Fiddler.FiddlerApplication.BeforeRequest += delegate(Fiddler.Session oS)
{
  Monitor.Enter(oAllSessions);
  oAllSessions.Add(oS);
  Monitor.Exit(oAllSessions);
};
```

Keep in mind that oAllSessions can quickly balloon out the memory use within your application because Sessions cannot be garbage-collected while they are referenced in the list. You should periodically trim the list to keep it of a reasonable size. Alternatively, if you only care about request URLs or headers, you could keep a List<> of those types rather than storing references to Session objects.

Getting Traffic to FiddlerCore

Like Fiddler itself, FiddlerCore runs as a local proxy instance, and it only sees traffic that is sent to it. If the RegisterAsSystemProxy flag is set when you call the FiddlerApplication.Startup method, FiddlerCore will automatically register as the system proxy, just like Fiddler does. If you do not configure FiddlerCore as the system proxy, you can manually configure most applications to point at your FiddlerCore instance. FiddlerCore offers the unique ability to register as the WinINET proxy for just the process in which it is running. This is a useful capability for scenarios where you have a Web Browser control in your .NET application and want to use FiddlerCore to only capture or modify the traffic from that Web Browser control (and any other WinINET APIs).

To make use of this capability, call the SetProxyInProcess method with your listening endpoint's address and port, and a proxy-bypass list:

```
Fiddler.URLMonInterop.SetProxyInProcess("127.0.0.1:7777", "<-loopback>");
```

When capture is complete, you may reset the current process back to the default system proxy:

```
Fiddler.URLMonInterop.ResetProxyInProcessToDefault();
```

Trusting the FiddlerCore Certificate

If your FiddlerCore application needs to decrypt HTTPS traffic, you can have your application automatically generate a root certificate and prompt the user to trust it:

```
private bool CreateAndTrustRoot()
{
  // Ensure root exists
  if (!Fiddler.CertMaker.rootCertExists())
  {
    bCreatedRootCertificate = Fiddler.CertMaker.createRootCert();
    if (!bCreatedRootCertificate) return false;
  }

  // Ensure root is trusted
  if (!Fiddler.CertMaker.rootCertIsTrusted())
  {
    bTrustedRootCert = Fiddler.CertMaker.trustRootCert();
    if (!bTrustedRootCert) return false;
  }

  return true;
}
```

If you prefer to trust the FiddlerCore root certificate on a machine-wide basis instead, call `createRootCert` and then call `GetRootCertificate` to retrieve the new root certificate. Then call the following method:

```
private static bool setMachineTrust(X509Certificate2 oRootCert)
{
  try
  {
    X509Store certStore = new X509Store(StoreName.Root,
                                        StoreLocation.LocalMachine);
    certStore.Open(OpenFlags.ReadWrite);
    try
    {
      certStore.Add(oRootCert);
    }
    finally
    {
      certStore.Close();
    }
    return true;
  }
  catch (Exception eX)
  {
    return false;
  }
}
```

Note that your application must be running with Admin-level privileges to add certificates to the machine-wide root certificate store.

Generating Responses

Fiddler's AutoResponder tab allows users to replay a previously captured Session. Hosters of FiddlerCore can reproduce the behavior of this feature in their applications. The following snippet identifies requests for replaceme.txt and returns a previously captured response stored in a Session object named SessionIWantToReturn.

```
Fiddler.FiddlerApplication.BeforeRequest += delegate(Fiddler.Session oS)
{
  if (oS.uriContains("replaceme.txt"))
  {
    oS.utilCreateResponseAndBypassServer();
    oS.responseBodyBytes = SessionIWantToReturn.responseBodyBytes;
    oS.oResponse.headers =
      (HTTPResponseHeaders) SessionIWantToReturn.oResponse.headers.Clone();
  }
};
```

Other Resources

See http://fiddler.wikidot.com/fiddlercore for more information on building FiddlerCore-based applications.

Appendices

APPENDIX A: TROUBLESHOOTING

Over the years, Fiddler has been refined to address most of the common problems users have encountered. However, there are some circumstances in which manual troubleshooting steps may be required.

Missing Traffic

The single most common complaint I hear from users is: "*Fiddler used to work but now it doesn't show anything. Please help!*"

In virtually all cases, the problem is that a filter is set that is causing the traffic to be hidden. Sometimes, the filter was set inadvertently, and sometimes the user merely set it a while ago and forgot about it.

Fortunately, it's easy to troubleshoot filters—just click the **Troubleshoot Filters** option on the **Help** menu. When Filter Troubleshooting is enabled, the Web Sessions list will include all Sessions that would ordinarily be hidden, rendering each filtered Session using the strikethrough font. The Comments column for each filtered Session shows which filter was responsible for hiding the traffic, allowing you to adjust filters as needed. For instance, these following Sessions were hidden because they were sent by a web browser process, and the status bar's Process Filter is set to show only **Non-Browser** traffic:

If you don't see the missing Sessions even after enabling Filter Troubleshooting, your next step is to try to visit `http://ipv4.fiddler:8888/` in the client application. If your client's traffic is being proxied by Fiddler, you will see an entry in the Web Sessions list and the browser will show an "echo" page:

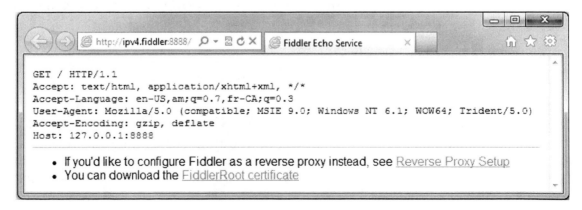

If you don't see this page, that suggests that the client application isn't correctly configured to have its traffic proxied. Ensure that you are not connected to the target network using Microsoft DirectAccess—that technology will bypass the local Fiddler proxy server.

Your next step should be to try the URL `http://localhost:8888/`, assuming the client and Fiddler are running on the same computer. If that URL cannot be reached, it means that your client application is unable to contact Fiddler, either because Fiddler is not properly running, or there is a firewall or other problem preventing Fiddler from receiving the traffic. You should check your firewall configuration, and see if you get different results from other clients or when running on a different computer.

Interference from Security Software

In rare instances, security software like firewalls, anti-malware, and antivirus programs can interfere with the proper download, installation, and running of Fiddler.

Problems Downloading Fiddler

Some enterprise firewalls or security gateways will block your ability to download software from the Fiddler websites (e.g. `getfiddler.com` and `fiddler2.com`); instead of a successful download, you'll instead see a blocking error page. This behavior is typically because these overzealous security suites consider network debugging software like Fiddler a "hacking tool" and thus not something needed by common users. In most cases, there's little an end-user can do to get around the block, short of protesting to their IT administrator or downloading Fiddler from an unblocked mirror website.

Problems Installing Fiddler

Some security programs running locally attempt to protect the system from setup programs; these products often change the access control lists on registry keys and filesystem locations which prevent successful install of Fiddler. In such cases, you will usually see a message from the Fiddler installer complaining "A system administrator must install this tool" despite the fact that you are, in fact, such an administrator. To address this problem, you can either temporarily disable the security software, or perform an XCOPY install of Fiddler, described on page 14.

Problems Running Fiddler

After Fiddler has been successfully installed, security software may still interfere with it.

Some security packages attempt to filter web-traffic using their own locally-running proxy server; for instance, some products from AVG and McAfee do this. The problem with such proxies is that they can overwrite the proxy settings that allow Fiddler to capture your traffic. Even if they properly chain to Fiddler, all traffic will be coming from that proxy process rather than the original client process, breaking Fiddler's Process Filters (e.g. nothing will show if Fiddler is configured to show only **Web Browser** traffic). You may be able to live with this limitation, or you may choose to disable the web filtering component of your security software.

Other packages impose firewall restrictions that prevent traffic from being sent to Fiddler or that prevent traffic from Fiddler from being sent to the Internet. By default, Fiddler's installer attempts to register an exception with the Windows Firewall, but this exception probably will not be respected by other firewalls. If you encounter this problem, you will either not see any requests in Fiddler (because the traffic didn't make it to Fiddler) or you will see all requests fail with HTTP/502 errors, the body of which will read:

```
[Fiddler] The socket connection to example.com failed. <br /> An attempt was
made to access a socket in a way forbidden by its access permissions.
```

You can typically use your firewall's configuration interface to add an exception for Fiddler.exe or its port 8888.

Lastly, you may find that security software prevents Fiddler from successfully registering as the system proxy server. When you click **Tools** > **WinINET Options** > **LAN Settings** while Fiddler is running, you should see the proxy settings set to 127.0.0.1:8888. If you don't see Fiddler properly listed, it's possible that your security software is blocking access to the proxy-configuration registry keys. To resolve this, you may be able to turn off a "registry protection" option in your software, or might possibly resolve the issue by running Fiddler as an Administrator.

Corrupted Proxy Settings

If Fiddler crashes or is terminated without shutting down properly, your system's proxy settings will likely remain pointed at Fiddler. If you subsequently start your browser or use other applications that respect the proxy settings, you will likely see connection errors.

To resolve this problem, simply restart Fiddler. On startup, Fiddler will detect that the system proxy settings were already pointed at Fiddler and note that fact. Later, when Fiddler is gracefully shut down, the proxy settings will be restored to the Windows default ("Automatically detect proxy") settings.

Alternatively, rather than restarting Fiddler, you can manually adjust your proxy settings by opening the Internet Options Control Panel from your system Control Panel or by clicking **Tools** > **Internet Options** in Internet Explorer. Click the **Connections** tab, then click the **LAN Settings** button at the bottom. Ensure that when Fiddler is not running, the proxy settings are not configured to point to 127.0.0.1:8888. If they are, adjust the proxy settings to point to your network's proxy, or clear all of the checkboxes if your network does not require a proxy.

If you have connection problems in Firefox when Fiddler isn't running, check Firefox's **Tools** > **Options** > **Advanced** > **Network** > **Connection Settings** screen to ensure that the settings are correct for your network.

Resetting Fiddler

In order to prevent data loss, reinstalling or uninstalling Fiddler will not remove its settings from the registry and filesystem. This means that you cannot resolve simple problems (for instance, a "missing column" or similar issue) by reinstalling Fiddler.

If you wish to reset Fiddler's configuration, hold the SHIFT key while starting Fiddler, and click Yes in the following prompt:

When started with the default settings, Fiddler will restore all UI elements to their default states and sizes, unhide any hidden tabs or columns, and reset other state as appropriate. It will not, however, uninstall any plugins or reset your FiddlerScript.

To reset your FiddlerScript, simply delete or rename the file %USERPROFILE%\My Documents\Fiddler2\CustomRules.js, if it is present. The next time Fiddler is started, the default SampleRules.js file will be loaded.

Troubleshooting Certificate Problems

In rare cases, you may find that Fiddler is unable to generate HTTPS interception certificates using the MakeCert.exe utility. This problem is accompanied by the error message:

```
--------------------------------------------
Creation of the interception certificate failed.
makecert.exe returned -1.
Error: Can't create the key of the subject ('JoeSoft')
Failed
--------------------------------------------
```

This problem might be resolved by resetting Fiddler's certificates. Click **Tools** > **Fiddler Options** > **HTTPS**. Untick the **Decrypt HTTPS Traffic** checkbox, then click the **Remove Interception Certificates** button to clear any Fiddler interception certificates from the Windows certificate store. Then, tick the **Decrypt HTTPS Traffic** checkbox again.

Warning: As the following instructions involve editing sensitive areas of your system, they should only be undertaken by experts.

You may be able to fix broken MakeCert.exe functionality by using the SysInternals Process Monitor utility to find MakeCert.exe file accesses within the folder path %USERPROFILE%\Application Data\Microsoft\Crypto\RSA\<keyname>\<filename> when Fiddler fails to generate a certificate. Moving the accessed files may restore the certificate store's functionality.

If problems persist, you may be able to avoid the problem by switching to the **Certificate Maker** plugin described on page 111. This plugin does not utilize the Windows Certificate APIs for certificate generation, and thus may resolve the problem.

Wiping all traces of Fiddler

Warning: As these instructions involve editing sensitive areas of your system, they should only be undertaken by experts.

To fully clear all remnants of Fiddler from your system:

1. Uninstall Fiddler using the **Add/Remove Programs** applet in the system control panel.
2. Uninstall any Fiddler plugins listed in the **Add/Remove Programs** list.
3. Delete the folders:
    *   `%PROGRAMFILES%\Fiddler2`
    *   `%USERPROFILE%\Documents\Fiddler2`
4. Use `RegEdit.exe` to remove the registry keys:
    *   `HKLM\Software\Microsoft\Fiddler2`
    *   `HKCU\Software\Microsoft\Fiddler2`
    *   `HKCU\Software\Eric Lawrence`
5. Use the Windows Certificate Manager (`CertMgr.msc`) to remove all of Fiddler's certificates from your Personal and Trusted Root Certification Authorities storage areas.
6. If you configured Firefox or Opera to trust Fiddler certificates, use the control panels in those products to remove the Fiddler certificates.
7. Inside IE's **Tools > Internet Options > Connections > LAN Settings**, ensure that none of the settings point to Fiddler.

Fiddler crashes complaining about the "Configuration System"

The following error message indicates that one of the .NET Framework's configuration files is corrupt:

```
----------------------------
Sorry, you may have found a bug...
----------------------------
Your Microsoft .NET Configuration file is corrupt and contains invalid data.
You can often correct this error by installing updates from WindowsUpdate and/or
reinstalling the .NET Framework.

Configuration system failed to initialize
Source: System.Configuration
at System.Configuration.ConfigurationManager.PrepareConfigSystem()
at System.Configuration.ConfigurationManager.GetSection(String sectionName)

System.Configuration.ConfigurationErrorsException: Unrecognized configuration
section system.serviceModel.
c:\WINDOWS\Microsoft.NET\Framework\v2.0.50727\Config\machine.config
```

The most common fix for this is to visit WindowsUpdate and install all available .NET Framework updates. If that doesn't work, try re-installing the .NET Framework. If that doesn't work, try editing the XML file (e.g. `machine.config`) specified by the error message to correct whatever the message is complaining about.

Fiddler randomly stops capturing traffic

The Microsoft Firewall client for ISA / Forefront TMG has an option to automatically reconfigure Internet Explorer settings. Unfortunately, this setting will cause Internet Explorer to detach from Fiddler at random times. To prevent this problem, disable **browser automatic configuration** in the Microsoft Firewall client applet.

If there's a Firewall Client icon in your system tray, right click it and choose **Configure...** from the popup menu. If you don't see the icon, type `forefront` in the Start Menu search box to find the applet. On the Web Browser tab, uncheck the **Enable Web browser automatic configuration** checkbox.

Fiddler stalls when streaming RPC-over-HTTPS traffic

The HTTP and HTTPS protocols are extremely popular data transports; even scenarios that would otherwise use a straight TCP/IP connection often use HTTP or HTTPS because these protocols are usually allowed to traverse firewalls. Fiddler may encounter problems if some traffic is masquerading as HTTP.

For instance, one scenario where you will encounter this is when using Microsoft Outlook with an Exchange Server configured to deliver mail using the RPC-over-HTTPS feature. You will see a request in Fiddler like so:

```
RPC_OUT_DATA /rpc/rpcproxy.dll?ex.example.com HTTP/1.1
Host: ex.example.com
Content-Type: application/rpc
Content-Length: 1073741824
```

Outlook is attempting to use the HTTPS protocol to establish a bytestream over which a bidirectional TCP/IP stream will be layered. The problem is that the client isn't *really* planning to send a one gigabyte request body—it's instead just sending a huge value to indicate that it *might* send a lot of data. Fiddler dutifully waits for the client to send the promised gigabyte of data before proceeding with the network request. Since the data is not forthcoming from the client, no connection is made, and Outlook will indicate that it's "*Trying to connect...*" forever. While enabling the **Stream** option in Fiddler's toolbar enables *responses* to stream to the client, Fiddler does not currently offer a way to stream incomplete *requests* to the server.

To enable Outlook's RPC-over-HTTPS feature to work correctly while Fiddler is running, you can:

1. Configure the target hostname to bypass Fiddler entirely: Add `exchange.example.com` to the **Bypass List** box on the **Tools** > **Fiddler Options** > **Connections** tab, or

2. Configure Fiddler to skip decrypting connections to the target host: Add `exchange.example.com` to the **Skip Decryption** box on the **Tools** > **Fiddler Options** > **Connections** tab, or

3. Configure Fiddler to skip decrypting of traffic from the client application: Use the dropdown box on the **Tools** > **Fiddler Options** > **Connections** tab to enable decryption **for browsers only**.

Appendix B: Command Line Syntax

`Fiddler.exe` accepts zero or more command-line arguments, consisting of zero or more option flags and a single filename of a SAZ file to load on startup.

```
fiddler.exe [options] [FileToLoad.saz]
```

Fiddler also registers itself in Windows' `AppPaths` key so that you can launch it by typing `fiddler2` in the Start > Run prompt instead of specifying a fully-qualified path to `fiddler.exe`.

Option Flags

Option flags may be preceded by either a / or - character.

Flag	Description
/?	Show the list of available command line arguments.
/viewer	Open a Viewer mode instance of Fiddler which can be used to display previously captured traffic but cannot capture new traffic.
/quiet	Launch in "quiet" mode, where prompts and alerts are suppressed, and the main window is minimized to the system tray. This mode is most often used when Fiddler is running as a part of an automated script.
/noattach	Do not register as the system proxy on startup, even if otherwise configured to do so. You can manually register Fiddler as the proxy for an individual application or set it as the system proxy using the option on the File menu.
/noversioncheck	Do not send a web service request to check for updates on startup.
/extoff	Do not load any Fiddler Inspectors or Extensions. This flag is used to troubleshoot problems related to buggy extensions.
/noscript	Do not load FiddlerScript. This flag is used to determine whether your FiddlerScript is causing some problem.
/port:####	Specify the port that Fiddler should listen on, overriding the default setting configured in the Fiddler Options window.

Examples

Launch Fiddler without attaching:

```
C:\program files (x86)\Fiddler2\fiddler.exe /noattach
```

Launch Fiddler with no UI, running on port 1234:

```
fiddler2 /port:1234 -quiet
```

Open a SAZ file in a new Fiddler Viewer instance:

```
fiddler2 -viewer C:\users\joe\desktop\Sample.saz
```

Appendix C: Session Flags

A `StringDictionary` field in each Session object contains flags that control the processing or display of the session.

Some flags are set by Fiddler itself, but most are set script or extensions. The list of supported flags grows with each update to Fiddler, and extensions may use their own flags (which have no meaning to Fiddler) to add state information to a given Session.

The flags can be accessed by `oSession.oFlags["flagname"]` or by using the default indexer on the Session object: `oSession["flagname"]`.

Flag names are case-insensitive strings, and most flag values are interpreted case-insensitively. Most of Fiddler's flags are simply checked for their *existence*, such that setting *any* value (even misleading strings like 0, `false`, and `heck no!`), enables the named behavior. To disable a flag, remove the flag from the Session like so:

```
oSession.oFlags.Remove("flagname");
```

Because most flags are simply tested for existence, a best practice is to use the flag's value to store a terse explanation of *why* the flag was set. For instance:

```
oSession["ui-hide"] = "hidden by Hide Images rule";
```

You can view a Session's flags by using the Properties item on the Web Sessions list's context menu.

Session Display Flags
The following flags control how a session appears within the Web Sessions list.

Flag Name	ui-hide
Explanation	The session will not appear within the Web Sessions list. One of the most commonly used flags, ui-hide is used by script or extensions to avoid cluttering the Web Sessions list with uninteresting traffic.
Supported Values	Any value will hide the Session. Typically, you should provide a terse explanation of *why* the Session was hidden, so that if the user activates the Troubleshoot Filters feature on the Help menu, the UI will explain why the Session was hidden. By default, Fiddler will not hide requests that it itself generated (e.g. using the Composer). However, if the ui-hide flag's value contains the word stealth, the Session will be hidden unconditionally.

Flag Name	`ui-bold`
Explanation	The Session's list item in the Web Sessions list is rendered using **bold** text.
Supported Values	Any value triggers the font formatting.

Flag Name	`ui-italic`
Explanation	The Session is rendered using *italicized* text.
Supported Values	Any value triggers the font formatting.

Flag Name	`ui-strikeout`
Explanation	The Session is rendered in ~~struck~~ text.
Supported Values	Any value triggers the font formatting.

Flag Name	`ui-color`
Explanation	The Session is rendered in text of the specified color.
Supported Values	The color string value may be a .NET `Color` constant like `red`, or may be a HTML-formatted color code, like `#ff0000`.

Flag Name	`ui-backcolor`
Explanation	The Session's background is rendered in specified color.
Supported Values	The color string value may be a .NET `Color` constant, like `red`, or may be a HTML-formatted color code, like `#ff0000`.

Flag Name	`ui-comments`
Explanation	This string, set by FiddlerScript, extensions, or the Comment button on the toolbar, is shown in the **Comments** column in the Web Sessions list.
Supported Values	The string that you'd like to display in the column.

Flag Name	`ui-customcolumn`
Explanation	This string, set by FiddlerScript or extensions is shown in the **Custom** column in the Web Session's list.
Supported Values	The string that you'd like to display in the column.

Breakpoint and Editing Flags

Breakpointing and editing features are triggered by setting flags during the processing of the Session.

Flag Name	`x-BreakRequest`

Explanation	When this flag is set on a Session before the request is sent to the server, Fiddler will pause the Session to allow you to use Inspectors to modify the request.
Supported Values	Any value will enable a request breakpoint. It is customary to set this string to a terse explanation about why this request was chosen to be breakpointed.

Flag Name	x-BreakResponse
Explanation	When this flag is set on a Session before the response is sent to the client, Fiddler will pause the Session to allow you to use Inspectors to modify the response. Response tampering is incompatible with streaming. The response breakpoint is only checked after a streamed response has been returned to the client.
Supported Values	Any value will enable a response breakpoint. It is customary to set this string to a terse explanation about why this response was breakpointed.

Flag Name	x-Unlocked
Explanation	This flag, set by Fiddler's **Unlock for Editing** option, allows you to use Inspectors to modify a completed Session as if it were paused at a breakpoint.
Supported Values	Any value will unlock the Session.

Networking Flags

The following flags control and log Fiddler's use of the network:

Flag Name	x-overrideHost
Explanation	Controls the hostname used for DNS resolution when deciding what address this request should be sent to. This flag will not change any of the Headers in the request itself.
Supported Values	Specify either an alternative hostname or an IP Address to which this request should be targeted. Setting this flag will have no effect if the request is sent to an upstream gateway, because the upstream gateway will perform its own DNS resolution.

Flag Name	x-OverrideGateway
Explanation	Controls which upstream gateway proxy, if any, this request is sent to.
Supported Values	Provide a string that specifies the target gateway proxy in the format ProxyHost:Port, for example, myproxy:8080. The provided address information will be used instead of any default gateway proxy. If you prefix the string with socks= the provided gateway will be used as a SOCKS proxy. For instance, the string socks=127.0.0.1:8118 can be used to send traffic to a locally running instance of the TOR Polipo SOCKS proxy. A value of DIRECT means that the request will be sent directly to the server, bypassing any gateway. This value is equivalent to setting the Session's bypassGateway boolean to true.

Flag Name	x-ReplyWithTunnel
Explanation	When set on a CONNECT tunnel's Session, this flag causes Fiddler to automatically respond with a 200 OK response without contacting the server or gateway. This flag is set by the AutoResponder to enable capture of HTTPS requests from a client even when the system is offline. Otherwise, the CONNECT's failure would prevent subsequent HTTPS requests from being sent by the client.
Supported Values	Any value will result in returning a 200 OK response to the CONNECT.

Flag Name	FTP-UseASCII
Explanation	When this flag is present, Fiddler will use ASCII mode rather than Binary mode when acting as a FTP gateway.
Supported Values	Any value will result in using ASCII mode when talking to the server.

Flag Name	x-HostIP
Explanation	Set by Fiddler, this flag contains the IP address of the server to which this request was sent.

Flag Name	x-OriginalURL
Explanation	Set by the AutoResponder, this flag contains the original request URL in the event that the URL was changed by an AutoResponder rule.

Flag Name	X-EgressPort
Explanation	Set by Fiddler, this flag contains the local port number used to establish the connection to the server or gateway proxy.

Flag Name	X-ServerSocket
Explanation	Set by Fiddler, this flag contains diagnostic information about the connection to the server or gateway proxy, including information about whether the connection was reused.

Flag Name	X-SecurePipe
Explanation	Set by Fiddler, this flag contains diagnostic information about the HTTPS connection to the server or gateway proxy, including information about whether the connection was reused.

Authentication Flags

The following flags control Fiddler's automatic authentication behavior:

Flag Name	x-AutoAuth
Explanation	If this flag is set, Fiddler will attempt to automatically respond to HTTP/401 challenges sent by servers and HTTP/407 challenges sent by upstream proxies. This flag supports the

	Digest, NTLM, and Negotiate protocols.
Supported Values	When set to (default), the current logon user's credentials will be used. To use different credentials, set the flag to a string in the format username:password. **Warning**: If Fiddler is configured to accept requests from other devices or user-accounts, use of (default) introduces a security vulnerability. That's because those requests will be authenticated using the credentials of the account in which Fiddler is running.

Flag Name	X-AutoAuth-Retries
Explanation	When the x-AutoAuth is set, this flag specifies the maximum number of attempts Fiddler will make to supply the credentials in response to HTTP/401 authentication challenges.
Supported Values	Any positive integer; the default value is 5.

Flag Name	X-AutoAuth-Failed
Explanation	This flag is set if Fiddler fails to successfully authenticate to the server because the X-AutoAuth-Retries limit was reached.

Client Information Flags

The following flags track information about the source of the request:

Flag Name	x-ProcessInfo
Explanation	Set by Fiddler, this flag contains the name and ID of the local process which issued the request to Fiddler.

Flag Name	x-ClientIP
Explanation	Set by Fiddler, this flag contains the IP address of the client that issued the request. Typically, this will be the current PC's IP address, unless remote connections have been permitted using the option in the **Fiddler Options** > **Connections** tab.

Flag Name	x-ClientPort
Explanation	Set by Fiddler, this flag contains the port number of the connection from the client that issued the request.

Performance Simulation Flags

Fiddler offers simple flags that allow you to roughly simulate limited-bandwidth connections like modems, DSL, or Satellite connections.

Flag Name	request-trickle-delay
Explanation	Set this flag to control the rate at which Fiddler writes the request headers and body to the server. Fiddler will ensure that every 1kb of data written to the server is delayed by the amount specified.
Supported Values	Specify this flag's value as an integer number of milliseconds. For instance, the value 300 will result in Fiddler sending the request to the server in 1kb chunks, with a 150ms delay

	before the chunk and a 150ms delay after the chunk.

Flag Name	`response-trickle-delay`
Explanation	Set this flag to control the rate at which Fiddler writes the response headers and body to the client. Fiddler will ensure that every 1kb of data written to the client is delayed by the amount specified.
Supported Values	Specify this flag's value as an integer number of milliseconds. For instance, the value 300 will result in Fiddler sending the response to the client in 1kb chunks, with a 150ms delay before the chunk and a 150ms delay after the chunk.

HTTPS Flags

The following flags are related to HTTPS handling in Fiddler. Several of the flags are set automatically by Fiddler to reflect information about the HTTPS connection, while others can be set by script or extensions to influence the connection.

Flag Name	`x-no-decrypt`
Explanation	When set on a CONNECT tunnel, this flag instructs Fiddler not to attempt to decrypt the HTTPS traffic that flows through the tunnel.
Supported Values	Any value will disable decryption for the CONNECT tunnel. Typically, you should provide a terse explanation of why the CONNECT's traffic will not be decrypted so that a user examining the CONNECT Session's properties can understand why its traffic is not being decrypted.

Flag Name	`x-OverrideCertCN`
Explanation	When HTTPS decryption is enabled, this value controls the hostname that is used for the self-signed certificate generated by Fiddler to send to the client when a CONNECT tunnel is created. This flag is most useful when you've used other flags to reroute HTTPS traffic to a different server and do not want the client to encounter an unexpected certificate error.
Supported Values	Specify the hostname to be sent to the client. For instance www.example.com.

Flag Name	`x-IgnoreCertCNMismatch`
Explanation	This value controls whether Fiddler validates that the server's certificate's Subject Common Name (CN) field matches the hostname expected for the target server. This flag is meaningful only for CONNECT tunnels and only when HTTPS decryption is enabled. Set this flag when you have rerouted HTTPS traffic to a different server and do not want Fiddler to complain that the server's certificate is invalid. Fiddler's Host Remapping tool sets this flag on CONNECT tunnels that it has rerouted.
Supported Values	Any value will disable Certificate Subject CN validation. Typically, you should provide a terse explanation of why Subject CN validation was disabled, so that a user examining the CONNECT Session's properties will understand why the flag was present.

Flag Name	`x-IgnoreCertErrors`

Explanation	When HTTPS decryption is enabled, this value controls whether Fiddler validates that the server's certificate is unexpired, chains to a trusted root, and is valid for the target hostname. This flag is meaningful only for CONNECT tunnels and only when HTTPS decryption is enabled. Set this flag when interacting with Test or Development servers which are using self-signed or otherwise invalid certificates. To enable this behavior globally (unsafe), tick the **Ignore server certificate errors** checkbox inside **Tools > Fiddler Options > HTTPS**.
Supported Values	Any value will disable warnings about Certificate Errors on the CONNECT tunnel. Typically, you should provide a terse explanation of why certificate errors are being ignored, so that a user examining the CONNECT session's properties will understand why the flag was present.

Flag Name	x-OverrideSslProtocols
Explanation	Controls what SSL and TLS versions will be advertised when talking to the server

Supported Values	Provide a semi-colon delimited string containing one or more of the following tokens:
	
	    ssl2
	    ssl3
	    tls1.0
	
	For example: ssl2;ssl3.
	
	The provided versions will be used instead of the default versions controlled by the CONFIG.oAcceptedServerHTTPSProtocols value (Ssl3 and Tls1.0 by default).

Flag Name	https-Client-Certificate
Explanation	Set this flag on a CONNECT tunnel to provide the location of a certificate file that Fiddler should use if the server prompts for HTTPS Client Authentication. The .CER file must have a matching private key in the Windows Certificate store. If this flag is not present, Fiddler will look for the file %USERPROFILE%\My Documents\Fiddler2\ClientCertificate.cer and attach any certificate it finds.
Supported Values	Specify a fully-qualified path to the file. If you're setting this property from script or C#, remember to escape backslashes by doubling them up. E.g. oS["https-Client-Certificate"] = "C:\\test\\someCert.cer";

Flag Name	https-Client-SessionID
Explanation	Set by Fiddler on a CONNECT tunnel, this flag reports the HTTPS Session ID sent by the client in the HTTPS handshake.

Flag Name	https-Server-SessionID
Explanation	Set by Fiddler on a CONNECT tunnel, this flag reports the HTTPS Session ID sent by the server in the HTTPS handshake.

Flag Name	https-Client-SNIHostname
Explanation	Set by Fiddler on a CONNECT tunnel, this flag contains the hostname sent by the client in a

	TLS Handshake's Server Name Indication TLS extension, if any.

Flag Name	X-Client-Cert
Explanation	Set by Fiddler when a given connection is secured by a client certificate, this string contains the client certificate's Subject Field and Serial number.

Flag Name	X-HTTPS-Decryption-Error
Explanation	This flag is set by Fiddler when it is unable to find or generate a self-signed HTTPS interception certificate.

Request Composer Flags

While these flags were designed for use by the Request Composer, your script or extensions may use them as well.

Flag Name	X-Builder-Inspect
Explanation	When this flag is present (set by the Composer when the **Inspect Session** option is enabled) the Session will be automatically inspected when added to the Web Sessions list.
Supported Values	Any value will trigger the inspection.

Flag Name	X-Builder-MaxRedir
Explanation	Controls the number of HTTP/3xx redirections Fiddler is willing to follow before giving up.
Supported Values	Any positive integer value. The default is 0.

Flag Name	X-From-Builder
Explanation	This flag is set if the request was built and issued by the Request Composer.

Other Flags

Flag Name	log-drop-request-body
Explanation	When this flag is set, Fiddler "forgets" the request body to save memory when Session processing completes.
Supported Values	Any value will cause the request body to be dropped after Session processing completes.

Flag Name	log-drop-response-body
Explanation	When this flag is set, Fiddler "forgets" the response body to save memory when Session processing completes.
Supported Values	Any value will cause the response body to be dropped after Session processing completes.

Flag Name	X-Fiddler-Stream1xx

Explanation	When the `fiddler.network.leakhttp1xx` preference is set to `true` (its default), Fiddler will stream any HTTP/1xx intermediate responses from the server to the client. This flag's value, if present, indicates which HTTP/1xx codes were returned.

Flag Name	`X-Fiddler-Streaming`
Explanation	When the `fiddler.network.leakhttp1xx` preference is set to `false`, Fiddler will "swallow" any HTTP/1xx intermediate responses from the server. This flag's value, if present, indicates which HTTP/1xx codes were swallowed.

Flag Name	`X-Divorced-ServerPipe`
Explanation	When set, this flag indicates that Fiddler was forced to use a different connection to the server than expected. This might occur, for instance, if FiddlerScript or an extension changed the target URL of a Session that had been designated to reuse an existing connection from a prior Session.

Flag Name	`X-CreatedTunnel`
Explanation	When set, this flag indicates that Fiddler was forced to generate a CONNECT tunnel to the server in order to process a Session. This might occur, for instance, if FiddlerScript or an extension changed a HTTP request to a HTTPS request, or an existing secure connection cannot be reused because it has been closed.

Flag Name	`X-Fiddler-Generated`
Explanation	Set by Fiddler, this flag is present if Fiddler itself generated the response with the `utilCreateResponseAndBypassServer` method.

Flag Name	`X-DNS-Failover`
Explanation	If present, this flag will contain a string indicating the number of times that Fiddler failed over to another DNS record when attempting to contact the host. A +1 is added to the string each time this occurs, up to the maximum number of DNS failover attempts.

Flag Name	`x-Original-Host`
Explanation	This flag is set if the inbound request violated the HTTP protocol by specifying a different hostname in the request URL and the `Host` request header. This flag will contain the original `Host` header value. The request's `Host` header will be overwritten with the hostname parsed from the request URL.

Flag Name	`x-UsedVirtualHost`
Explanation	This flag is set to the virtual hostname value that was parsed from an inbound request; e.g. `ipv4.fiddler` or `localhost.fiddler`.

Flag Name	`X-Fiddler-Aborted`
Explanation	This flag is set when the Session is aborted by calling its `Abort` method. From the Fiddler UI, right-clicking an in-progress Session and choosing **Abort Session** from the context

	menu will call `Abort`.

Flag Name	`X-TTFB`
Explanation	Legacy flag reports the number of milliseconds until the first byte was read from the server.

Flag Name	`X-TTLB`
Explanation	Legacy flag reports the number of milliseconds until the last byte was read from the server.

Flag Name	`X-ReplyWithFile`
Explanation	Set this flag to instruct Fiddler to load the specified file and use it to respond to the request instead of sending the request to the server.
Supported Values	Supply either a fully-qualified filepath to the file to load. If only a bare filename is supplied without a path, Fiddler will look for the specified filename in the `\ResponseTemplates` or `\Captures\Responses\` folders.

Flag Name	`X-RepliedWithFile`
Explanation	When Fiddler reacts to `X-ReplyWithFile` by loading the specified file, the `X-ReplyWithFile` flag is copied to the `X-RepliedWithFile` flag.

Flag Name	`X-ResponseBodyTransferLength`
Explanation	This flag stores the response body byte count computed immediately after the response is read from the network, prior to any unchunking, decompression, or manipulation of the response from script or extensions.

Flag Name	`x-RequestBodyLength`
Explanation	If the `log-drop-request-body` flag is set, Fiddler "forgets" the request body to save memory when Session processing finishes. The `X-RequestBodyLength` flag records the request body byte count at the point that the body is dropped.

Flag Name	`X-ResponseBodyFinalLength`
Explanation	If the `log-drop-response-body` flag is set, Fiddler "forgets" the response body to save memory when Session processing finishes. The `X-ResponseBodyFinalLength` flag records the response body byte count at the point that the body is dropped.

Flag Name	`X-Format-JS`
Explanation	This flag controls the automatic reformatting of JavaScript performed by the JavaScript Formatter extension.
Supported Values	When this flag is set to a value of 0, the JavaScript Formatter extension will not format the response body, even if the **Make JavaScript Pretty** option is enabled on the Rules menu. Any other value will cause the JavaScript response body to be formatted, even if the **Make JavaScript Pretty** option is not enabled on the Rules menu.

Appendix D: Preferences

Fiddler's Preferences system allows you to control myriad aspects of Fiddler's behavior. This appendix contains a list of the Preferences that affect Fiddler and its default set of extensions.

Network Preferences

The following preferences control Fiddler's network behavior:

Name	`fiddler.network.timeouts.dnscache`
Default	150000 (2.5 minutes)
Explanation	Number of milliseconds for which Fiddler should cache DNS lookup results.

Name	`fiddler.network.timeouts.serverpipe.reuse`
Default	120000 (2 minutes)
Explanation	Number of milliseconds for which Fiddler is willing to leave a server connection idle. A connection which has been idle for this time without being reused will be closed.

Name	`fiddler.network.timeouts.clientpipe.receive.initial`
Default	60000 (1 minute)
Explanation	Number of milliseconds for which Fiddler is willing to wait for a client to begin sending a request on a newly established connection. After this timeout expires, Fiddler will close the connection from the client.

Name	`fiddler.network.timeouts.clientpipe.receive.reuse`
Default	30000 (30 seconds)
Explanation	Number of milliseconds for which Fiddler is willing to wait for a client to begin sending a request on a previously used connection. After this timeout expires, Fiddler will close the connection from the client.

Name	`fiddler.network.timeouts.serverpipe.receive.initial`
Default	60000 (1 minute)
Explanation	Number of milliseconds for which Fiddler is willing to wait for a server to begin sending a response on a newly established connection. After this timeout expires, Fiddler will close the connection to the server.

Name	`fiddler.network.timeouts.serverpipe.receive.reuse`
Default	60000 (1 minute)
Explanation	Number of milliseconds for which Fiddler is willing to wait for a server to begin sending a response on a previously used connection. After this timeout expires, Fiddler will close the connection to the server.

Name	fiddler.network.egress.IP
Default	
Explanation	Set this preference if your computer has multiple outbound connections and you need requests to be sent on a particular outbound connection. This preference is rarely used, but is sometimes needed if you have particular routing needs. For instance, if you have tethered a 3G phone to your PC, you may want Fiddler to send outbound requests from its IP address so that traffic is sent from the 3G connection. Warning: If you set this preference to an IP address that is not currently bound to one of your network connections, all outbound requests will fail.

Name	fiddler.network.auth.ReuseMode
Default	0
Explanation	This preference controls how Fiddler is willing to reuse server connections upon which an authentication (HTTP header authentication or HTTPS client certificate authentication) has taken place. The default value of 0 requires "Process Affinity." Fiddler will only reuse the authenticated connection to service requests that originated from the same process that authenticated the connection originally. The value 1 requires "Client Connection Marriage." Fiddler will only reuse the authenticated connection to service requests that originated from the same client connection that authenticated the connection originally. The value 2 allows "Arbitrary reuse." Fiddler will reuse the authenticated connection to service any request from any client. **Warning**: This value will yield better performance but unexpected and insecure behavior.

Name	fiddler.ftp.UseBinary
Default	true
Explanation	When set to true, Fiddler (acting as a FTP gateway) will use BINARY mode for file transfers. When set to false, Fiddler will use ASCII mode instead. To control this option on a per-request basis, set the FTP-UseASCII flag on the Session object.

Name	fiddler.ftp.UsePassive
Default	true
Explanation	When set to true, Fiddler will use the PASV option when acting as a FTP gateway. When set to false, Fiddler will make active FTP connections, which are not compatible with most firewalls.

Name	fiddler.network.sockets.ClientReadBufferSize
Default	8192

Explanation	This preference controls the size, in bytes, of the buffer used to read from client connections.

Name	`fiddler.network.sockets.ServerReadBufferSize`
Default	`32768`
Explanation	This preference controls the size, in bytes, of the buffer used to read from server connections.

Name	`fiddler.network.proxy.RegistrationHostName`
Default	`127.0.0.1`
Explanation	This preference controls the hostname used to register as the system proxy. There are some cases where you will need to register as the system proxy using a different hostname. For instance, the Windows Phone Emulator requires that the hostname be set to the machine name of the current machine.

Name	`fiddler.network.dns.fallback`
Default	`true`
Explanation	A DNS server may return multiple addresses for a single hostname resolution. This allows "failing over" if one or more servers is offline. When this preference is set to `false`, Fiddler will fail a connection if the first IP address cannot be reached. When this preference is set to `true`, Fiddler will try up to `MaxAddressCount` addresses before giving up.

Name	`fiddler.network.dns.MaxAddressCount`
Default	`5`
Explanation	A DNS server may return multiple addresses for a single hostname resolution. This preference allows you to control the maximum number of addresses returned, which in turn limits the number of DNS fallbacks that are permitted when `fiddler.network.dns.fallback` is `true`.

Name	`fiddler.network.leakhttp1xx`
Default	`true`
Explanation	This preference controls whether Fiddler will automatically pass `HTTP/1xx` messages through to the client connection as they are read from the server. `HTTP/1xx` responses are "non-final" headers-only responses and they are not shown in Fiddler's UI. `HTTP/100` Continue responses are sent by a server in response to a client sending an `Expect: Continue` header on POST requests.

Name	`fiddler.network.streaming.AbortIfClientAborts`
Default	`false`
Explanation	This preference controls whether Fiddler will close the server connection if the client

connection closes while a response is being streamed from the server to the client.

The default value of `false` ensures that Fiddler will attempt to read the entire response from the server even if the client that originally requested the data closes its connection.

Set this preference to `true` if you would like Fiddler to close the server connection when the client connection closes during streaming. This configuration can significantly reduce the amount of memory used by Fiddler by aborting downloads that the client application has cancelled.

Name	`fiddler.network.streaming.ForgetStreamedData`
Default	`false`
Explanation	When set to `true`, Fiddler will "forget" response data from the server as soon as that data is sent to the client. This precludes you from using Fiddler to examine streamed responses, but significantly decreases memory usage when streaming video or other large responses through Fiddler.

Name	`fiddler.network.gateway.DetermineInProcess`
Default	`false`
Explanation	Fiddler uses the WinHTTP library for proxy auto-configuration support (either via WPAD or a manually-specified PAC script). When this preference is set to `true`, Fiddler will direct WinHTTP to perform proxy determination in-process rather than calling out to the WinHTTP service.

Name	`fiddler.network.gateway.UseFailedAutoProxy`
Default	`false`
Explanation	By default, Fiddler will begin to ignore an automatically-detected upstream proxy script if it returns errors; requests will instead be sent directly to the target. Set this preference to `true` to disable that optimization and always attempt to use a proxy script even if it is non-responsive.

Name	`fiddler.proxy.pacfile.UseFileProtocol`
Default	`true`
Explanation	When the **Use PAC Script** option is enabled on the **Fiddler Options** > **Connections** tab, Fiddler will register as the system proxy by providing a proxy auto-configuration script URL. By default, the URL points to the `BrowserPAC.js` file in your `Documents` folder. When this preference is set to `false`, Fiddler will instead register using a HTTP URL, in the format `http://127.0.0.1:8888/proxy.pac`. You must then respond to inbound requests for the script using the AutoResponder or FiddlerScript.

Name	`fiddler.proxy.pacfile.text`
Default	`return 'PROXY 127.0.0.1:8888';`

Explanation	This preference controls the body of the `FindProxyForURL` function stored in the `%UserProfile%\My Documents\Fiddler2\Scripts\BrowserPAC.js` file.

HTTPS Preferences

The following preferences control Fiddler's behavior when interacting with HTTPS requests.

Name	`fiddler.network.https.StoreServerCertChain`
Default	`false`
Explanation	When set to `true`, Fiddler will walk the entire certificate chain provided by the server and add information about each certificate in the chain to the text shown in the Response Inspector for the `CONNECT` tunnel.

Name	`fiddler.network.https.CheckCertificateRevocation`
Default	`false`
Explanation	When set to `true`, Fiddler will perform a revocation check to determine whether the server's certificate has been revoked by the issuer. While validation enhances security, it will slow down HTTPS connection establishment.

Name	`fiddler.network.https.SetCNFromSNI`
Default	`false`
Explanation	When set to `true`, Fiddler will use the Server Name Indication TLS extension from the client's HTTPS handshake to set the CN field of the certificate used in the HTTPS handshake with the client. When set to `false`, the CN field will be set using the request's `Host` header. This preference can be handy if you have a client which sends a `Host` header that contains a literal IP address rather than the hostname of the target server. This may occur, for instance, if you've used `iptables` to send traffic to Fiddler from an Android device that does not accept a proxy setting.

Name	`fiddler.network.https.NoDecryptionHosts`
Default	
Explanation	A semi-colon delimited list of hostnames for which HTTPS decryption should not take place. This preference is exposed by the textbox on the **Fiddler Options** > **HTTPS** tab.

Name	`fiddler.network.https.BlindTunnelIfCertUnobtainable`
Default	`true`
Explanation	If Fiddler is configured to decrypt HTTPS traffic, but a certificate could not be generated to secure a connection, Fiddler will treat the connection as a blind tunnel if this preference is set to `true`. When set to `false`, Fiddler will fail the HTTPS connection if the certificate cannot be obtained.

Name	`fiddler.CertMaker.CleanupServerCertsOnExit`
Default	`false`

Explanation	If HTTPS-decryption is enabled, Fiddler's default certificate maker will add certificates to the user's certificate store. When this preference is set to `true`, all such certificates will be removed when Fiddler shuts down. This preference is not used by FiddlerCore; instead call `CertMaker.removeFiddlerGeneratedCerts(false);` before your application exits.

Name	`fiddler.CertMaker.Assembly`
Default	`%Program Files%\Fiddler2\CertMaker.dll`
Explanation	When this preference is set, Fiddler will attempt to load specified assembly when a certificate is needed to secure a HTTPS connection. If the specified assembly cannot be found or does not contain a `public class` that implements the `ICertificateProvider2` interface, Fiddler's default certificate provider will be used instead.

Name	`fiddler.CertMaker.Root.ExtraParams`
Default	
Explanation	Specifies any extra parameters that should be passed to `makecert.exe` when the Fiddler root certificate is generated.

Name	`fiddler.CertMaker.EE.ExtraParams`
Default	
Explanation	Specifies any extra parameters that should be passed to `makecert.exe` when generating end-entity certificates for HTTPS servers.

Name	`fiddler.CertMaker.OfferMachineTrust`
Default	`false` except on Windows 8.
Explanation	Set this preference to `true` to configure Fiddler to offer to use an elevated process to add the root certificate to the per-Machine Trusted Root certificate store. By default, Fiddler prompts you to add its Root Certificate to the per-*User* Trusted Root certificate store. If you plan to use Fiddler across multiple user-accounts, or need Windows 8-style Metro applications to trust Fiddler's root certificate, the Root must instead be stored in the per-*Machine* Trusted Root certificate store.

Name	`fiddler.network.https.cacheclientcert`
Default	`true`
Explanation	Controls whether Fiddler will cache, for the lifetime of the Fiddler process, the default client certificate upon its first use. Caching ensures that you will not be prompted with a PIN request if your certificate requires one. However, caching also means that you cannot use a different certificate without restarting Fiddler or using script to `null` the property `FiddlerApplication.oDefaultClientCertificate`.

Name	`fiddler.config.path.defaultclientcert`
Default	`%USERPROFILE%\My Documents\Fiddler2\ClientCertificate.cer`
Explanation	If a HTTPS server demands a client certificate, Fiddler will look for a client certificate file in this location.

Name	`fiddler.network.https.clientcertificate.ephemeral.prompt-for-missing`
Default	`true`
Explanation	This preference controls whether Fiddler will prompt the user if a server demands a client certificate but no certificate location was specified in the Session's flags and no certificate is present in the default location.

Name	`fiddler.network.https.RequestClientCertificate`
Default	`false`
Explanation	When this preference is set to `true`, Fiddler will request a client certificate every time a client attempts to establish a HTTPS connection. Set this preference to test client software to see how it handles client certificate demands.

Fiddler UI Preferences

Preferences under the `Fiddler.UI` branch track the state of options and settings that are shown within the Fiddler user interface, including the toolbar.

Name	`fiddler.ui.toolbar.visible`
Default	`true`
Explanation	This preference controls whether the toolbar is displayed.

Name	`fiddler.ui.toolbar.ShowLabels`
Default	`true`
Explanation	Controls whether optional text labels are shown on toolbar's buttons.

Name	`fiddler.ui.StayOnTop`
Default	`false`
Explanation	Controls the **View > Stay on Top** menu checkbox. When set to `true`, Fiddler will remain on top of all other windows on the system.

Name	`fiddler.ui.font.size`
Default	`8.25`
Explanation	Controls the default font size for text in Fiddler. It can be adjusted using the **Tools > Fiddler Options > Appearance > Font Size** dropdown.

Name	`fiddler.ui.LastView`
Default	`Statistics`
Explanation	Stores the last active View tab when Fiddler is shutdown. That tab is subsequently reactivated the next time Fiddler is started.

Name	`fiddler.inspectors.HideList`
Default	
Explanation	Stores the list of Inspectors which should be hidden. You can hide an Inspector by right-

	clicking on it and choosing **Hide Inspector** from the menu. Unhiding an Inspector by editing this preference requires that you restart Fiddler.

Name	`fiddler.filters.ResetOnRestart`
Default	`false`
Explanation	When set to `true`, Fiddler will reset all filters each time the debugger is launched. This option is helpful if you're in the habit of applying filters, using them for a while, closing Fiddler, restarting it days later, forgetting you've applied filters, and then spending frustrated hours trying to figure out why Fiddler isn't showing you traffic.

Name	`fiddler.ui.rules.KeepOnly`
Default	`0`
Explanation	When set to a non-zero value, Fiddler will automatically trim the Web Sessions list to the specified number of Sessions. This preference backs the **Keep** dropdown on the toolbar.

Name	`fiddler.ui.rules.HideImages`
Default	`false`
Explanation	Stores the **Rules** > **Hide Images** menu option.

Name	`fiddler.ui.rules.HideConnects`
Default	`false`
Explanation	Stores the **Rules** > **Hide CONNECTs** menu option.

Name	`fiddler.ui.rules.RemoveEncoding`
Default	`false`
Explanation	Stores the **Rules** > **Remove all Encodings** menu option and the **Decode** toolbar toggle.

Name	`fiddler.ui.rules.ForceGZIP`
Default	`false`
Explanation	Stores the **Rules** > **Apply GZIP Encoding** menu option.

Name	`fiddler.ui.rules.BufferResponses`
Default	`true`
Explanation	Stores the **Stream** toolbar toggle.

Name	`fiddler.ui.ephemeral.rules.RequireProxyAuth`
Default	`false`
Explanation	Stores the **Rules** > **Require Proxy Authentication** menu option.

Name	`fiddler.ui.inspectors.request.AlwaysUse`
Default	
Explanation	Use this preference to always choose a particular Request Inspector when activating a Session. Set the preference to the Inspector tab's title text, e.g. `Raw`.

Name	`fiddler.ui.inspectors.response.AlwaysUse`
Default	
Explanation	Use this preference to always choose a particular Response Inspector when activating a Session. Set the preference to the Inspector tab's title text, e.g. `WebView`.

Name	`fiddler.reissue.AutoAuth`
Default	`false`
Explanation	When set to `true`, Fiddler will attempt to automatically respond to authentication challenges when you reissue a request from the Web Sessions list.

Name	`fiddler.reissue.AutoRedirCount`
Default	`0`
Explanation	Specifies the maximum number of redirections Fiddler will perform if a HTTP/3xx redirect response is returned when a Session is reissued using the context menu or toolbar. When the redirection limit is exceeded, Fiddler will ignore the `Location` header specified on the final redirect.

Name	`fiddler.differ.UltraDiff`
Default	`true`
Explanation	The UltraDiff option is used when comparing two Sessions. When set to `true`, Fiddler reorders the headers of both Sessions such that headers that exactly match in both Sessions are listed first, then headers with different values are listed, then headers that are entirely different are listed last. When set to `false`, this reordering does not occur.

Name	`fiddler.differ.Params`
Default	`"{0} {1}"`
Explanation	Specifies the command line arguments to supply to the file comparison tool when the Compare command is invoked. {0} is replaced with the first filename and {1} is replaced with the second filename.

Name	`fiddler.differ.ParamsAlt`
Default	`"{0} {1} -p"`
Explanation	Specifies the command line arguments to supply to the file comparison tool when the Compare command is invoked while holding the SHIFT key. The default value adds the -p parameter to instruct WinDiff to use its "break on punctuation" mode.

Name	`fiddler.filters.ephemeral.DebugMode`
Default	`false`
Explanation	Stores the **Help > Troubleshoot Filters...** menu option. When set to `true`, Sessions that would normally be hidden are instead shown in the Web Sessions list using a strikethrough font.

Name	`fiddler.ui.ephemeral.rules.BreakOnRequest`
Default	`false`
Explanation	When set to `true`, Fiddler will automatically break on each request.

Name	`fiddler.ui.ephemeral.rules.BreakOnResponse`
Default	`false`
Explanation	When set to `true`, Fiddler will automatically break on each response.

Name	`fiddler.ui.SessionList.UpdateInterval`
Default	`80`
Explanation	This preference contains the number of milliseconds for which Fiddler should accumulate new Web Sessions before showing them in the Web Sessions list. **Warning**: Setting a lower value will force Fiddler to repaint the Web Sessions list more often, and can dramatically slow down Fiddler. You may wish to increase the value from the default when running on a slow PC or through a Remote Desktop connection.

Name	`fiddler.ui.CtrlX.PromptIfMoreThan`
Default	`0`
Explanation	When set to a positive integer, you will be prompted when pressing CTRL+X before clearing more than the specified number of Sessions from the Web Sessions list.

Name	`fiddler.ui.CtrlX.KeepMarked`
Default	`false`
Explanation	When set to `true`, hitting CTRL+X to clear the Web Sessions list will leave behind any Sessions which are marked. The same behavior can be triggered by clicking the **Remove** > **Complete and Unmarked** item in the toolbar.

Name	`fiddler.session.prependIDToSuggestedFilename`
Default	`false`
Explanation	This preference controls whether the session's ID number is prepended to the automatically generated filename used to save Sessions, Requests, and Responses to disk. For instance, when saving Session #4's response to disk, the default filename of `download.exe` becomes `4_download.exe` when this preference is set to `true`.

Name	`fiddler.find.ephemeral.LastSearch`
Default	
Explanation	Stores the last search term supplied to Fiddler's **Edit** > **Find Sessions** prompt. An extension *might* choose to use this value to pre-fill its own inline search box for convenience.

FiddlerScript Preferences

Name	`fiddler.script.AutoRef`
Default	`true`

Explanation	When this Preference is set to `true`, Fiddler will automatically determine which assemblies to reference based on the `import` statements at the top of the FiddlerScript file. When set to `false`, library references must be manually provided in the **Fiddler Options > Extensions** tab.

Name	`fiddler.script.LibPath`
Default	
Explanation	Specify a fully-qualified path that contains assemblies your FiddlerScript will use. For instance, set the value to `C:\src\library dlls\` and when your FiddlerScript is next compiled, Fiddler will look for referenced assemblies in the `Library DLLs` folder.

Name	`fiddler.script.CompileToFilename`
Default	
Explanation	Set this preference to a fully-qualified `.DLL` filename and upon next compilation, your FiddlerScript will generate an assembly of the provided name. Use this option to create an assembly that you can load into Reflector or another code-inspection tool to inspect the compiled output. **Warning:** When you use this preference, your FiddlerScript will not execute until the preference is removed and you recompile your script.

TextWizard Preferences

Name	`fiddler.textwizard.InputEncoding`
Default	UTF-8
Explanation	Specify a character set from which %-encoded characters will be decoded by the TextWizard. The string value provided must be an `Encoding` name recognized by the .NET Framework; valid values can be found at `http://fiddler2.com/r/?EncodingNames`.

Name	`fiddler.textwizard.OutputEncoding`
Default	UTF-8
Explanation	Specify a character set to which characters will be %-encoded by the TextWizard. The string value provided must be an `Encoding` name recognized by the .NET Framework; valid values can be found at `http://fiddler2.com/r/?EncodingNames`.

Request Composer Preferences

Name	`fiddler.composer.FollowRedirects`
Default	true
Explanation	Controls whether the Composer will automatically follow a redirect when the server returns one for a request sent by the Composer. Set this preference using the Composer's **Options** tab.

Name	`fiddler.composer.FollowRedirects.Max`
Default	10
Explanation	Controls the number of redirects that the Composer is willing to follow before giving up. This preference sets the `x-Builder-MaxRedir` flag on the new Session.

Name	`fiddler.composer.AutoAuth`
Default	`true`
Explanation	Controls whether the Composer will automatically attempt to respond to Authentication challenges sent by servers. Set this preference using the Composer's **Options** tab.

Name	`fiddler.composer.AutoAuthCreds`
Default	`(default)`
Explanation	Controls which credentials are used when the Composer attempts to respond to Authentication challenges sent by servers. This preference sets the `x-AutoAuth` flag on the new Session. When set to `(default)`, the current logon user's credentials will be used. To use different credentials, set the preference to a string in the format `username:password`.

Name	`fiddler.composer.InspectSession`
Default	`true`
Explanation	Controls whether the Inspectors will be automatically activated when you send a request using the Composer. Set this preference on the Composer's **Options** tab. This preference sets the `x-Builder-Inspect` flag on the new Session.

Path Configuration

Fiddler and FiddlerCore use a variety of paths on the filesystem when loading and storing content or invoking utilities. Some paths may be configured using the user-interface, but some can only be controlled using preferences.

Name	`fiddler.config.path.captures`
Default	`%USERPROFILE%\My Documents\Fiddler2\Captures\`
Explanation	Path under which captured requests and responses will be stored.

Name	`fiddler.config.path.differ`
Default	`Windiff.exe`
Explanation	Path to the file comparison tool used when comparing two Sessions.

Name	`fiddler.config.path.defaultclientcert`
Default	`%USERPROFILE%\My Documents\Fiddler2\ClientCertificate.cer`
Explanation	Path to the client certificate which will be used to respond to any certificate demands during HTTPS handshaking.

Name	`fiddler.config.path.requests`
Default	`%USERPROFILE%\My Documents\Fiddler2\Captures\Requests`
Explanation	Path under which captured requests will be stored.

Name	`fiddler.config.path.responses`
Default	`%USERPROFILE%\My Documents\Fiddler2\Captures\Responses`

Explanation	Path under which captured responses will be stored.

Name	`fiddler.config.path.templateresponses`
Default	`%ProgramFiles%\Fiddler2\ResponseTemplates\`
Explanation	Path under which Template Responses used by the AutoResponder are stored.

Name	`fiddler.config.path.TextEditor`
Default	`notepad.exe`
Explanation	Path to the editor to launch when viewing textual content.

Miscellaneous

Name	`fiddler.updater.CheckFreshness`
Default	`true`
Explanation	When set to `true`, you will be prompted for permission to check for a new version each time you launch a version of Fiddler built over 200 days ago. When set to `false`, this prompt will not be shown.

Name	`fiddler.websocket.ParseMessages`
Default	`true`
Explanation	When set to `true`, Fiddler will attempt to parse bytes transmitted over WebSocket connections into WebSocket messages.

Name	`fiddler.websocket.ShowRawBytes`
Default	`true`
Explanation	When set to `true`, Fiddler will display the bytes of the WebSocket messages in the Log tab.

Name	`fiddler.debug.extensions.ShowErrors`
Default	`false`
Explanation	When set to `true`, any exceptions raised when Fiddler calls into extensions will be shown in a notification window. When set to `false`, exceptions raised when calling into extensions will be silently discarded.

Name	`fiddler.debug.extensions.verbose`
Default	`false`
Explanation	When set to `true`, all extension-related messages will be logged on Fiddler's Log tab and any exceptions raised when Fiddler calls into extensions will be shown in a notification window. Set this preference to `true` when developing and debugging Fiddler extensions.

Name	`fiddler.SAZ.AES.Use256Bit`
Default	`false`
Explanation	When set to `true`, Fiddler will store password-protected SAZ files using 256-bit encryption instead of the default of 128-bit encryption. The higher level of encryption is much slower and is probably unnecessary if your adversary is not a government intelligence agency.

Name	`fiddler.script.delaycreate`
Default	`true`
Explanation	When set to `true`, Fiddler will create the `CustomRules.js file` from the default `SampleRules.js` file only when you attempt to edit the script using **Rules > Customize Rules**. This ensures that if you never edit the script, you always have the latest script when you perform build-to-build upgrades.

Extension Preferences

Many Fiddler Inspectors and extensions offer Preferences that control their behavior. The following is a list of commonly used Preferences for these modules.

Raw Inspector

Name	`fiddler.inspectors.request.raw.TruncateBinaryAt`
Default	128
Explanation	When the AutoTruncate feature is enabled, the Raw Inspector will display at most the specified number of bytes of a Request body that is believed to be binary in nature.

Name	`fiddler.inspectors.request.raw.TruncateTextAt`
Default	262144
Explanation	When the AutoTruncate feature is enabled, the Raw Inspector will display at most the specified number of bytes of a Request body that is believed to be textual in nature.

Name	`fiddler.inspectors.response.raw.TruncateBinaryAt`
Default	128
Explanation	When the AutoTruncate feature is enabled, the Raw Inspector will display at most the specified number of bytes of a Response body that is believed to be binary in nature.

Name	`fiddler.inspectors.response.raw.TruncateTextAt`
Default	262144
Explanation	When the AutoTruncate feature is enabled, the Raw Inspector will display at most the specified number of bytes of a Response body that is believed to be textual in nature.

JavaScript Formatter

Name	`fiddler.extensions.JSFormat.AutoFormat`
Default	`false`
Explanation	When set to `true`, the JavaScript Formatting extension will attempt to automatically auto-format all script files before they are returned to the client application. When set to `false`, you must manually format JavaScript files using the **Make JavaScript Pretty** context menu item in the Web Sessions list.

Certificate Maker

The Certificate Maker add-on (`http://fiddler2.com/r/?FiddlerCertMaker`) offers many flags that enable it to generate certificates which are compatible with a wide variety of platform, including iOS and Android devices. In its default configuration, iOS-compatible certificates are generated.

Name	`fiddler.CertMaker.BC.Debug`
Default	`false`
Explanation	When set to `true`, the Certificate Maker plugin will emit logging information to the Log tab.

Name	`fiddler.CertMaker.BC.ReusePrivateKeys`
Default	`true`
Explanation	When set to `true`, the Certificate Maker plugin will use the same private key for each certificate it generates. This is obviously insecure, but harmless when debugging locally.

Name	`fiddler.CertMaker.BC.LogPrivateKeys`
Default	`false`
Explanation	When set to `true`, the Certificate Maker plugin will emit Private keys to the Log tab.

Name	`fiddler.CertMaker.BC.AddCRL`
Default	`false`
Explanation	When set to `true`, the Certificate Maker plugin will add a Certificate Revocation List URL to the certificates it generates. The CRL added is hardcoded to point to `http://www.fiddler2.com/revocationlist.crl`, a nonexistent URL that you can intercept in Fiddler or FiddlerCore.

Name	`fiddler.CertMaker.BC.EE.CriticalAKID`
Default	`true`
Explanation	When set to `true`, the end-entity certificates generated by the Certificate Maker plugin will have the `AuthorityKeyID` extension marked as `Critical`.

Name	`fiddler.CertMaker.BC.EE.CriticalBasicConstraints`
Default	`true`
Explanation	When set to `true`, the end-entity certificates generated by the Certificate Maker plugin will have the `BasicConstraints` extension marked as `Critical`.

Name	`fiddler.CertMaker.BC.EE.CriticalEKU`
Default	`true`
Explanation	When set to `true`, the end-entity certificates generated by the Certificate Maker plugin will have the `ExtendedKeyUsage` extension marked as `Critical`.

Name	`fiddler.CertMaker.BC.Root.SetAKID`
Default	`false`
Explanation	When set to `true`, the Certificate Maker plugin will add an `AuthorityKeyID` to the root

	certificate which points at itself.

Name	`fiddler.CertMaker.BC.Root.CriticalBasicConstraints`
Default	`true`
Explanation	When set to `true`, the root certificate generated by the Certificate Maker plugin will have the `BasicConstraints` extension marked as `Critical`.

Name	`fiddler.CertMaker.BC.Root.CriticalKeyUsage`
Default	`true`
Explanation	When set to `true`, the root certificate generated by the Certificate Maker plugin will have the `KeyUsage` extension marked as Critical.

Name	`fiddler.CertMaker.BC.Root.CriticalAKID`
Default	`false`
Explanation	When set to `true`, the Certificate Maker plugin will mark the root certificate's `AuthorityKeyID` as `Critical`.

INDEX

A

Android
  HTTPS Decryption, 111
AppContainers, 90
Apple
  HTTPS Decryption, 111
  iOS, 95
  Mac OSX, 91
audio and video
  previewing, 144
  streaming, 102
authentication
  Auth Inspector, 125
  automatic, 117
  channel-binding, 118
  client certificates, 119
  loopback, 89, 119
  methods, 116
  problems, 118
  WinHTTP, 118
AutoResponder
  action text, 50
  drag-and-drop, 52
  FARX files, 52
  match condition, 48
  regular expressions, 51

B

breakpoints
  Breakpoint bar, 73
  Filters tab, 41
  overview, 72
  resuming, 74
  using QuickExec, 73

C

caching
  Inspector, 127

capturing
  .NET Framework, 86
  browsers, 84
  devices, 94
  DirectAccess, 99
  FTP, 115
  Java, 87
  loopback, 88
  Mac OSX, 91
  other PCs, 93
  PHP/CURL, 88
  reverse proxy, 96
  VPNs/Modems, 99
  Win8 apps, 90
  Windows Phone, 95
  Windows RT, 95
  WinHTTP, 86
certificates
  CertMgr.msc, 108
  troubleshooting, 276
  trusted root, 107
  Windows 8, 108
clipboard
  pasting from, 24
  pasting to, 19
Clone Response, 21
code samples
  assigning sessions to Inspectors, 233
  extension example, 240
  implementing OnValidateServerCertificate, 262
  removing HTTP encodings, 235
  scripts to manipulate requests, 200
  scripts to manipulate responses, 202
  transcoder example, 250
  trusting a root certificate, 269
columns, 16
  adding from code, 192
COMETPeek, 21
  overview, 103
Composer
  automatic breakpoints, 59

options, 56
overview, 56
parsed, 57
raw requests, 57
sequential requests, 57
uploading files, 58
cookies
Inspector, 128
CPU architecture and bitness, 100

E

EnableLoopback.exe, 90
encoding
decoding programmatically, 235
Decoding using UI, 142
Decoding with Transformer, 141
headers, 82
HTTP Chunking, 140
HTTP Compression, 140
text encoding overview, 82
TextWizard, 54
execaction
driving FiddlerScript, 183
export
HTML5 AppCache, 171
HTTPArchive format, 172
MeddlerScript, 173
Raw Files, 173
Visual Studio WebTest, 174
WCAT Script, 174
extensions
AnyWHERE, 160
assemblies, 245
best practices, 208
building in .NET, 207
Content Blocker, 154
delay-loading, 208
Developing, 238
directory, 149, 150
example code, 240
FiddlerScript tab, 156
for Performance analysis, 149
for Security analysis, 149

Gallery tab, 152
installing, 226
JavaScript Formatter, 151
options, 79
overview, 149
SAZClipboard, 159
third-party, 149
Traffic Differ, 155

F

FiddlerApplication overview, 262
FiddlerCap, 165
FiddlerCore
common tasks, 268
getting started, 258
overview, 257
StartupFlags, 260
FiddlerHook, 84
FiddlerScript
automation, 183
ClassView sidebar, 157
cross-process messaging, 184
Editing, 156
engine, 221
examples, 200
extending menus, 186
FiddlerObject, 196
general functions, 181
JScript.NET, 177
overview, 177
referencing assemblies, 199
resetting, 179
session-handling functions, 180
standalone editor, 157
filtering
Filters tab, 39
Find, 61
fonts
previewing, 144
FTP
overview, 115

H

headers
   Inspector, 129
HTTPS
   Certificate Maker plugin, 111
   certificate pinning, 113
   certificate validation, 113
   client certificates, 119
   configuring devices, 111
   configuring other clients, 110
   configuring remote computers, 110
   CONNECT tunnels, 106
   decryption, 106
   handshake failures, 112
   limiting decryption, 109
   options, 78
   overview, 106
   protocol versions, 112

I

IFiddlerExtension, 238
import and export
   export formats, 170
   import formats, 170
   overview, 170
   Transcoders, 246
Inspectors
   assemblies, 237
   Auth, 125
   Caching, 127
   Cookies, 128
   developing, 229
   Headers, 129
   HexView, 132
   ImageView, 134
   JSON, 135
   Raw, 136
   SyntaxView, 137
   TextView, 139
   Transformer, 140
   WebForms, 143
   XML, 145

installation, 13

J

JavaScript
   formatting, 151

K

keyboard shortcuts
   general, 15
   hotkeys, 36
   Web Sessions list, 18

L

Log
   macro commands, 221
loopback
   authentication, 89
   bypass, 88
   capturing, 88
   Windows 8, 90

M

memory
   conserving, 100
   overview, 100
   usage, 28
Menus
   Copy submenu, 19
   Edit menu, 23
   extending with extensions, 240
   extending with FiddlerScript, 186
   File menu, 23
   Help menu, 27
   Mark submenu, 20
   Performance submenu, 25
   Replay submenu, 20
   Rules menu, 24
   Save submenu, 19
   Select submenu, 21
   Tools menu, 26

View menu, 26
Web Sessions context menu, 18

N

NetMon, 3
NSIS installer, 226

O

object model
  BitFlags, 218
  FiddlerApplication events, 262
  FiddlerApplication methods, 265
  FiddlerApplication properties and fields, 266
  FiddlerScript engine, 221
  Log, 220
  Preferences, 223
  session objects, 214
  SessionStates, 217
  TextWizard, 220
  Timers, 219
  Web Sessions list, 212

P

P3P, 128
Parallels, 91
performance
  add-ons, 149
  Caching Inspector, 127
  simulation, 25
  Timers object, 219
Preferences
  about:config, 83
  IFiddlerPreferences, 223
  observing, 225
  overview, 83
  programming with, 223
  Reference List, 291
protocols
  references, 6
  support, 9
proxy server, 7

client applications, 84
SOCKS, 98
upstream chaining, 97

Q

QuickExec
  commands, 31
  default FiddlerScript commands, 33
  extension integration, 239
  general commands, 32
  overview, 31
  selecting sessions, 31

R

reverse proxy, 96

S

SAZ Files
  encrypting, 164
  overview, 163
  saving with FiddlerCap, 165
searching
  Find Sessions window, 61
security
  add-ons, 149
selecting sessions
  with QuickExec, 31
sessions
  aborting, 21
  comparing, 70
  comparing multiple, 155
  inspecting in a new window, 22
  properties, 22
  rerouting, 67
  unlocking, 22
settings
  Appearance tab, 81
  command-line, 280
  Connections tab, 79
  Extensions tab, 79
  Fiddler Options, 77

FTP, 115
HeaderEncoding, 82
Preferences, 83
status bar
overview, 30
streaming
COMET, 103
minimizing memory usage, 101
Timeline, 45
vs. buffering, 102
System Requirements, 13

hiding text, 30
overview, 29
TOR
chaining to, 98
Transcoders, 246
example code, 250
progress events, 249
supporting options, 248

V

viewer mode, 169

W

T

Tabs
adding from extensions, 245
Composer, 56
FiddlerScript, 156
Filters, 39
Gallery, 152
Inspectors, 123
Log, 60
Statistics, 37
TextWizard
character encoding, 55
invoking from code, 220
overview, 54
threading
IAutoTamper, 239
Transcoders, 250
timing
Statistics tab, 37
toolbar

Web Sessions list
colors, 16
columns, 16
icons, 16
overview, 15
WebSockets
Log tab, 60
overview, 104
windows
About box, 28
Fiddler Options, 77
Find Sessions, 61
Windows 8 Metro
capturing, 90
Windows Phone
HTTPS Decryption, 111
Windows RT, 95